SO-ARH-608

The Book of Forest and Thicket

Trees, Shrubs, and Wildflowers of Eastern North America

John Eastman

Illustrated by Amelia Hansen

STACKPOLE
BOOKS

Text copyright © 1992 by John Eastman

Illustrations copyright © 1992 by Amelia Hansen

Published by
STACKPOLE BOOKS
Cameron and Kelker Streets
P.O. Box 1831
Harrisburg, PA 17105

All rights reserved, including the right to reproduce this book or portions thereof in any form or by any means, electronic or mechanical, including photocopying, recording, or by any information storage and retrieval system, without permission in writing from the publisher. All inquiries should be addressed to Stackpole Books, Cameron and Kelker Streets, P.O. Box 1831, Harrisburg, Pennsylvania 17105.

Printed in the United States of America

First Edition

10 9 8 7 6 5 4 3 2 1

Cover design by Mark Olszewski

Library of Congress Cataloging-in-Publication Data

Eastman, John Andrews.
    The book of forest and thicket : trees, shrubs, and wildflowers of eastern
North America / John Andrew Eastman : illustrated by Amelia
Hansen. — 1st ed.
        p.   cm.
    ISBN 0-8117-3046-8
    1. Forest flora—East (U.S.) 2. Forest ecology—East (U.S.)
I. Title.
QK115.E28   1991
581.974—dc20   91-28395
                                                                            CIP

To
Faythe M. Butler
and
Jack Olsen.
They made trails.

Objects are concealed from our view not so much because they are out of the course of our visual ray as because we do not bring our minds and eyes to bear on them; for there is no power to see in the eye itself, any more than in any other jelly. We do not realize how far and widely, or how near and narrowly, we are to look.

Henry D. Thoreau

If you can see, you can see with your nose and smell with your ears.

Frederick Franck

Contents

Acknowledgments

For reading the manuscript with critical eyes and providing many valuable suggestions, I especially thank ecologist Dr. Richard Brewer, professor of biology at Western Michigan University; forest pest specialist Roger Mech and state silviculturist William J. Mahalak, both of the Michigan Department of Natural Resources; and Dr. Willard M. Rose, botanist and director of the Kalamazoo Nature Center, Kalamazoo, Michigan. Final responsibility for the accuracy and interpretation of factual material remains, of course, my own.

Working with illustrator Amelia Hansen was a joy from start to finish. The privilege of engaging this talented artist as my consultant and collaborator was a stroke of luck for which I shall always be grateful.

Of vital help in collecting and photographing specimens in a variety of areas and habitats was Jacqueline Ladwein, teacher, naturalist, and cherished friend.

For my companion Susan Woolley Stoddard, who typed endless text drafts so efficiently and who has enlarged my life in so many caring ways, words fail—for the fourth time—to express my gratitude.

Others who contributed in important ways to this project include Joy Andrews, Sally Atwater, Jennifer Byrne, Don Hennig, Greg Kowalewski, Janea Little, and William J. Mills.

Introduction

It is one thing to recognize a plant or animal. It is another to know where to look for it, to become familiar with its ways of life, to achieve a sense of its links to other organisms and its existence as a community dweller.

Providing the name and identifying the features of a plant or animal are the concerns of field guides. Many excellent ones now exist. But as environmental awareness increases and more of us become vitally interested in the "planet part of ourselves," we develop a need to reach beyond that first step. We want to know something more. We want to understand this life form not only as an individual but also as an interdependent element of its habitat.

That's the focus of this book: to explore the details of certain organisms and their communities (including the human community) and to advance beyond the scope and intentions of the field guide.

Plants form the ultimate base of the food and energy chains upon which all organisms depend. Forest and edge plants, the subjects of this book, are the foundation of particular plant habitats. Forests may be broadly divided into woodlands composed of coniferous, deciduous, or mixed species (the terms forest and woodland are used interchangeably in this book). Or, on the basis of moisture, they can be classified as moist, mesic, or dry. Forest plants are stratified into various, rather distinct levels: tall trees, understory trees and shrubs, a ground layer of low shrubs and herbs, and the all-important subsurface flora of fungi.

Except on wooded shorelines fronting lakes or streams, a forest is almost always bounded by an edge. Edges are border zones, transition areas, between forest and open land, including openings in the forest itself. Dominant edge species consist mainly of shrubs and small trees that generally tolerate much less shade than forest plants. Edge plants are often pioneering species, characteristic of young stages in plant succession. Edges are by definition unstable. They form the "front line" of the forest and are major players in the process by which open land becomes forested.

The plants covered here characterize most forest and edge habitats of northeastern and north-central North America. Accounts focus not only on features of the plant itself but also on its existence as a community hub for other organisms and processes. Plant and animal coactions—that is, the effects of one species upon another—range through parasitic, commensal, competitive, and mutualistic relationships. Most often the interactions are not rigidly exclusive to the organisms involved, yet some species have evolved highly specific coactions. Examples from all parts of this continuum abound in this book.

Such host-specific organisms as leaf-spot fungi, powdery mildews, aphids, and scale insects are almost universally present on plants. Thus, except in cases where these organisms are especially conspicuous or important, they are generally omitted in the separate accounts. Many other common associates, such as lichens, mosses, and many kinds of fungi, seed plants, and insects, are not host-specific or coactive to a sufficient degree to warrant inclusion. Such organisms are nevertheless important habitat residents.

Herb, *shrub*, and *tree* are general and ultimate size designations; shrubs and trees are woody, herbs are not. Technical biological terms, though kept to a minimum, are usually defined at the places they occur in the text. A short list of recurring terms appears in the glossary at the end of the book. Latin names are added only for plant and invertebrate animal species, since these are the organisms whose common or popular names most often lead to confusion. I have personally inspected all the plants as well as the large majority of other organisms mentioned. With few exceptions, the illustrations were drawn from field specimens I collected or photographed.

Thorough treatments, of course, really don't exist in science. The totality of accomplished field investigations to date into the lives and associates of many plants—even some very common ones—often amounts to very little. This book scratches at only a few of the known and more visible surfaces. Plenteous opportunity exists for individual observers to add to our understanding by the simple investment of time and notice. The aim of this book is to help one take such time and notice.

If you enjoy being outdoors, enjoy finding, watching, enlarging your own scope of vision and vision of life . . . this book, my friends, is for you.

Anemone, Wood *(Anemone quinquefolia).* Buttercup family. Herb in moist woods and dry or mesic prairie. Its white, solitary flower and deeply divided three- or five-part leaves identify this delicate spring perennial.

Other names: Windflower, mayflower, nimble weed, wood flower.

Close relatives: Thimbleweeds *(Anemone)*; hepaticas *(Hepatica)*; buttercups *(Ranunculus)*; baneberries *(Actaea)*; rue anemone *(Anemonella thalictroides).*

Lifestyle: An examination of the bisexual flower shows that its apparent petals (usually five or six) are actually sepals (bracts that underlie the petals in most wildflowers); real petals are absent.

Wood anemone, one of the earliest spring flowers, thrives colonially in the sunlit woodland floor, which will later be shaded by the tree canopy. The light-sensitive flowers close at night or on cloudy days and are thus limited to insect pollinators that are active in the daytime. (Many other white flowers attract night-flying moths.) The flowers last about two weeks.

Flowerless anemone plants often have a single leaf of five leaflets; the flowering plants show three sets of three leaflets. This difference reveals the plant's means of energy conservation. It concentrates its dominant growth activity on either vegetative or reproductive forms.

Associates: *Spring.* Look for wood anemones at the same times and places as other woodland ephemerals, including hepaticas, spring beauty, and trout lily.

Golden-brown, pilelike growths on leaf surfaces indicate the feeding of *Eriophyes* mites.

Pollinators are primarily early-appearing wild bees and beelike flies.

Lore: Anemones are linked in mythology with the wind (the name derives from *anemos,* the Greek word for "wind"); just why remains obscure, unless this name refers to the flower's windlike, ephemeral existence.

They are also linked with images of human sadness. In various accounts, these flowers sprang from Venus's tears over the dead Adonis ("Where a tear has dropped, a wind-flower blows"); or, in England, from the blood of Danes slain in battle. To the ancient Chinese, anemone was a "death flower" and was used in funeral rites. A meadow species of this little flower was probably the biblical "lily" (as in "consider the lilies of the field"), with which Solomon's glory could not compare.

Ash, White *(Fraxinus americana).* Olive family. Tree in dry to moist woods. Its opposite, feather-compound leaves, deeply notched leaf scars, and narrow, winged seeds shaped like canoe paddles are good field marks.

White ash twigs are slightly compressed, especially at the leaf nodes. The grooved leafstalks are opposite on the twig.

Other name: American ash.

Close relatives: Forsythias *(Forsythia)*; privets *(Ligustrum)*; lilacs *(Syringa)*.

Lifestyle: White ash flowers are wind-pollinated and unisexual, with male and female flowers appearing on separate trees before the relatively late leaves emerge. Usually more male than female trees flower. The fruits are winged samaras or "keys" and may remain on the female tree in drooping clusters through winter.

This tree always grows singly or in small groups, often on well-drained sites along streams and on north and east slopes. Its straight, columnar trunk displays characteristic narrow, diamond-shaped bark fissures. Slightly flattened at the U-shaped leaf scars, the twig has a knobby, bonelike appearance. In the fall, starch accumulates near the terminal buds, later providing a quick surge of energy in early spring for flowering. The foliage, turned a distinctive maroon or reddish green, drops early in autumn.

White ash is moderately shade tolerant (less so as it ages), fast growing, and long-lived. It is, however, very sensitive to drought, especially in spring and early summer.

Associates: Look for white ash among those hardwood species found in dry or mesic oak–hickory forests; it appears less commonly in beech–maple woodlands.

Spring, summer. Beneath and around white ash trees are good places to hunt in early spring for morel mushrooms, especially the common morel *(Morchella esculenta)*, the thick-footed or gigantic morel *(M. crassipes)*, and the black morel *(M. angusticeps)*.

High sugar and nitrogen levels in its fallen leaves provide a rich humus for earthworms.

This tree is a favorite host of oystershell scale insects *(Lepidosaphes ulmi)*, tiny brownish sap-suckers that mass on twigs. Stunted or yellowed foliage often indicates their presence.

The ash flowergall mite *(Aceria fraxinivorus)* attacks male flowers only, leaving gall clusters that blacken and remain over winter.

Inspect the leaves for a large, green, smooth caterpillar with a rear projecting horn; this is probably the larva of either the waved sphinx *(Ceratomia undulosa)* or the great ash sphinx *(Sphinx chersis)*. Another common moth to watch for is Grote's sallow *(Copivaleria grotei)*. The adult is olive green and black.

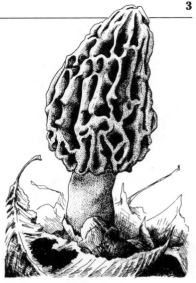

The black or narrowhead morel grows in early spring from the leaf litter beneath ash as well as other trees. Other morels beneath ash may include the common and thick-footed morels.

A reddish brown insect that closely mimics the paper wasp *(Polistes)* may be the lilac or ash borer moth *(Podosesia syringae)*, one of this tree's most destructive pests; large, scarlike outgrowths on the trunk may indicate where the caterpillars have burrowed.

Masses of whitish, caterpillarlike larvae consuming foliage in early spring likely are brown-headed ash sawflies *(Tomostethus multicinctus)*, which may defoliate entire trees.

Summer, fall. Look beneath the tree for an olive-brown pore mushroom with an off-center stem. This is probably the shallow-pore, *Boletinellus merulioides.*

Another wasplike borer, similar in appearance to the ash borer, is the banded ash clearwing *(Podosesia aureocincta)*.

Ash trees are favorite hosts of the fall webworm *(Hyphantria cunea)*, a tiger moth caterpillar that builds communal, tentlike nests enclosing the foliage at branch tips. The unsightly nests may expand to encompass several branches. They commonly remain on the tree over winter as ragged masses of silken webbing. Insect raiders on webworm nests include two hornet species, the sandhills hornet *(Vespula arenaria)* and the bald-faced hornet *(V. maculata)*. The hornets sting and carry away the caterpillars to feed to their own larvae. A small ichneumon wasp *(Hyposoter pilosulus)* enters the nest to parasitize caterpillars by inserting eggs into them; dead caterpillars in the nest may have hosted these parasites. Allegheny mound ants *(Formica exsectoides)* also raid the nests.

Winter. Dried remains of oystershell scale insects sheltering their egg masses may be visible on the bark. Blackish gall clusters of the ash flowergall mite may also remain.

All year. A large, woody bracket fungus, *Phellinus perenniporia*, often grows on dead or dying ash trees. This dark, hoof-shaped fungus is the exterior fruiting portion of a heartwood rot and indicates interior decay.

Lore: This tree's name is said to originate from the bark's ashy color.

Ash is a workhorse wood—durable material for tough tasks. Tool handles, oars, tennis rackets, skis, and furniture are some of its uses. The famed Louisville Slugger baseball bat comes from white ash stands in northern Pennsylvania and western New York. In furniture making, it is sometimes substituted for oak because of its similar color and grain.

Native Americans made canoe paddles, snowshoe frames, and sleds from ash, and it is still used for these items. It is also an excellent fuel wood and campfire starter, burning even when green because of its flammable sap.

Fall webworm nests enclosing the tips of branches are familiar sights in summer and fall, especially on ash and black walnut trees. Other insects often parasitize these nests.

In Norse mythology ash was "Ygdrasil," the tree that supported the universe. In America both natives and early pioneers were convinced that white ash leaves, when stuffed in boots or leggings, were highly offensive to rattlesnakes and prevented bites. When swallowed, a decoction of ash buds or bark was said to be a sure remedy for snakebite. No medical evidence supports these claims. Aphrodisiac effects have been claimed for the seeds.

Aspen, Quaking *(Populus tremuloides).* Willow family. Tree in open woods and thickets. Aspen is recognized by its rounded, triangular leaves and smooth whitish or greenish bark. The teeth on leaves of the closely related largetooth aspen *(P. grandidentata)* are larger and less numerous.

Other names: Trembling aspen, smalltooth aspen, poplar, popple.

Close relatives: Eastern cottonwood *(P. deltoides)*; white poplar *(P. alba)*; willows *(Salix).*

Lifestyle: Sun-loving aspen fronts the woods. The basic aspen unit is not an individual tree but a clone of trees—all arising from the same lateral root system, all of the same sex, all genetically alike. A single clone may include more than a hundred separate stems (called *ramets* or *suckers*) and may spread to more than eighty feet. A clonal group can be distinguished from a distance by its profile, that of a parabola or mound, with the oldest and tallest stems in the middle.

The flowers of both male and female clones are hanging catkins that emerge before the leaves. Pollination is accomplished by wind. Ramets begin flowering about age fifteen, producing abundant seed crops every fourth or fifth year. Aspen seeds remain viable for only a short time; they need bare, high-calcium soil with plenty of moisture for germination.

But most aspen reproduce vegetatively (that is, by means of the suckers rather than by seed). The rise of ramets from an existing root system is stimulated by clear-cutting, by browsing, or in most cases, by ground fires that destroy standing ramets.

Clonal root systems may survive indefinitely; some may be among the oldest living organisms on the planet. (A clone in Minnesota has been aged at about eight thousand years.) But individual ramets generally begin to deteriorate at thirty-five to forty-five years, though they may live to eighty. Because aspen is intolerant of shade, the spreading crown of an aging clone weeds out the shaded ramets below.

Long, flattened leafstalks, flexible as ribbons, account for the characteristic flutter of aspen leaves in a breeze. Aspen leaves have evolved some remarkable defenses against insect feeders. Triggered by an attack of insects, the leaves manufacture phenol compounds that act as natural insecticides against foraging populations.

Aspens in cold climates often show thicker, whiter bark on the south side, giving a subtle two-toned appearance to the trunks. The whiter bark provides a more reflective surface on the sun-exposed side so that the tree won't thaw on that side.

Associates: A pioneering species because of its sunlight requirement, aspen typically forms one early part of a conifer–hardwood relationship. Among northern hardwoods, for example, aspen frequently associates with the more shade-tolerant balsam fir, and both trees are gradually replaced by climax hardwoods.

Several other plants provide clues about aspen habitat: Sweetfern generally suggests a low-quality soil for aspen, whereas a tall, vigorous growth of bracken fern *(Pteridium aquilinum)* indicates suitable conditions for aspen. Witch hazel and mapleleaf viburnum also indicate good aspen sites.

Quaking and largetooth aspens are often found growing in close proximity, and occa-

Tightly crumpled, distorted leaves forming galls at twig tips indicate the presence of poplar vagabond aphids, which use the galls as feeding and egg-laying sites.

sionally they hybridize, although largetooth aspens generally prefer drier sites and usually flower a week or more later. Many plant and animal associates of aspen are common to the entire poplar genus.

Spring, summer. In very early spring, look on the ground near aspen trees for two mushrooms: the early morel *(Verpa bohemica)*, the false or beefsteak morel *(Gyromitra esculenta)*, and the black morel *(Morchella angusticeps)*.

A common whitish mushroom appearing in fan-shaped, overlapping clusters on aspen trunks, branches, and stumps is the oyster mushroom *(Pleurotus ostreatus)*, a wood decomposer.

More than three hundred insect species feed on aspen. One of the most conspicuous, the poplar vagabond aphid *(Mordwilkoja vagabunda)*, is detected by crumpled, bunchy leaves forming bladderlike galls at the twig tips. These galls, turning blackish by midsummer, host successive generations of the aphids, which return to lay eggs. Oval, cracked twig swellings indicate feeding by larvae of a longhorned beetle, *Mecas ornata.*

Spindle-shaped swellings on small branches may be caused by a clear-winged moth caterpillar, *Memythrus tricintus.*

Oval black spots on older trunks are often the overgrown egg niches of the poplar borer, *Saperda calcarata,* one of the largest longhorned beetles. The adult insect has orange stripes, and its marks on the trunk may persist through the life of the tree.

Masses of black, spiny caterpillars, each with a center row of red spots, are mourning cloak butterfly larvae *(Nymphalis antiopa),* which may defoliate entire branches. It produces two broods; spring caterpillars are the first progeny of adults that hibernated over winter.

Aspen's foremost insect pest, often defoliating acres of trees, is probably the forest tent caterpillar *(Malacosoma disstria).* Irruptions of this insect, at approximate ten- to sixteen-year intervals, are recorded back to 1790. Masses of bluish caterpillars feed on the leaves, leaving silken mats on trunks or branches. The adult female moth encircles twigs with shiny, square-cornered bands of eggs. Often during outbreaks, a large gray flesh fly *(Sarcophaga aldrichi),* which parasitizes the caterpillar cocoons, becomes abundant.

The gypsy moth is another destructive foliage feeder (see Red Oak).

Numerous other moth caterpillars feed on aspen leaves, including the big poplar or modest sphinx *(Pachysphinx modesta)*, with a short rear horn, and the poplar tentmaker *(Ichthyura inclusa)*, which webs several leaves together. The large aspen tortrix *(Choristoneura conflictana)* is a leaf-rolling caterpillar that causes periodic widespread defoliation.

Large viceroy butterfly caterpillars *(Limenitis archippus)*, with two hornlike projections behind the head, are also seen.

Hairy woodpeckers often excavate nest holes in living aspens. Yellow-bellied sapsuckers prefer trees infected with *Phellinus* heartrot.

For porcupines, aspen foliage is a choice summer food. The thin branch tips where the most nutritious leaves are crowded cannot support the animal's weight, so it often nips these twigs, holding them in its paws until it eats the leaves. Look for these nipped twigs, often with leafstalks intact and only the blades eaten, beneath the trees. Earlier in the season, aspen catkins provide the protein-starved porcupine its first green food of the year.

A Nectria canker resembles a concentric target. *Its shape is a result of differential growth of wood tissue and the canker fungus as both enlarge, eventually weakening the trunk.*

Black bears often climb into the treetops after aspen leaves, an important spring food source.

Late summer, fall. Mushrooms growing beneath aspens at this time may include the reddish orange aspen scaberstalk *(Leccinum aurantiacum)*; the pinkish-gray yellow foot *(Tylopilus chromapes)*; and *Suillus subaureus.* All are pore fungi. The yellowish, many-branched crown coral mushroom *(Clavicorona pyxidata)* is common on decaying aspen, as are several gill mushrooms. The oyster mushroom may also reappear in late fall.

Winter. On twigs, look for egg masses of the forest tent caterpillar.

Aspen is an important winter wildlife food. Twigs and foliage are heavily browsed by white-tailed deer, elk, and moose. Snowshoe hares gnaw the bark.

Buds and catkins are favored foods of the ruffed grouse, and these birds often forage in aspen groves. (Once in the woods I found evidence of owl predation; all that remained was

Gnawed trunks and abundant wood chips on the ground are marks of beaver work on aspen. Aspen provides the main food and construction resources for these animals.

scattered grouse feathers and a neat pile of aspen buds. The owl had eaten all of the bird except the contents of its crop.) Ruffed grouse range closely coincides with that of aspen.

All year. Two common canker fungi that attack living aspens are *Hypoxylon mammatum* and *Nectria galligena. Hypoxylon*, the major disease of aspen, appears as yellowish, sunken areas on the trunk marked by vertical cracks or black, blisterlike patches. *Nectria*, also called target canker, resembles a concentric target eaten into the tree. This canker enlarges only during cool weather; its intermittent growth, together with an edge of callus formed by the tree as it tries to heal the canker, produces the typical target appearance. Both cankers kill the tree by weakening the trunk until it eventually breaks off.

The false tinder fungus *Phellinus tremulae*, a hoof-shaped bracket found on trunks and indicating heartrot, causes more loss of timber than any other hardwood destroyer. It frequently occurs on aspen.

Except during winter months, aspen is harvested by beavers for food. They also use harvested trees as a building material for lodges and dams. (One study showed that an acre of aspens could support a colony of five beavers for three years.) Depletion of aspens seems to be the main reason for abandonment of beaver colonies.

Lore: Aspen parkland forms a wide transition between prairie and boreal forest regions. Indeed, quaking aspen has the widest continental range of any tree in North America, growing from the tree line in Canada to northern Mexico.

Aspen's major commercial use is pulpwood for book and magazine papers; its clonal sprouting and fast growth make this tree a valuable cash crop. The soft, weak wood also provides materials for crating, matches, excelsior, and interior trim.

Native Americans used aspen primarily for medicinal purposes. Like the related willows, bitter aspen bark contains salicin, an ingredient of modern aspirin. Solutions of the bark were used much as we use aspirin, for treating colds, fevers, coughs, menstrual pain. The Crees also used the sweetish inner bark for food, and the Chippewas tapped the tree for sap.

Asters (*Aster* spp.). Composite family. Herbs. Various species of this perennial occupy almost every sort of wet and dry habitat, though most are sunloving and grow in open or edge areas. Prominent woodland species include the white wood aster *(A. divaricatus)*, with white ray flowers and an often zigzag stem; the heart-leaved or blue wood aster *(A. cordifolius)*; Lowrie's aster *(A. lowrieanus)*, with winged leafstalks; and the large-leaved aster *(A. macrophyllus)*, with violet or white ray flowers and large, coarse basal leaves.

Other names: Wild aster, Michaelmas daisy.

Close relatives: Goldenrods *(Solidago)*; fleabanes *(Erigeron)*; and all other composites.

Lifestyle: More than sixty-five North American species exist, and they widely hybridize.

The bisexual flower heads are dominantly female since the ray flowers bear only pistillate (female) flower parts; the tubular disk flowers in the center bear both stamens (male) and pistils. A hand lens helps show this flower arrangement.

In woodland asters, there is a much greater proportion of stem and foliage to flower clusters, in contrast to the reverse situation seen in meadow asters. Such divergent ratios reflect the plant's concentration of energy; in woodland asters, the reproductive parts are less vital than the vegetative structures necessary to maintain their population stability in shaded forest environments.

The roots are good soil binders.

Associates: *Summer.* The needle blister rust *(Coleosporium asterum)* appears as bright, orange-yellow pustules on leaf undersides. This club fungus parasitizes two- and three-needle pines as alternate hosts.

Several species of gall gnat larvae produce galls on flowers, buds, leaves, and stems.

A common insect on asters (as well as on many other plants) is the buffalo treehopper *(Stictocephala)*, which sucks plant juices.

Skeletonized leaves may indicate the presence of butterfly caterpillars that forage in groups on the plants. The Harris' checkerspot *(Melitaea harrisii)*, orange and black, often feeds on flat-topped white aster *(A. umbellatus)*. The silvery checkerspot *(M. nycteis)* is recognized by its dark and orange stripes and its barbed spines. The tawny crescent *(Phyciodes batesii)*, spiny and darkly nondescript, feeds mainly on the wavy-leaved aster *(A. undulatus)*. And the extremely common pearl crescent *(P. tharos)*, found feeding on New England aster *(A. novae-angliae)*, is spiny and black with yellow dots and side stripes. Also look for the latter's layered egg masses on the leaves.

Honeybees *(Apis mellifera)* forage on several aster species.

Although a few bird species consume the seeds and several mammals graze the foliage, asters are not major food plants for wildlife.

Lore: The word *aster* comes from a Greek word meaning "star," as in *asterisk.* The flower was considered a sacred emblem in the pantheon of Greek divinities.

Young leaves of the large-leaved aster, said to make palatable cooked greens, were eaten by the Chippewas. For human food, however, the most important woodland asters are two major nectar and honey producers: the heart-leaved aster and the whorled or wedge-leaved aster *(A. acuminatus)*.

Balsam Fir *(Abies balsamea)*. Pine family. Tree in moist woods, bottomlands. This conifer has flat, unstalked needles with two white stripes beneath. Its form is typically steeple shaped.

Close relatives: Firs *(Abies)*; Douglas fir *(Pseudotsuga menziesii)*; spruces *(Picea)*; hemlocks *(Tsuga)*; tamaracks *(Larix)*; pines *(Pinus)*.

Lifestyle: The leaves (needles) usually appear horizontally two-ranked (except for needles higher in the tree or exposed to direct sunlight—these project in all directions like spruce needles), but they are actually spirally arranged around the twig. Balsam needles have a broad circular base and, when removed, leave the twig smooth. They remain on the tree about four years. Chemicals in the needles give this tree a unique defense against insect feeders; they mimic a growth hormone that interferes with normal insect metamorphosis. Obviously this defense doesn't work against *all* insects. Resins in the cone apparently have some deterrent effect against seed feeding by crossbills and red squirrels.

Both male and female cones occur on the topmost branches of a single tree. Although the tree produces seed annually, an abundance of cones appears only at two- to four-year intervals.

This tree is highly shade tolerant in the forest understory, but its shallow root system—seldom deeper than three feet—makes it vulnerable to drought.

Balsam gall midge larvae, which feed inside the galls, produce round swellings on the needles. Also look for small, parasitic wasps that invade the galls.

Associates: Balsam usually grows in

mixed stands with white spruce, quaking aspen, and white birch.

Spring, summer. Curled or twisted needles and swollen twig ends are signs of aphids, several species of which prey on this tree.

Swollen galls at the needle bases are formed by balsam gall midge larvae *(Dasineura balsamicola)*; when galls are present, look for tiny black wasps *(Platygaster)* that parasitize the larvae.

Notched needles may indicate feeding of the hemlock looper *(Lambdina fiscellaria)*, a greenish yellow geometer moth caterpillar. These caterpillars feed from the top of the tree downward. The brownish adult moths deposit eggs on bark and needles.

Balsam's chief insect pest—and a normal part of its ecology—is the spruce budworm *(Choristoneura fumiferana)*, a reddish brown tortricid moth caterpillar. Signs include defoliated or top-killed trees or browning needles loosely webbed together, which give the tree

Blisters on balsam bark contain the clear resin known as Canada balsam. Sometimes the blisters break and the flowing resin evaporates on the trunk, leaving whitish residues.

a tangled, messy appearance. Later the brownish pupa wraps itself lengthwise to a twig by fine silken strands. Epidemics of these needle eaters have killed thousands of trees in spruce and balsam stands. During such outbreaks, watch for dramatic increases in local bird populations attracted to the abundant food supply. Cape May warblers, uncommon at other times, will often show up during budworm years.

In dead or dying balsam firs, piles of sawdustlike chaff around the tree base indicate wood-feeding larvae of the balsam fir sawyer *(Monochamus notatus)*, a longhorned beetle.

Tufts of dead needles along with defoliated lengths of twig usually suggest the gregarious feeding of larval sawflies. Balsam fir sawfly larvae *(Neodiprion abietis)*, green with brown stripes, resemble moth caterpillars.

Yellow-rumped warblers frequently nest in balsam fir, and evening grosbeaks often nest in the tops of fifteen- to twenty-foot trees. The nests of both may remain long after the birds have left.

Winter. Balsam needles are a favorite food of spruce and sharp-tailed grouse. Look for partially denuded twigs with needle bases still attached.

Neatly edged, gnawed patches of bark are signs of porcupine feeding.

Cropped twigs with raggedly bitten ends give away the white-tailed deer that have browsed them. Since balsam is a "starvation food" for deer, these signs may indicate a poor supply of preferred deer browse in the area. For moose, on the other hand, balsam is a favorite and nourishing food. A flat-bottomed browse line of foliage, generally quite high, results when deer or moose stretch to feed.

All year. A bracket fungus on the upper trunk may signify red heartrot *(Stereum sanguinolentum)*, one of balsam's chief invaders.

Lore: Clear, aromatic resin accumulates on balsam bark beneath raised blisters, which are easily punctured with a fingernail. This is Canada balsam, a pharmaceutical ingredient, once used for cementing microscope lenses and mounting specimens on microscope slides. Woodsmen used this resin as a wound plaster and waterproof cement. Sweetened, it once sold as a confection. Not the tastiest stuff, balsam pitch is nevertheless a concentrated, nourishing food and can provide an emergency ration if needed.

Native Americans inhaled the melted pitch as a headache remedy and treated burns and wounds with it. Mixed with bear grease, it also served as a hair dressing.

Balsam's weak, soft wood is used as pulpwood and crate stock. It's ideal for starting a fire by friction, but as fuel, it spits sparks. This tree's main economic value, however, owes largely to Christmas; some thirty percent of all trees cut and sold for the holiday season are balsams. Shock shearing—removal of lower branches and knife-scarring of bark—stimulates bud development and thicker foliage. The balsam holds its aromatic needles indoors much longer than spruce.

Baneberry, White *(Actaea alba).* Buttercup family. Herb in rich woods. This plant is most conspicuous in late summer, when its oblong terminal clusters of china-white berries on red stalks, each berry tipped with a dark spot, decorate the forest floor.

Other names: Doll's eyes, cohosh, necklaceweed, white beads, toadroot.

Close relatives: Buttercups *(Ranunculus)*; anemones *(Anemone)*; hepaticas *(Hepatica).*

Lifestyle: The white, bisexual flowers, blooming in May and June, contain no nectar but produce plenty of pollen, which attracts bees.

All parts of this perennial, especially roots and berries, contain a poisonous cardiac glycoside.

Associates: *Spring.* Most of the bees seen on baneberry flowers are halictid species (which include the "sweat bees" that hover around our faces and arms on warm days).

These semicolonial ground nesters collect pollen for feeding their larvae.

Summer, fall. Baneberry is not a major food for wildlife. Only a few eaten berries may cause severe dizziness and nausea in humans, but ruffed grouse, yellow-bellied sapsuckers, and American robins consume at least small numbers of berries, as do white-footed mice and red-backed voles, with no ill effects.

Observers note that toads seem attracted by the plant's odor.

Lore: This plant's name warns of a baneful experience for those who partake of its fruit. But those black-tipped white berries also gave the plant its other familiar name, doll's eyes; the berries were said to resemble the ceramic eyes that peer from the heads of old-fashioned china dolls. The berries yield a black dye when crushed and mixed with alum.

A few Native American tribes very cautiously drank decoctions of leaves and roots to ease the pain of rheumatism, to induce milk secretion, and to stop excessive menstrual flow.

White baneberry fruits ("doll's eyes") are conspicuous features of the forest herb layer in late summer. Though poisonous to humans, they are eaten by several birds and mammals.

Barberries *(Berberis* spp.). Barberry family. Low shrubs in dry woods, thickets. Usually wider than tall, these spiny, stiff-branched bushes display bright red berries in the fall. Varieties of ornamental Japanese barberry *(B. thunbergii),* widely planted for hedge borders, often escape to woods and thickets. The European barberry *(B. vulgaris)* also frequently escapes from yards and gardens. American barberry *(B. canadensis),* our only native species, is found mainly in the Appalachians.

Other name: Pepperidge bush.

Close relatives: Mayapple *(Podophyllum peltatum);* blue cohosh *(Caulophyllum thalictroides).*

Lifestyle: Its yellow, bisexual flower is probably barberry's most curious feature. This flower has a spring trap—it does not capture the insect but rather explodes a pollen shower

The horizontal alignment of barberry stems and leaves exposes the foliage to maximum sunlight. The three-pronged spines at leaf bases help protect the plant from browsers.

upon it. The male stamens, tipped with pollen containers (anthers), are held under tension by the enclosing curve of the petals. As the insect probes in the orange nectaries at the base of each petal, its movements cause the stamen filament rising from each gland to spring inward, hitting either the insect or the central female pistil, releasing a cloud of pollen over the insect. A bee may be thus "flogged" as many as six times before it gets out, for each stamen can spring independently. You can trigger this action by inserting a pin or toothpick into the base of the flower and watching it snap inward. The mechanism resets itself in several minutes.

Barberry does best in full sunlight but is also moderately shade tolerant. Note that the leaves are sized and spaced differently along the spur branches, so that the entire shrub presents a uniform foliage surface to the sun.

Associates: *Spring.* American and European barberry leaves are original hosts for the wheat black stem rust *(Pucinia graminis)*, which is highly injurious to wheat *(Triticum aestivum)*. The rust appears as orange-red spotting on upper leaf surfaces and as yellowish waxy masses on leaf undersides. After parasitizing barberry, the rust spores are released to the wind. Those that germinate on wheat go through a several-stage process, ending with a spore release in early spring that may infect a barberry leaf and thus renew the cycle.

Summer, fall. The barberry looper *(Coryphista meadii)* is an inchworm-type moth caterpillar that skeletonizes leaves and may defoliate entire shrubs.

Webbed twigs and leaves indicate barberry webworms *(Omphalocera dentosa)*, white-spotted moth caterpillars.

There is some indication that barberry seeds are dispersed by ants.

Winter. Unsightly web masses remaining on the ends of shoots are remnant signs of the barberry webworm.

The scarlet, fleshy berries are usually consumed only when other foods are scarce; ring-necked pheasants are probably the foremost feeders. Yet most wild barberry plants have probably originated from seeds dispersed in bird droppings.

Lore: In North America, determined efforts have been made to eradicate American and European barberries, especially in wheat-growing areas. Consequently the rust-resistant

Japanese barberry is seen most frequently today, usually in hedges, gardens, or as escapes in thickets.

Though tart with malic and citric acids, the ripe berry is edible. Rich in pectin, it makes fine jelly and preserves. Europeans once cultivated barberry for its fruit.

For medieval Italians, it was not the berry but the thorn that mattered most. The sets of three-pronged spines (which in this plant are modified leaves) signified the Trinity. This "Holy Thorn" was believed to have formed part of the crown of thorns placed on Jesus at the crucifixion (see also Hawthorns).

The yellow wood and bark contain berberine, an alkaloid that produces a yellow dye. Berberine is also a mild astringent and antiseptic. Some Native American tribes applied a mash of pulverized roots to mouth sores. A tea made of roots and stems was taken for stomach ulcers.

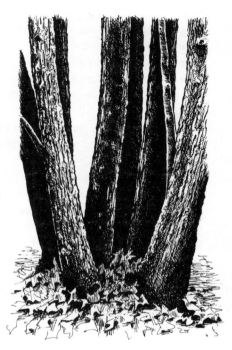

Multiple trunks that began as sprouts from an older tree or stump are a frequent growth form of basswood. The long, oval shape of the foliage crown is often distinctive from a distance.

Basswood, American *(Tilia americana).* Linden family. Tree in moist woods. The large, heart-shaped leaves with lopsided bases, the cream-yellow, fragrant flowers, and the pea-size nutlets attached to distinctive leafy wings are the key identifying marks.

Other names: Linden, lime tree, whitewood.

Lifestyle: This tree sprouts prolifically from its stumps; a characteristic growth form is a circular clump of trunks surrounding the remnants of a stump.

Bisexual flowers oozing with nectar appear after the leaves emerge in June.

The flowers draw hordes of bees and other insects that create a "humming tree" audible from many yards away. Flower clusters hang from specialized, ribbonlike bracts, which remain and often dangle the nuts into midwinter. Due to their hard seed coats, the nuts do not germinate quickly, but they can remain viable for several years. Basswood begins flowering at about age fifteen, thereafter producing a seed crop almost every year.

Roots plunge deep and wide; this tree is rarely upended by wind. Twigs, somewhat zigzagged, produce a rounded crown of leaves that overlap like roof shingles. In the fall those big leaves turn mottled yellow and drop, adding a rich assortment of minerals—calcium, magnesium, nitrogen, potassium, phosphorus—to the soil. Basswood buds, lopsided on the twig and red or sometimes two-tone red and green, provide a jot of color during winter's monochrome.

Shade tolerant when young, basswood becomes less so as it ages.

Associates: Look for basswood in mixture with other hardwoods, especially sugar maple and white ash.

Spring, summer. Basswood's broad leaves form tablet sheets for the distinctive signs and marks of a host of organisms. By midsummer, the result is an "experienced" foliage often torn, sticky, perforated, and otherwise used by life.

Leaf mines are common. Small, rectangular tent mines on leaf undersides are made by larvae of the polygon leaf miner *(Lithocolletis lucetiella)*. In contrast to most leaf miners, this one feeds from the leaf edge in, like a floor painter working toward the center of the room. Circular tent mines on leaf upper sides are formed by *Lithocolletis tiliacella*, another tiny gracilariid moth. Large, blisterlike, conjoining mines on leaf undersides result from larval feeding of the basswood leaf miner *(Baliosus ruber)*, a leaf beetle; the reddish, wedge-shaped adult beetles skeletonize leaves. Small blotch mines of *Brachys* larvae, a buprestid beetle, are formed on veins toward the leaf's outer perimeter. You can sometimes hear them inside the mines when they twitch their bodies rapidly.

Basswood leaf galls, also numerous, include top-shaped swellings on upper surfaces caused by the linden gall mite *(Eriophyes abnormis)*; hairy, circular galls or light brown patches near leaf veins, also caused by gall mites *(E. tiliae* or *E. liosoma)*; and wartlike galls on leaf surfaces, indicating the gall gnat larva *Cecidomyia verrucicola.*

Look for yellow and black linden aphids *(Eucallipterus tiliae)*, often abundant on leaf undersides. A side effect of aphid feeding is a black, crustlike growth appearing on leaves and twigs, the sooty mold fungus *Fumago vagans*, which colonizes the aphids' honeydew secretions.

Several moth caterpillars called inchworms or loopers include the yellowish spring cankerworm *(Paleacrita vernata)* and the elm spanworm *(Ennomos subsignarius)*. Also called the snowwhite linden moth and linden looper, the elm spanworm has bright red head and tail segments. The delicately beautiful, pure white adult moths often migrate for long distances. (The house sparrow was brought to America in 1850 as a biological control on these and similar spanworms). A related linden looper *(Erannis tiliaria)* is bright yellow with longitudinal lines.

Camouflaged caterpillars of the night-feeding yellow-banded underwing moth *(Catocala cerogama)* are often abundant on basswood.

A colorful caterpillar with white tufts on the back and a pair of pencillike horns at the head is the white-marked tussock moth, a pest of many shade trees (see Gray Dogwood). Rolled leaves in late summer are signs of the basswood leafroller *(Pantographa limata)*; this bright green tortricid moth caterpillar feeds on the inner rolls of the tube it constructs.

Swellings on basswood twigs may be galls formed by larvae of the linden bark gall fly *Agromyza tiliae.* Linden twig gall gnat larvae *(Cecidomyia citrina)* make galls on twigs, leaf stalks, or terminal buds.

The linden looper, also called elm spanworm, is an inchworm-type moth caterpillar common on basswood, elm, and several other trees. Infestation of this insect was the reason for importing house sparrows to America, a biological control measure that failed.

Bees are basswood's main pollinators. Look and listen at hollows in old trees; they provide superb animal dens and hive space for wild honeybees *(Apis mellifera)*.

Basswood leaves are a favored summer food of porcupines.

Fall. Counterpart of the spring cankerworm is the fall cankerworm *(Alsophila pometaria)*. Like most geometrid caterpillars, they often drop from foliage on a silken thread, then climb up again.

The basswood leafroller moves to another leaf in the fall, not rolling this one but merely folding in the edge. Here, in the fallen leaf, it passes the winter.

Trees injured by fire, wind, or ice often become infected by various heartrot fungi. A common one on basswood is the yellow cap *(Pholiota adiposa)*, a scaly, yellowish mushroom.

Winter. Look for neatly girdled twigs remaining on the tree or on the ground; a deeply cut groove surrounds the twig, and transverse slits in the bark are obvious on both sides of the groove. This is the work of an adult longhorned beetle *(Oncideres cingulata)*, the twig girdler; in late summer and fall, it lays eggs on the twig tips before grooving the twig.

Basswood twigs are relished by cottontail rabbits and white-tailed deer; the bitten-off ends will tell which animal nipped it (see Blackberry). Cottontails and porcupines may also gnaw the bark.

All year. The saprot polypore *(Polyporus resinosus)*, a woody pore fungus growing shelflike on the tree, indicates heartrot in the trunk.

Lore: "Say your vows under linden boughs." In ancient mythology this tree symbolized wedded bliss and conjugal love among the gods.

Early French explorers in America called this tree *bois blanc* ("white wood"), also giving the name to two islands in the Great Lakes region where basswood grew. The tree's English name is a corruption of "bast wood," referring to the fibrous inner bark, or bast, which was used for cordage and matting. Berlin's famous avenue Unter den Linden was named for the rows of European basswood *(T. vulgaris)*, a smaller species, that lined it.

Native Americans shredded the bark of young shoots for twine, matting, and baskets. Pioneer farmers used twisted sections of the tough bark as binding for hauling logs.

Hardly a finer honey exists than that produced from basswood flowers; gourmets regard its slightly minty flavor as exquisite. The flowers have other uses as well. Euell Gibbons, who made a profession of sampling pine trees, catkins, and corms for food, advertised the pleasures—not only in the cup but also in the bath—of a hot tea called *tilleul* steeped from dried basswood blossoms. Tilleul is a mild sedative and, like countless herbal teas, is reputed to calm your hysteria, balm your body, and ease your insomnia and cramps. The leaf buds can also be eaten.

Carvers like to use this soft wood. Commercially, basswood is the main source of excelsior shavings and is also used in light articles, such as crates, comb honey frames, berry baskets, and yardsticks. Exported basswood lumber is used for house flooring in Japan, since shoes are not worn indoors and pillows are used instead of chairs.

Beech, American *(Fagus grandifolia)*. Beech family. Tree in moist woods. Its smooth, steel-gray bark and the leaves with parallel veins extending to the even, marginal teeth make it immediately recognizable.

Close relatives: American chestnut *(Castanea dentata)*; oaks *(Quercus)*.

Lifestyle: Unisexual, wind-pollinated flowers appear on the same tree soon after the leaves emerge. The yellowish green male flowers hang in globular clusters on long stems, while the short-stemmed female flowers are urn shaped. The triangular nuts—usually two encased in a small, prickly bur—are known as *mast*, but many nuts contain no meat or seed.

A dozen or more saplings often sprout from the roots of a mature tree; probably most forest stands are colonized mainly by this means. Slow growing, shallow rooted but with a deep taproot, and very shade tolerant, beech begins producing seed at about age ten, and good mast crops generally occur only once in three to five years. Beech thrives best on limy soils with upper-level soil moisture. Its presence often indicates—and helps maintain—a rich forest-surface flora. A single tree may live for three hundred to four hundred years.

Beech is as thin-skinned as it looks; the tree is highly vulnerable to frost cracking and fire damage. Roots are susceptible to drought and to such damage as occurs when vehicles are driven near the trees. Beech's smooth trunk also tempts those who like to carve their initials on bark (an excellent way of introducing wood-rot fungi into a tree). Because beech saplings are so highly light-responsive *(phototropic)*, even small differences of light intensity may pull the stem to one side or another, accounting for the crooked trunks of many beeches.

Sharp-pointed, inch-long buds unroll like spindles to produce the potash-rich, calcium-poor leaves. In autumn the leaves turn a lustrous "clear leather color, like a book bound in calf," said Thoreau. Many young beeches hang on to their leaves, which bleach to almost white, over winter.

Associates: Beech typically grows in association with sugar maple, a partnership that forms one of the chief climax forest types of the northern deciduous biome. Beech–maple forests may exist in almost pure stands, but often they also contain American basswood, yellow birch, Eastern hemlock, and occasional others.

Ecologists have found that in many beech–maple forests, one of the two species dominates the canopy while the other dominates the understory, which then slowly rises to replace the canopy species. Seedlings of each species seem to thrive best under the canopy of the other. Thus these forests maintain a continual state of oscillation between the two canopy-dominant species. You won't see this process operating in every beech–maple woodland, but check it out. Just as often, perhaps, you'll see fairly pure stands of one tree in close proximity to stands of the other, with beech preferring drier upland sites.

Spring, summer. A pore mushroom with a red-orange cap growing beneath beeches may be a bittersweet bolete *(Tylopilus ballouii)*. On the tree itself may grow silky sheath mushrooms *(Volvariella bombycina)* and slimy armillarias *(Armillaria mucida)*, both gill fungi. Look for overlapping masses of whitish, fan-shaped gill mushrooms with inrolled edges growing on rotting or dead wood; these are oyster mushrooms *(Pleurotus ostreatus)*. Shiny black fungous beetles often inhabit the gills of this species.

Another insect-fungus association on beech is the beech scale *(Cryptococcus fagisuga)* and the bark canker *(Nectria coccinea)*. The yellowish scale insects—all females—secrete a cottony "wool," which coats masses of them. The minute wounds they cause in the inner bark tissue provide entry for the canker spores, which produce clusters of white or red pustules, then deeply depressed cankers, in branches and twigs. This canker is absolutely dependent on the scale insects and can invade the tree only after they have fed on the spot for a year.

A leaf-eating moth caterpillar, the saddled prominent *(Heterocampa guttivitta)*, shows a brown saddle on its greenish body and a long-pointed tail.

Wherever beech grows you are likely to find beech-drops, a parasitic plant that derives its nourishment from beech roots. The lower flowers on the stem remain closed and are self-fertilized. The base of the plant (inset) has many threadlike rootlets.

One always looks for rare or unusual associates, and a prize sighting for the beech-watcher is a small, brownish butterfly with bluish green underwings. The early hairstreak *(Erora laeta)* is well camouflaged and flies fast. Look for it alighting on bare ground along trails or around the trees themselves. The caterpillars are small, green, and grublike.

Beech trees are favored sites for the cavity nests of tufted titmice and the open nests of Acadian flycatchers. Red-shouldered hawks often build their large nests in high crotches of the tree.

Fall. The oyster mushroom also fruits in the fall.

One of beech's most conspicuous associates is an odd, stiff-stemmed little plant that needs no green chlorophyll because it is parasitic upon beech roots. Leaves of beechdrops *(Epifagus virginiana)* are scalelike, and the plant itself is a ripe brown, like autumn beech leaves. The tiny flowers, yellowish or reddish, appear in the fall showing brown or purple stripes. Look for the low *cleistogamous* flowers, which never open but are self-fertilized and produce an abundance of seed.

The moth caterpillar known as the beech leaftyer *(Psilocorsis faginella)*, pinkish white in color, webs several leaves together and skeletonizes them before pupating over winter.

Depending on the size of the mast crop, beech attracts most of its bird and mammal users in the fall. Accumulations of green beechnuts beneath the tree often indicate foraging by blue jays, important dispersers and cachers of beechnuts; they drop unsound nuts to the ground after plucking them. Other frequent consumers are wood ducks, ruffed and spruce grouse, wild turkeys, tufted titmice, and rose-breasted grosbeaks. An integral part of beech ecology we will never see was the passenger pigeon. It existed in huge numbers before market hunting and forest depletion rendered it extinct by 1900. Beech and acorn mast was its staple food. Pigeons in flocks of thousands descended on these trees, devouring the sweet nuts; Aldo Leopold described their coming as "a biological storm."

So vital a food is beech mast to resident squirrels and chipmunks that a poor mast year will visibly thin their population. Eastern chipmunks store vast quantities of the nuts deep in underground burrows; gray and fox squirrels bury them singly, usually near the source. Red squirrels bury large and small caches of the nuts or store them in burrows, brush piles, or stone walls. The squirrels, including chipmunks and flying squirrels, don't wait for the nuts to drop but often go into the tree canopy to sever them (flying squirrels are active only at night and do their foraging then). The black bear, where present, is also a heavy beechnut consumer, loading up on calories for winter hibernation.

Winter. Signs of gray and fox squirrel activity, especially the excavated holes where they have retrieved buried nuts, are frequently obvious in the snow near beech trees. Bits of nutshell may be seen since the squirrel usually eats on the spot.

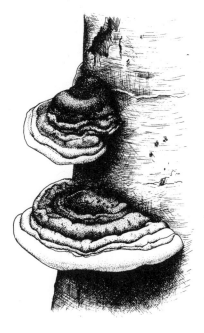

A porcupine den in the base of a beech tree is often marked by piles of scat. Gnawed patches may sometimes girdle the trees, killing them. Beech's thin bark offers easy feeding if not ideal nourishment.

Bracket fungi (Phellinus) are signs of rot inside the trunk. The concentric rings indicate periods of ample moisture, not yearly growth. Annual growth lines are visible in vertical cross-sections.

A conspicuous winter feeder is the porcupine. Look for neatly gnawed patches of bark, sometimes quite large and (if high on the trunk) next to a limb where the animal sits while feeding. Its gnawing occasionally girdles and kills the tree. Hollow-butt beeches are also favorite porcupine denning sites; piles of the distinctive, oblong scat pellets immediately identify the resident. Porcupines seem to defecate almost continuously; I have seen two-foot piles of scat dropped from inside beech dens, spilling out the ground entrance and almost plugging it up.

All year. Shelf or bracket fungi, indicating heartrot inside the trunk, are visible anytime. *Phellinus,* either rusty-hoof *(P. fomentarius)* or the false tinder fungus *(P. tremulae)*—see Quaking Aspen), is common. The large artist's fungus *(Ganoderma applanatum)*, with a smooth white undersurface on which pictures or writing may be etched, may also be seen. These pore fungi may grow from wounds in living trees as well as on dead trunks.

Dead stems of beechdrops can be found beneath the tree at any season.

Claw prints of black bears may remain on smooth-barked beech trees for several years. Bears climb the trees in the fall to consume ripening nuts, often leaving slash piles of broken branches in the tree.

More interesting by far than carved initials on the smooth, thin bark is the graffiti left there by foraging, tree-climbing mammals. The size and spacing of claw marks can identify the creature; like knife carvings, these marks remain evident for years. In black bear country, the old prints of bears are a common sight. Bears often leave messy accumulations of dead, broken branches called bears' nests high in the tree crotches where they have fed.

Lore: Deplore as we may the graffiti vandalism on trees, writing on beech bark is an ancient custom. *"Crescent illae, crescetis amores"* (as these letters grow, so may our love), wrote Latin swains. The connection between this tree and writing itself is an old one. The words *beech* and *book* apparently derive from the same Anglo-Saxon root, and in Europe at least, beech bark provided one of the earliest writing surfaces.

The "beechwood" of antiquity was a forest dark with menace and mystery (might not the curiously "eyed" appearance of bark spots and fissures in a beechwood at dusk suggest the forest watching you?), inspiring a rich tradition of European folklore. Beech is the environment of Grimm fairy tales, of Robin Hood's merry men, and of Tolkien's hobbits.

If you must shelter beneath a tree during a lightning storm, a beech might be your best choice; the oil in the wood is reputed to resist electricity. (Don't choose a very tall or isolated tree to test this theory.)

Beech lumber is used for flooring, handles, food containers, and butchers' blocks. It was especially favored for use as "bentwood" in furniture making because it was easily bent after steaming and held its shape. Bent "maple" furniture was often actually beech. For clean-burning fuel, there is hardly a better wood.

The nut, of course, is sweet and nourishing (about twenty-two percent protein), though small and hard to extract from its leathery shell. Once a primary food of gathering cultures, beechnuts were especially important in the Iroquois diet. A superior vegetable oil can be squeezed from beechnuts, and the roasted crushed kernels make a good coffee beverage.

Bellworts *(Uvularia* spp.). Lily family. Herbs in moist woods, thickets. These spring ephemerals show nodding, bell-like, yellow flowers. Parallel-veined leaves occur in different arrangements for three main species: perfoliate bellwort *(U. perfoliata)*, large-flowered bellwort *(U. grandiflora)*, and wild oats or sessile bellwort *(U. sessilifolia)*.

Other names: Merrybells, straw bell.

Close relatives: Lilies *(Lilium)*; Canada mayflower *(Maianthemum canadense)*; Solomon's seals *(Polygonatum)*; trilliums *(Trillium)*; trout lilies *(Erythronium)*; greenbriers *(Smilax)*; onions *(Allium)*.

Lifestyle: Perfoliate and sessile bellworts prefer acid soils, but the large-flowered species thrives best in limy soils. Bellworts rarely gang together like spring beauty or violets. Instead, these solitary plants rise inconspicuously from slender perennial rhizomes amidst the mosaic of the showier crowds.

Probably because its flower dangles rather than presenting "wide-open sex" to the sun, bellworts give an impression of modesty. The bisexual flowers nevertheless attract pollinating insects with a slight fragrance emanating from the nectaries at the flower base. Rough, dustlike orange particles on the perfoliate's inner flower surface may aid an insect's foothold.

As a six-parted lily, the bellwort is older on the evolutionary scale than the attention-grabbers around it. Yet its method is manifestly adequate for its reproduction. Bellwort will never carpet the earth after all, and in that subtlety and grace lies its interest.

Associates: *Spring.* Bellwort's flower associates include most of the common spring woodland ephemerals, depending on the bellwort species and its particular soil preference. Look for sessile bellwort where jack-in-the-pulpit grows.

The chief pollinators are bumblebees *(Bombus)*.

Yellowish blister galls on bellwort leaves may indicate the presence of a gall gnat larva *(Cecidomyia)*.

Lore: Linnaeus, that great Swedish Adam who founded the system of scientific naming, chose bellwort's generic name because its drooping flower reminded him of the uvula that hangs from the upper palate of the human mouth (biologists, if unromantic, are hardly unimaginative).

Native Americans made an infusion from the rhizome as a backache treatment and as a massage lotion for sore muscles.

The young shoots (minus leaves) are edible when boiled like asparagus, as is the rhizome.

Bindweed, Hedge *(Convolvulus sepium)*. Morning glory family. Trailing vine in thickets, hedgerows. White or pink bell-like flowers and arrowhead-shaped leaves are its most distinctive features. Field bindweed *(C. arvensis)* is similar but has smaller flowers and leaves and usually grows in more open areas.

Other names: Great bindweed, wild morning glory, bell-bind, lady's nightcap.

Close relatives: Wild potato vine or manroot *(Ipomoea pandurata)*; sweet potato *(I. batatas)*; garden morning glory *(I. purpurea)*; dodders *(Cuscuta)*.

Lifestyle: This colorful trailing vine requires full sunlight, and its underground parts are almost as sprawling as the visible vine. Its perennial rhizome can send up new shoots many feet from the original plant, while its taproot may plunge ten feet. Any piece of the rhizome that gets cut off, as in digging or plowing, can reproduce the plant. The twining tips rotate about once every two hours, rapidly advancing until they find a support surface, usually another plant. In contrast to most twining vines, these tips turn counterclockwise.

Bindweed, so dependent on adjacent plants for support, releases poisons that may inhibit or retard the growth of such plants (a process called *allelopathy*). Plants of the amaranth family, including green amaranth or pigweed *(Amaranthus retroflexus)*, are especially affected; you will seldom find these herbs associated with bindweed. So potent is the toxin buildup in the soil that after several years bindweed eventually eliminates itself. Later, after the toxins break down, bindweed may reappear. If its site remains undisturbed, the plant will finally succumb to shading.

Bands of white or pink on the petals lead insects to the five nectaries at the flower base;

the large, showy blossom itself emits little fragrance. Flowers generally close early in the day but may open on moonlit nights when nocturnal pollinating moths can easily spot the white petals. The seed simply falls out of the pealike seed capsules and may remain viable for two decades or longer on the ground. It will also pass intact through bird or mammal digestive systems.

Associates: *Spring, summer.* Remember Edgar Allan Poe's story *The Gold Bug*? Look for that insect (not a bug but the golden tortoise beetle, *Metriona bicolor*) on hedge bindweed. The turtle-shaped adult insect may be brilliant brassy gold or may change hues to iridescence or dull yellow. Before the flowers appear, look for pinlike or larger holes in the leaves, indications of this beetle's larval feeding. The brownish, spiny larva, called a *peddler*, can easily be mistaken for a speck of mud or debris; it heaps excrement and cast-off skins on a forked tail that comes to resemble a parasol or pack, shielding the insect from predators.

Golden tortoise beetles are common feeders on hedge bindweed. Depending upon certain environmental factors, this chameleonlike beetle can change colors.

Bumblebees *(Bombus)* and honeybees *(Apis mellifera)* are the main pollinators, but watch too for sphinx moths *(Sphinx)* early or late in the day.

Caterpillars of the common spragueia moth *(Spragueia leo)* feed on the leaves.

Spindle-shaped stem galls indicate gall gnat larvae *(Lasioptera convolvuli).*

Lore: Its twining stems spiraling around other plants presumably gave this plant its common name. Its roots or rhizomes, like others of its family, have been noted for their purgative properties in herbal annals. Since a "good purge" is no longer considered a health benefit, bindweed has little current medicinal value to offer us.

Birch, White *(Betula papyrifera).* Birch family. Tree in dry or moist forests, edges. Its creamy-white bark, often peeling in strips or sheets, makes this a distinctive tree.

Other names: Canoe birch, paper birch.

Close relatives: Yellow birch *(B. alleghaniensis)*; hazelnuts *(Corylus)*; American horn-beam *(Carpinus caroliniana)*; hop hornbeam *(Ostrya virginiana)*; alders *(Alnus)*.

Lifestyle: This is essentially a boreal forest species; it doesn't thrive where average July temperatures exceed seventy degrees Fahrenheit. Red-brown saplings don't develop the papery white bark for their first decade or so. The leaves provide the best key mark at this time; their undersides are hairy in the vein angles.

Unisexual flowers, which develop in the fall, open just before the leaves emerge in spring. The male catkins, producing about 5,500,000 grains of pollen each, are long and droopy, the female ones shorter, more erect, and conelike. Female catkins are wind polli-nated.

White birch is a fire-dependent species. The small winged seeds need bare earth or rotten logs to germinate. Birch isn't a cloning tree, but its stems sprout prolifically from fire-killed stumps, and seedlings may form pure stands in fire-cleared or cut-over areas.

Along with quaking aspen, white birch marks an early, transitional phase in forest development. Although it grows best in moist bottomland openings, it is adaptable to dry, sandy soils. The tree grows fast, is relatively short-lived (sixty to eighty years), and is eventually shaded out by the succession of more stable forest species. Its shallow root system makes it vulnerable to wind-throw, and it is also very susceptible to ice damage.

Note the thin, horizontal markings in the bark; these are the lenticels—openings that admit air into the trunk. Once removed, the papery bark never rejuvenates on the tree but is replaced by dark tissue. The white, sun-reflective bark, made up of six to nine layers, is probably a cold-climate adaptation, preventing premature warming on sunny winter days.

Associates: Among its most frequent companion trees are pines, oaks, quaking aspen, and red maple. I have often found it growing near balsam fir.

Spring, early summer. During birch flowering, look for spider webs in the foliage. Recent research indicates that certain orb weavers, when young, are pollen feeders. *Araneus diadematus*, the cross or garden spider, for example, spins webs that catch floating pollen—a sort of "aerial plankton"—then eats the webs, including snared pollen. Birch pollen is a highly nutritious food for the spiderlings.

Several orders of insects encompassing hundreds of species forage on birch leaves. For most of them, white birch is only one of several food plants.

Corrugated leaf surfaces may indicate spiny witch hazel gall aphids *(Hamamelistes spinosus)*, which hatch on witch hazel, then produce six generations on birch, and finally return to lay eggs on witch hazel.

The moth caterpillars that feed on birch are too many to name. One that seems especially partial to birch, the forest tent caterpillar (see Quaking Aspen), occurs in cyclic outbreaks, sometimes defoliating acres of trees. The birch casebearer *(Coleophora fuscedinella)*, a yellowish green caterpillar, cuts holes in leaves and constructs a small cylindrical case from which it feeds. The birch skeletonizer *(Bucculatrix canadensisella)* makes twisted, whitish linear mines and skeletonizes leaves.

Leafmining insects leave their signatures by their patterns of feeding beneath the leaf epidermis. The moth larvae *Lithocolletis* and *Parornix* are common birch miners. Look too for kidney-shaped, translucent blotch mines of the birch leafminer *(Fenusa pusilla)*, a serious pest. These sawfly larvae gradually enlarge their mines until half the leaf is brown and blighted.

An efficient way to see some of the moths that lay eggs on birch is to paint patches of bark with a sugar solution, which lures the insects. Your white birch checklist could include any of the following common moths: the elm sphinx *(Ceratomia amyntor)*; the large ruby tiger *(Phragmatobia assimilans)*; the birch dagger *(Acronicta betulae)*; the chocolate prominent *(Peridea ferruginea)*; hooktips *(Drepana)*; and the infant *(Archiearis infans*—look for it flying on warm days near birch).

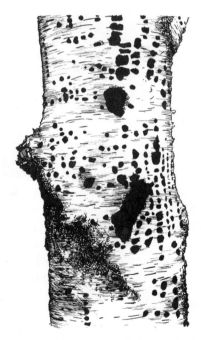

White birch's most serious insect pest is the bronze birch borer *(Agrilus anxius)*, a buprestid beetle that kills trees by larval girdling beneath the bark. Signs of its presence include reddish brown trails on bark below the point of wilting and lumpy, loosened bark caused by its tunneling.

A pitted area of holes drilled in regular horizontal rows, usually fairly high on the tree, indicates the feeding site of the yellow-bellied sapsucker. After drilling the holes, the sapsucker returns at intervals to lick up the exuded sap and any insects attracted to the flow. The ruby-throated hummingbird is a secondary feeder. Though not the only tree "tapped" by sapsuckers, white birch is a favorite.

Rows of drilled holes in trees indicate sap feeding by the yellow-bellied sapsucker. These sites are good places to watch for other birds as well as insects that come to feed from the flowing sap wells.

A tough, hoof-shaped bracket conk on birch is the false tinder fungus, the fruiting body of a heartwood rot. It is also common on aspen. The brackets enlarge and darken with age.

Several birds, notably Philadelphia vireos and black-throated green warblers, use birchbark strips for exterior nest construction.

Late summer, fall. Now is the time to look for birch-associated mushrooms. Two birch scaberstalks (*Leccinum scabrum* and *L. holopus*) are grayish or yellowish brown, scaly-capped boletes, either scattered or in groups beneath birches. Gilled mushrooms include the bright yellow-capped *Russula lutea* and the powderpuff milkcap *(Lactarius torminosus)*, a pinkish mushroom with inrolled edges; its underground mycelia form symbiotic mycorrhizae with birch roots.

Old birch logs are favored habitats for land snails.

Common foragers on the catkins include black-capped chickadees, common redpolls, pine siskins, and fox sparrows.

Winter. Squared-off crusty bands circling the twigs are the overwintering egg masses of the forest tent moth.

Pay attention now to buds and bark. Cropped buds may indicate feeding of ruffed, sharp-tailed, or spruce grouse; gnawed bark or cropped twigs may be signs of snowshoe hare, cottontail rabbit, porcupine, white-tailed deer, or moose. Size of tooth marks and telltale ends of bitten-off twigs (see Blackberry) should reveal the forager's identity.

All year. Tough, shelflike fungi are frequently seen on birch trunks, especially dead or dying ones. Leathery or woody brackets with banded upper surfaces and gill-like chambered pores beneath are probably birch maze-gills or lenzites *(Lenzites betulina)*. Hoof-shaped brackets are probably *Phellinus tremulae*, the false tinder fungus (see Quaking Aspen); a single *Phellinus* conk may signify fifteen linear feet of heartwood rot. Fruiting bodies of brown cubical rot *(Polyporus betulinus)* show smooth grayish caps with incurved margins and a porous undersurface. *Poria obliqua* emerges in black, clinkerlike masses from wounds or cankers.

A severe disease of birch is *Nectria* canker, a fungous invader that appears as dark, target-shaped depressions in the trunk. *Melanconium betulinum* is also a frequent canker. Fungus-infected trees are common foraging sites for hairy and downy woodpeckers.

White birch leaf litter, with its high sugar and nitrogen levels, is a preferred habitat of earthworms.

Lore: Probably no tree served the northern Native American tribes in so many ways as white birch. It provided sugar in the form of sap, transportation through the use of bark for canoes, medicine for stomach upsets, and dyes from the root. The Chippewas, among others, regarded the tree as sacred, strongly associated with the legendary teacher-deity-trickster figure Winabojo, who blessed the tree for the benefit of humanity. Old branch scars on the trunks are Winabojo's "thunderbirds."

The light, waterproof bark was the basic raw material for a host of domestic items, including decay-proof containers, utensils, matting for covering wigwams, torches, scrolls for

The Chippewas regarded "winged" branch scars on white birch as marks of favor from Winabojo, the tribe's deity. The scars signified the eaglelike thunderbirds that caused him to seek protection inside a hollow birch.

ritual ceremonies, and reliable tinder in the wettest weather. Except for the extensive bark sheets needed for canoes, the removal of bark did not kill the tree.

For a canoe, the tree was felled, usually in spring, when the bark was heaviest and strongest. Builders made a lengthwise cut along the trunk, then pried off the bark. This sheet was stretched around a frame of white cedar, sewn with roots of black spruce, Eastern tamarack, or jack pine, and sealed with spruce pitch. Birchbark canoes were extremely durable owing to their lightness and flexibility. (In Siberia, birch bark has been found clinging to excavated petrified wood. Long-downed birch trees in a forest often reveal the wood rotting inside the dry, still-intact bark.) Tribes established shady, level areas as regular boat yards, where generations of canoe builders worked. These were also the crafts of French voyageurs; birchbark transported them throughout northeastern North America. John McPhee theorized that the hull structure was modeled on the thoracic skeleton of vertebrates.

Today birchbark canoes are mainly an antiquarian's art, but the bark itself is still used for shelter and even clothing by northern Canadians and Scandinavians. The inner bark is edible as emergency food. A tea made of twigs and young leaves is mildly sedative and diuretic and can be used on skin rashes and acne. White birch produces excellent sap for making syrup, though not in the quantity or sweetness of sugar maple.

Modern commercial uses of white birch involve only the wood, from which small items like handles, dowels, and spools are manufactured. It is also increasingly used as pulpwood.

Birch makes an excellent firewood. As tinder in wet weather, birch bark can be a camper's best friend. No day is so damp that this bark won't flare into a blaze.

Birch, Yellow *(Betula alleghaniensis)*. Birch family. Tree in moist woodland. Its most distinctive feature is its lustrous, shiny yellowish or silver-gray bark, peeling in small ragged curls.

Other names: Gray birch, curly birch.

Close relatives: White birch *(B. papyrifera)*; hazelnuts *(Corylus)*; American hornbeam *(Carpinus caroliniana)*; hop hornbeam *(Ostrya virginiana)*; alders *(Alnus)*.

Lifestyle: This tree differs from white birch not only in appearance of the bark but also in its much wider shade and soil tolerances. Like that tree, however, it rarely forms pure stands, and in aspects of flowering and preference for cool mean temperatures, the two species are similar.

Because it often germinates on rotting stumps, yellow birch frequently shows a stilt-rooted growth form; that is, the tree perches on stiltlike roots above an empty gap where a stump has rotted away. Sprawling and twisting where they meet the ground, these thick, horizontally striped roots resemble shiny serpents.

Yellow birch must have a "clear deck" for

Stilt rooting is characteristic of yellow birch. The tree germinates especially well on rotting stumps, and after the stump perch decays, the tree remains standing on its thick props.

sprouting—either a stump or bare ground. It will not germinate in heavy leaf litter. Most mature yellow birches probably germinated after forest fires. Sniff the leaves, which turn bright yellow in fall—they're slightly aromatic. Large seed crops come at about three-year intervals, after which seedlings may form dense carpets. Smothering, competition, and mammal browsing, however, leave few survivors.

Associates: A common tree associate is Eastern hemlock, but yellow birch is also found with maples, American beech, American basswood, and Eastern white pine, among others. Although most of the plant and animal associates noted for white birch can also be found with yellow birch, the following organisms generally seem to prefer the latter.

Spring. A grayish, rectangular bug with gauzy wings is probably the birch lace bug *(Corythuca)*, a sap feeder. Look on leaf undersides for miniature stalactites of oozing plant juices covering its eggs. A peppered appearance on the leaf indicates fecal pellets of the nymph.

The maple looper *(Parallelia bistriaris)* is an inchworm caterpillar that feeds on foliage. Multihued caterpillars with humps and spiny warts are probably those of the banded purple or white admiral butterfly *(Limenitis arthemis)*. They often produce small balls of woven leaf scraps on the leaves.

Mature yellow birches are sometimes nesting sites for red-shouldered hawks.

Winter. Seed catkins, which often remain on the tree, provide an important food resource for resident birds.

Yellow birch saplings are a favorite browse of white-tailed deer; indeed, where deer are numerous, young trees will probably not survive. Look for the characteristic ragged ends of deer-nipped twigs.

All year. The target canker *Nectria galligena* is a common fungous infection of yellow birch (see Quaking Aspen). *Poria obliqua,* an associated pore fungus, often covers old cankers with matlike, spreading cushions.

Lore: The shreddy bark of yellow birch is highly combustible in any weather. This birch shares with the black birch *(B. lenta)* the odor and flavor of wintergreen in its twigs. The chemical ester involved is the same as in wintergreen. Both birches were used to make "birch beer," a root-beerlike beverage still popular in some areas. Steeped in hot water, the twigs make a refreshing tea that was well known to Native Americans. Yellow birch lumber is widely used for furniture and for high-quality veneer.

Bittersweet, American *(Celastrus scandens).* Staff-tree family. Climbing vine in open woods, thickets. Easily overlooked when green in spring and summer, this vine gives

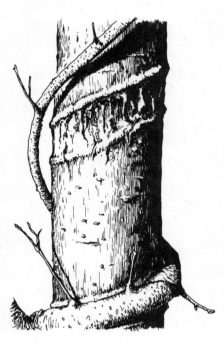

The ridged scar circling this tree trunk marks the place where a large American bittersweet vine once climbed. A living bittersweet vine now spirals up the tree.

a brilliant display of scarlet and orange fruits in fall and winter. The closely related Oriental bittersweet *(C. orbiculatus)*, widely planted as an ornamental, often escapes to woods and thickets.

Other names: False bittersweet, climbing bittersweet, waxwork, staff-tree.

Close relatives: Burning bush *(Euonymus atropurpureus)*; mountain lover *(Pachystima canbyi)*.

Lifestyle: Unlike many climbing vines, bittersweet has no tendrils to cling with; instead it spirals tightly around host stems. So snug is its clasp and so rapid its growth that it may strangle its tree or shrub support. More often, though, the wood of the host tree will simply grow around the vine, gradually embedding it. Occasionally you may observe a tree that shows the twining scars where a bittersweet climbed before it died out. It probably died out because of dense shading; this vine, though moderately shade tolerant, prefers full sun and will climb twenty to forty feet or higher to get it. Bittersweet may also sprawl and drape over the ground or low shrubbery.

Greenish white flowers are mostly unisexual on separate vines, though female plants often bear a few male flowers as well. The plant is insect pollinated and forms clones. Conspicuous fruit capsules consist of scarlet seeds partially enclosed by orange pods *(arils)*, an immediate identity mark.

Associates: *Spring, summer.* Bittersweet is seldom overrun by insect feeders, but the few that do forage on this plant may cause considerable injury and loss of vigor.

Masses of sap-sucking euonymus scale insects *(Unaspis euonymi)* may encrust stem and leaves.

Brown foliage tips may indicate the presence of a curiously humped insect, a blackish and yellow thorn mimic called the two-spotted treehopper *(Enchenopa binotata)*. Treehoppers spend their entire lives on the stems, sucking juices. Along the stems in late summer, look for cottony domes of froth deposited by female treehoppers over deep egg slits in the bark; these protective caps harden and last until the insect eggs hatch the following spring.

Fall. Although the fruits are mainly dispersed by birds, bittersweet is not a favorite wildlife food. Seeds are occasionally eaten by game birds, songbirds, and squirrels. The primary consumer (of seeds and buds) is probably the ruffed grouse.

Lore: Because of the ornamental appearance and durability of its fruits, this vine was once widely collected and sold for Christmas decorations. A generation of stern warnings against cutting has saved it; if the plant was ever in serious danger, it certainly thrives now.

Domes of hardened froth on the underside of bittersweet stems protect the incisions where two-spotted treehoppers have laid eggs. These insects are sap feeders, common wherever bittersweet grows.

Celastrin, found in the root and bark, is poisonous to humans, but mild decoctions were used as a physic and a wash for skin rashes by Native Americans. The fruit is also toxic.

This vine's common name, curiously, has nothing to do with the taste buds. English colonists in America noted the not-very-similar resemblance of its fruits to the unrelated common nightshade plant familiar to them—the "true bittersweet"—and simply attached the label. Today *bittersweet* is now only a secondary name for the nightshade, and nightshade's namesake has become the "true" bittersweet, without a verbal clue to its own respectable botany. So much for descriptive accuracy in naming.

Blackberry, Common *(Rubus allegheniensis).* Rose family. Prickly, arching

shrub in thickets, forest edges. Its white flowers, stoutly ridged, reddish canes, and black, juicy fruits identify it. This is the most common blackberry of more than a hundred alleged species—a complex, widely hybridizing group divided by technical characters, causing much disagreement among plant specialists.

Other names: Bramble, highbush blackberry.

Close relatives: Raspberries *(Rubus)*; roses *(Rosa)*; cherries *(Prunus)*; mountain-ashes *(Sorbus)*; hawthorns *(Crataegus)*; shadbushes *(Amelanchier)*.

Lifestyle: This is the thicket of arching brambles that rip clothes, scratch skin, and snag the berry picker into total immobility. To a botanist the sharp barbs that do the damage are prickles rather than thorns, a distinction less than significant on the receiving end. Despite the formidable barriers, however, browsing mammals nip the prickly canes, and numerous fruit eaters raid the thickets.

From a perennial rootstock rises a cane with a two-year lifespan. The first year it produces only leaves; the second year it bears flowers and fruit. If it survives a third year, it is decadent and dies, often arching its tip to the ground and there establishing roots for a new plant. This results in extensive networks of old and new roots, plus thickets resembling rolls of barbed wire. Thus all plants of a thicket may share the same genetic stock.

The insect-pollinated, bisexual flower produces a cluster of aggregated small drupes—

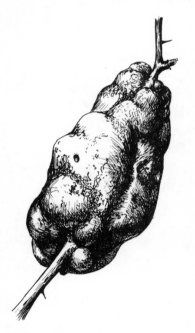

Blackberry stems host several gall-making insects. A common, conspicuous gall is that of the blackberry knotgall wasp, whose larvae created this large, knobby growth.

the blackberry. Fruits are first green, then turn red and finally darken and sweeten to ripeness, usually in September. Green fruits contain large amounts of tannic acid, as do all parts of the plant, and won't ripen once picked. The ripe fruits will dry on the plant if not picked.

Leaves in autumn turn bright red: "a streak of blood in the grass," said Thoreau.

Blackberry is intolerant of shade but in full sunlight will grow on all but the wettest soils.

Associates: Most of the fungi and animals associated with raspberries are also frequent on blackberry. The following are more exclusive to or common on blackberry.

Spring, summer. Bright orange spots on leaf undersides together with bunched or dwarfed shoots indicate orange rust *(Gymnoconia peckiana)*, a club fungus that is probably blackberry's most serious plant disease.

A variety of gall-making insects, mostly tiny wasps *(Diastrophus)* and gnats *(Lasiop-*

tera), create characteristic swellings on stems and leaves. The blackberry knotgall wasp *(D. nebulosus)*, for example, causes knotty, furrowed swellings up to six inches long on stems.

Curled, distorted leaves may indicate the presence of blackberry psyllids *(Trioza tripunctata)*, common yellow-brown sucking insects also known as jumping plant lice.

Caterpillars of the large ruby tiger moth *(Phragmatobia assimilans)*, among others, feed on blackberry. The blackberry looper caterpillar *(Chlorochlamys chloroleucaria)* forages on the fruits.

A fly-catching wasp *(Hypocrabro stirpicolus)* often tunnels into blackberry stems, constructing cells for eggs and stored flies.

Blackberry flowers, with their large petals and deep nectaries, seem to invite bumblebees *(Bombus)*, probably their most effective pollinators, but smaller solitary bees often gather pollen and aid fertilization.

Blackberry thickets are favored sites for birds, such as chestnut-sided warblers and common yellowthroats, that nest in dense shrub cover. Cottontail rabbits locate their well-camouflaged ground nests here, too.

Fall. In fruiting season look for land turtles, which relish low-hanging fruits. The common ones are Eastern box turtle, wood turtle, and Blanding's turtle.

Rubus species are among the most valuable wildlife food plants. The birds and mammals that use these shrubs are innumerable (see Raspberries).

Winter. Look for zipperlike scars on stems; these are egg scars of the black-horned tree cricket *(Oecanthus nigricornis)*.

Rubus twigs are relished by cottontail rabbits and white-tailed deer. Rabbits clip off the stems at an oblique angle; a ragged end indicates deer browsing.

Lore: Blackberry fruits provide an extremely rich source of vitamin C. Also, unlike most fruits edible by humans, they have a mild constipating effect and can be a pleasant remedy for diarrhea. Tea made from the dry leaves or young twigs is also effective for this

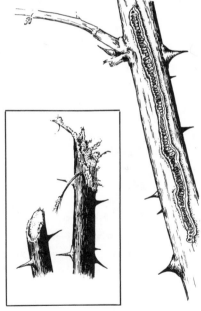

Egg scars of the black-horned tree cricket resemble zippers. The inset shows two browsed stems: the angular bite of a cottontail rabbit (left) and the ragged twig end left by a white-tailed deer (right).

purpose. Native Americans brewed a medicinal tea from the roots. Ripe fruits, of course, are best known as ingredients for jams, jellies, juice, pies, and wines.

Cultivated varieties of this and similar species, genetically developed for large fruit and high yield, supply the market brands of blackberry.

Bloodroot *(Sanguinaria canadensis).* Poppy family. Low herb in moist, humus-rich woodland. Its showy, white flower, only briefly appearing in early spring colonies, is always partially clasped by a single, pale green, lobed leaf, which lasts much longer.

Other names: Red puccoon, Indian paint.

Close relatives: Celandine *(Chelidonium majus)*; poppies *(Papaver)*; prickly poppies *(Argemone).*

Lifestyle: The bisexual flower of this spring ephemeral is usually gone by the time seasonal warmth convinces us that spring is not just another winter thaw. This flower produces prodigious amounts of pollen and is usually self-pollinated, a process called *autogamy.* This ensures maximum chances for seed production despite unreliable appearance of insect pollinators in early spring. A single flower usually lasts about two days.

Cloning stems rise from a thick perennial rhizome. During the flowering season of two to three weeks you may find stems of the same clone in virtually all phases of development. As the oblong seed case develops, the leaf grows taller to shelter it.

This plant's name, of course, arises from the orange-red juice of stem and rhizome.

Associates: *Spring.* Bloodroot's early flowering associates may include hepaticas, trout lily, Dutchman's breeches, and spring beauty.

Despite bloodroot's reliance on autogamy and cloning, its flower shows most of the typical structural invitations and devices for insect pollination. This, when it occurs, is accomplished most often by pollen-collecting bees, notably the solitary halictids and andrenids plus bumblebees *(Bombus)* and honeybees *(Apis mellifera).* Pollen-eating syrphid flies ("flower flies") are also frequent visitors.

When mature seed cases are present, look for ant activity; bloodroot seeds are dispersed by ants, and the plant may owe its distribution largely to these seed collectors and storers.

Lore: Bloodroot's staining juice, highly toxic if ingested, contains the alkaloid sanguinarine. Native Americans used it not only as a dye for baskets and clothing but also as an insect repellent and facial paint. The Iroquois used it to treat ringworm. Commercially sanguinarine is useful as an antiplaque agent for toothpastes and mouthwashes.

A tea made of the root was a favorite rheumatism treatment among tribal nations of the Mississippi region. American pioneer families used drops of the juice on lumps of sugar for coughs and colds—an uncertain, rather hazardous remedy.

Blueberries (*Vaccinium* spp.). Heath family. High or low shrubs in a variety of dry and moist habitats. Many of the almost thirty species found in eastern North America are bog or wetland dwellers. The most common woodland and edge species include the deerberry *(V. stamineum)*; the velvetleaf blueberry *(V. myrtilloides)*; the late lowbush or sweet blueberry *(V. angustifolium)*; the early low or dryland blueberry *(V. vacillans)*; and the common highbush *(V. corymbosum)*. Blueberries all have warty twigs and bear small, whitish, bell-shaped flowers and sweet purplish or blue-black fruits.

Close relatives: Bilberries, cranberries *(Vaccinium)*; huckleberries *(Gaylussacia)*; heaths *(Erica)*; heather *(Calluna vulgaris)*; wintergreen *(Gaultheria procumbens)*; trailing arbutus *(Epigaea repens)*; laurels *(Kalmia)*; rhododendrons *(Rhododendron)*.

Lifestyle: Although the names blueberry and huckleberry are often used interchangeably, the two are distinct. Huckleberries don't have warty twigs and the fruit contains only ten seeds; blueberry fruit has more than a hundred. Other less obvious differences also occur.

Woodland blueberries, which grow best in dry, sandy sites, often on acidic soil of low nutrient content, are moderately shade tolerant. The dangling, bell-like flowers are bisexual and insect pollinated. I have occasionally found the late lowbush blueberry flowering into October, though this is far from typical—most flowering occurs in spring.

Blueberries are cloning plants, and different clones often exhibit slight differences in leaf and berry shape and color. Hybrids abound, so any given blueberry shrub may show combined characters of two or more species and thus can be difficult to identify beyond the generic level.

Note in winter the two-tone, red-green twigs.

Associates: Common tree associates include oaks, pines, and white birch.

Spring. Blueberry leaves are alternate hosts for two sorts of club fungi. Short, bunchy twigs with a "witch's broom" appearance may be infected by *Pucciniastrum goeppertianum*, whose alternate hosts are firs. Eastern hemlock is the alternate host for hemlock or blueberry leaf rust *(P. vaccinii)*, which produces yellow pustules on the leaves and may defoliate the plant.

Blueberry plants host so many insects that only some of them can be mentioned. The chief pollinators are bees. Inside the flower, bees often vibrate their wings vigorously, shaking loose the pollen. Look for flowers punctured at the base, where bees occasionally bypass their pollination task by biting through the flower wall to "rob" the nectaries. Watch too for bees landing on discolored leaves and licking them; this behavior transmits *Monilinia*, a fungous disease of the fruits.

Other important nectar feeders and pollinators are blackflies *(Simulium)*, those biting scourges of the North.

Larvae of blueberry stemgall wasps cause these common, bunchy galls on blueberry twigs. The galls often distort subsequent twig growth. A witches'-broom fungus may cause similar distortion.

Leaf feeders include several conspicuous butterfly and moth caterpillars. Green, slug-like caterpillars may be elfins *(Incisalia)*. The small, brownish adult elfins, among the earliest spring butterflies, also visit the flowers, as do short-tailed swallowtails *(Papilio brevicauda)*. A dark, yellowish-green caterpillar with white, downy sides is probably a pink-edged sulphur *(Colias interior)*. Large, green caterpillars with sphinxlike postures and rear projecting horns are sphinx moth larvae; common ones on blueberry include the pawpaw sphinx *(Dolba hyloeus)* and the huckleberry sphinx *(Paonias astylus)*.

On stems, look for green or brownish kidney-shaped swellings, often bending the twig at a ninety-degree angle. These are caused by larvae of the blueberry stemgall wasp *(Hemadas nubilipennis)*.

Nashville warblers commonly nest on the ground beneath low blueberry shrubs.

Summer. Fruit foragers are blueberry's main summertime users. While you pick your own handfuls, watch for some equally eager diners.

Blueberries are among the most important seasonal foods for ruffed and spruce grouse. Prominent berry foragers among songbirds include tufted titmice, red-eyed vireos, gray catbirds, brown thrashers, American robins, Swainson's thrushes, veeries, scarlet tanagers, rufous-sided towhees, and orchard orioles.

White-footed mice, least chipmunks, and striped skunks are also frequent berry eaters. But blueberry's foremost mammalian forager (excluding *Homo*) is probably the black bear, which consumes mouthfuls of leaves and twigs along with berries.

Look for small, hard, whitish "mummy berries," the bane of commercial blueberry growers. Mummy berries are loaded with an ascomycete fungus *(Monilinia)*, which produces small, mushroomlike cups beneath the plant in early spring. These release spores that infect the leaves, attracting bees with a sweetish taste and strong ultraviolet light reflection. The bees, in turn, carry conidia spores from the leaves into the flowers they pollinate. The fungus penetrates the flower's ovaries, thus resulting in the so-called mummy berries.

Winter. Inside the persistent blueberry stem galls you may find groups of wintering wasp larvae. Two types of tiny flies also inhabit these galls as *inquilines* (that is, "guest" organisms that inhabit abodes made by others).

Blueberry twigs are relished by cottontail rabbits and white-tailed deer. The nipped ends tell which animal's teeth have cropped them (see Blackberry).

Lore: Blueberry was a primary food plant for Native Americans. They dried the berries, then pounded them together with strips of dried venison to make pemmican, a durable winter staple. The Chippewas placed the flowers on hot stones and inhaled the fumes as a remedy for "craziness." They believed this cure had been handed to them by Winabojo himself, the great Chippewa deity-prankster figure.

Though blueberry grows on almost every continent, only the United States and Canada cultivate it as a fruit crop. *V. angustifolium* and *V. corymbosum* are the most important species for commercial berry growing, and systematic breeding has produced many large-fruited varieties. Farmers in New England and elsewhere burn their blueberry fields periodically to rejuvenate decadent plants, which can be quickly shaded out by taller vegetation; the second year after burning usually produces a maximum crop. For pies, jellies, and jams, the wild fruits taste much superior to us berrypickers than the cultivated varieties.

Box Elder *(Acer negundo).* Maple family. Tree in bottomlands, floodplains, fencerows, open or disturbed sites. Its opposite compound leaves (usually consisting of three leaflets), crooked and divergent trunks, and clusters of winged, maplelike seeds identify this tree.

Other name: Ash-leaved maple.

Close relatives: Maples *(Acer)*; unrelated to elderberries.

Lifestyle: This maple is often regarded as a weed tree because of its prolific sprouting and its tendency to lean, shed branches, and generally ignore human standards for an attractive tree. Farmers and city planners, however, needed a tree that would grow fast and reliably just about anywhere; thus today we see old box elders lining city streets, shading yards and farmsteads, and rising from vacant lots and old fields.

Box elder differs from other maples in its flowering. The others have bisexual flowers, at least in part, but box elder flowers are unisexual and grow on separate trees. The wind-pollinated flowers emerge before or with the leaves, and the winged samaras often hang on the tree through winter.

This is also the only shade-intolerant maple, requiring full sun to sprout and mature.

Warty galls on box elder leaves are produced by several species of mites, as shown here, and gall gnats. Though its three harmless leaflets resemble poison ivy foliage, box elder is a maple.

Roots are shallow and wide spreading, and brittle twigs and branches usually litter the ground beneath these trees.

Associates: In its natural habitat, box elder's common tree peers include silver maple, Eastern cottonwood, willows, sycamore, and Northern hackberry. Many fungi and animals associated with box elder are also common to other maples (see Red Maple, Sugar Maple).

Spring, summer. A large, white, hairy-capped mushroom growing on logs or living trunks may be the silky sheath *(Volvariella bombycina)*, easily confused with some species of deadly *Amanita.*

On leaves, look for several sorts of galls. Mites *(Eriophyes, Phyllocoptes)* produce warty swellings, and the box elder leaf gall gnat *(Contarinia negundifolia)* causes roundish galls.

The box elder bug *(Leptocoris trevittatus)*, a blackish hemipteran with red markings, feeds on the female flowers and foliage; its nymph stages are bright red.

Fall. Box elder bugs sometimes congregate in huge masses—not only on female box elder trees, but also in houses or other enclosures—seeking sheltered places to hibernate. Their presence in such places may be a nuisance, but they don't eat anything.

Winter. Box elders with samaras still hanging on the tree are good places to watch for evening and pine grosbeaks. These birds relish the seeds—an important winter food. Their heavy bills neatly dissect the seed from its outer covering, which they discard along with the winged key.

Especially numerous in the fall, box elder bugs assemble on the trees and in other places before hibernating. Their black and red colors make them conspicuous.

All year. A common bark canker is the coralspot *(Nectria cinnabarina)*, a fungus that attacks box elder trees near wounds or branch stubs, producing dieback of twigs and foliage.

Lore: This tree's common name provides a constant reminder, by omission, of its poor-relation status to the long-lived, "respectable" maples. Certainly it bears no resemblance to the true elders *(Sambucus)*, and the word *box* apparently refers to its usage as a hedge tree. The wood, soft and weak, elicits little commercial demand; one source cites its main value as material for "cheap furniture and easily broken toys."

Yet several varieties are still planted, especially in the Northwest, for ornamental and landscaping purposes. Like all maples, it produces sweet sap in spring, but the syrup is of a blander, milder sweetness and flavor than that from sugar maple. Nevertheless, Crow tribes made sugar from box elder sap.

Buckeye, Ohio *(Aesculus glabra)*. Horse-chestnut family. Tree in moist woods, bottomlands, along stream banks. Its five palmate leaflets and its large, lustrous brown seed enclosed in a leathery capsule distinguish this buckeye, which ranges no farther north than western Pennsylvania and southern Michigan.

Close relative: Horse chestnut *(A. hippocastanum)*.

Lifestyle: This is one of the earliest trees to leaf out in spring and to drop leaves in the fall. The yellowish green, insect-pollinated flowers, appearing after the leaves, are sometimes bisexual, sometimes unisexual. When the latter, male and female flowers are usually borne on separate trees.

The palmate leaflet arrangement, similar to that of horse chestnut, is a feature of Ohio buckeye. Relatively few insects forage on buckeye leaves. The foliage is toxic to many animals.

Ohio buckeye is a "moderate" tree: moderately shade tolerant, moderately fast growing, moderately long-lived. It's extreme only in its smell; bruised leaves, twigs, and bark emit a rank, foul odor.

Associates: Lowland species in river bottoms—box elder, sycamore, Northern hackberry—are the chief woodland associates of Ohio buckeye, which also grows in mixed stands with American elm, sugar maple, American beech, and other deciduous trees. Buckeye

Eastern leafy mistletoe is a shrubby evergreen parasite sometimes seen on buckeye. It is most visible in winter when the tree is leafless. Mistletoe may become a destructive plant pest in some forests.

remains relatively freer of insect pests and diseases than most. (A common thistle butterfly called the buckeye, *Precis lavinia*, was named for the eyespots on its wings and has no associative relationship to the tree.)

Spring, summer. A common fungus that forms large, reddish brown patches on leaflets is the buckeye leaf blotch *(Guignardia aesculi).*

During early spring, watch for ruby-throated hummingbirds hovering at the flowers to seek nectar.

Fall. Fox squirrels sometimes feed on buckeye seeds, one of the few animals to do so. The tree may partially owe its local distribution patterns to seed burials by these mammals.

All year. Inspect branches for growth of the Eastern leafy mistletoe *(Phoradendron serotinum)*, a shrubby, parasitic evergreen that is fairly common on buckeye.

Lore: When Ohio pioneers noted the split seed capsule, partially exposing the pale, circular scar of attachment (the *hilum*), they thought it resembled the half-opened eye of a deer—hence the tree's common name. Ohioans not only adopted the name for themselves and their sports teams but also designated the Ohio buckeye as state tree.

Buckeye, however, has little current utility for Ohioans or anybody else. Foliage, twigs, and seeds contain a narcotic alkaloid that is toxic to livestock and other animals (nectar of the California buckeye, *A. californica*, is poisonous even to bees).

Native Americans, aware of this toxic property, threw crushed seeds and branches into ponds, stunning fish that could then be harvested for food (this practice is now illegal).

The soft, weak wood has found uses for boxing material, paper pulp, and most notably, artificial limbs.

Buckthorn, Common *(Rhamnus cathartica).* Buckthorn family. Shrub or small tree in dry, upland hedges, open woods, thickets. Its twigs tipped with sharp thorns and its black, berrylike fruits are the best field marks. This native of Eurasia, imported as a hedge plant and widely escaped from cultivation, is the only thorned species. The alder-leaved buckthorn *(R. alnifolia)* and European or glossy buckthorn *(R. frangula)* prefer wetter habitats.

Other names: European buckthorn (properly *R. frangula*), hartsthorn, waythorn, rhineberry.

Close relatives: New Jersey tea *(Ceanothus americanus)*; supplejack *(Berchemia scandens)*; common jujube *(Ziziphus jujube)*.

Lifestyle: This shrub often frustrates quick identification by novice naturalists. For example, are common buckthorn leaves opposite or alternate on the stem? The answer is yes. The leaves are not either-or, but both. Buckthorn is the only North American shrub that displays this characteristic. Opposite leaves occur on or near the twig tip; farther back on the twig, the leaves are increasingly "out of synch."

The flowering is likewise variable. Some flowers are bisexual, some unisexual on the same or different plants. Flowers are yellowish green, inconspicuous, but fragrant and insect pollinated. The fruit, a drupe, usually contains four seeds (other buckthorns have two or three), but this number too is variable.

Common buckthorn tolerates both shade

Common buckthorn leaves pose identification problems for observers unfamiliar with the plant. This opportunistic shrub is rapidly becoming a weed in many areas because of its ample tolerances.

and sun with equal aplomb and can also adapt to most soils. Such ample tolerances mean that this plant has become something of a weed, a frequent indicator of environmental changes wrought by humans.

Associates: *Spring, summer.* Yellowish pustules on buckthorn leaves spell trouble for nearby grain farmers. The alien buckthorn species are alternate hosts of oat crown rust *(Pucinia coronata)*, a severe fungous disease of oats.

A rolled-up portion of leaf near the tip probably shelters the caterpillar of *Anchylopera braunae*, a tortricid moth, which feeds on ends of the roll as it continues to curl toward the leaf base.

Bird and animal consumption of the fruit is apparently insignificant, at least in eastern North America. In the West, the fruits of certain *Rhamnus* species are much more important to birds. Yet common buckthorn probably owes its expanding distribution to birds, so obviously the fruit is eaten to some extent.

Lore: You're not likely to eat many of these fruits, loaded as they are with acrid glycosides. If you do, you'll become extremely nauseated, for they are strongly cathartic. Veterinarians, however, still use *Rhamnus* substances, especially as a purgative for dogs.

The yellow inner bark (another distinctive mark of this species) has been used to produce dyes, but this shrub's main human use is in hedgerows for landscaping. As a hedge, it provides a degree of wildlife cover but also a regular source of seed dispersal, parenting buckthorn thickets all over the countryside.

Bunchberry *(Cornus canadensis).* Dogwood family. Low shrub in cool, moist, acid woods. Four white, petallike bracts surmounting a whorl of six leaves identify this low flower, which is replaced by a tight cluster of scarlet berrylike drupes in late summer.

Other names: Dwarf cornel, low cornel, herb dogwood.

Close relatives: Dogwoods *(Cornus)*; gums *(Nyssa).*

Lifestyle: The bisexual flowers are greenish and tiny, clustered in the center of the four conspicuous bracts. They are insect pollinated. It is virtually a dwarf version of flowering dogwood; the flower of these two species is unlike that of the other shrubby dogwoods.

Cloning stems rise from a perennial woody rhizome that sometimes covers many yards, giving rise to colonies. Note that stems without flowers are often four-leaved instead of six-leaved, a variable pattern possibly reflecting the flowering stem's greater energy needs (see Wood Anemone).

Associates: Look for this smallest of the dogwoods in the same areas that host partridgeberry, twinflower, goldthread, and woodland ferns—mainly coniferous forests.

Spring. Bees and small flies are the chief pollinators. Most insects that specialize on flowering dogwood could probably feed on bunchberry, but since bunchberry's habitat is usually somewhat moister and it occupies a different forest stratum, there probably isn't much overlap.

This plant doesn't rank high as an important wildlife food. Nashville warblers sometimes nest beneath it.

Late summer, fall. Woodland birds, especially veeries and Philadelphia and warbling vireos, consume the fruits.

Lore: Ripe bunchberry fruits are edible, either raw or cooked, but they are extremely subtle if not insipid in flavor. Native Americans used them in puddings and sauces. They also made a tea of the leaves for various ailments.

Buttercups *(Ranunculus* spp.). Buttercup family. More than thirty species of this herb occupy mostly wet or meadow habitats in northeastern North America. The few common woodland species include the kidneyleaf or small-flowered buttercup *(R. abortivus),* the hooked buttercup *(R. recurvatus),* the hispid buttercup *(R. hispidus),* and the early buttercup *(R. fascicularis).* Recognize them by yellow, wet-shiny, five-petaled flowers and deeply cut palmate leaves.

Other names: Crowfoot, spearwort.

Close relatives: Anemones *(Anemone);* hepaticas *(Hepatica);* columbines *(Aquilegia);* baneberries *(Actaea).*

Lifestyle: Buttercups represent one of the most ancient flowering plant groups that survive from the early Cenozoic era. They are some of the easiest flowers for identifying male and female parts; male stamens surround the domed, central female pistils, a simple arrangement that more highly evolved plants have modified in numerous complexities and variations. At the inner base of each shiny petal exists a tiny flap, the nectary, the flower's invitation and reward to pollinating insects. Each flower lasts for about a week and opens only in daytime—or not at all if the weather is rainy.

This perennial overwinters as a small, basal rosette of leaves, which the flower stalk rises from in spring. Notice the small seeds, called *achenes,* which may germinate in either spring or fall. Some observers have thought they resemble tiny frogs in shape (the Latin genus name means "a little frog").

Associates: *Spring.* Flowers are pollinated by bees, small flies, and butterflies.

The leaves are often a staple for ruffed grouse chicks.

Fall, winter. Although a variety of birds and small mammals consume the seeds, buttercups are not important food plants. Wild turkeys and snow buntings are two of the more frequent seed foragers.

Lore: The reflected glow of buttercup petals under a smooth chin identifies a lover of butter. (Did this childhood game ever identify a cholesterol hater?) But from chin to mouth is definitely not a recommended move. All buttercups contain an irritant called ranunculin. This acrid glycoside can cause a skin rash in allergic individuals and severe illness if swallowed. Livestock generally avoid the plant, though cattle can develop something like an addiction to it, consuming it until it kills them. Wild animal foliage grazers are apparently not affected by the poison. Once the plant is dry (as in hay), the toxins disappear and it becomes harmless.

Illinois tribes pulverized the roots and used them in a solution to treat cuts and wounds, and the Montagnais inhaled the odor of crushed leaves for headache. The plant's juice has occasionally been used in medicine as a blistering agent.

Butternut leaf scars have been likened to camel faces topped with a furry hairline. Marks within the scar are bundle scars of the vascular system, which supplied the leaves with water and nutrients.

Butternut *(Juglans cinerea).* Walnut family. Tree in moist, lowland forests, bottomlands, also on dry limestone soils. Its pinnately compound leaves, greenish male catkins, and sticky-downy, lemon-shaped nut—together with its habitat—identify this native walnut.

Other names: White walnut, oilnut.

Close relatives: Walnuts *(Juglans)*; hickories *(Carya).*

Lifestyle: Unisexual flowers—the male catkins drooping, the female flowers in small, erect clusters—appear on the same tree when the leaves emerge. They are wind pollinated. The fringed lip *(stigma)* of the female pistil is bright red, as in hazelnuts. Female flowers are borne on shoots of the current season (that is, toward the twig ends), while the male flowers appear lower, on the previous year's growth.

On twigs, look for the "camel face" of the leaf scars—a fuzzy brow surmounts the three U-shaped groups of bundle scars that resemble eyes and a happy-face smile. Butternut leaves appear late in spring, drop early in autumn. This tree is a smaller, more stunted version of black walnut; it is less massive and more resistant to cold. Like its cousin, however, it is shade intolerant and fast growing, and has a taproot plus deeply set lateral roots—wind seldom tips these trees. Butternut is quite short-lived, seldom achieving more than a hundred years, and its stiff, brittle branches break easily. A canker disease that afflicts most mature butternut trees often produces a ragged, stag-headed appearance on the crown, with many dead limbs littering the topmost portions.

Twigs and leaves ooze a waxy, aromatic sap, and all green parts of the tree wear a downy, velvetlike coat of fuzzy hairs. Parts of the tree secrete the allelopath juglone, though to a lesser extent than black walnut.

Associates: Butternut never grows in pure stands. Single trees occur in mesic hardwood mixtures of American basswood, sugar maple, American elm, red oak, and others. Most insect associates common to black walnut may be found on butternut.

Spring, summer. One of butternut's foremost leaf feeders is the walnut caterpillar moth (see Black Walnut).

The butternut curculio, also called the walnut weevil *(Conotrachelus juglandis)*, feeds on foliage and deposits eggs in twigs and leaf petioles. This beetle, showing a long, down-curved snout, is dark brown with white markings.

Leaf undersides covered with masses of white wool and leaves eaten from the sides inward, leaving only the midrib intact, probably indicate the presence of butternut woolly-worms *(Blennocampa caryae)*. These caterpillarlike sawfly larvae are green beneath their long, white filaments.

Late summer, fall. Look for slits in the twigs just below the buds and for the adult two-spotted treehoppers *(Enchenopa binotata)* that make these cuts and lay eggs in them. These treehoppers resemble brown thorns in shape, with two yellow spots and a high, curved horn projecting forward above the head.

Crescent-shaped slits in the nut husks are egg deposits of the butternut curculio.

Gray and fox squirrels are probably the main nut harvesters. Their burials of nuts for winter storage account for the distribution of most butternut trees.

All year. Few trees are as vulnerable to fungous infections. Multiple wounds result from easy breakage in wind and ice; thus butternut trees become frequent hosts for various heartrot fungi, which are often indicated by shelflike brackets (the fruiting bodies) on trunks and limbs. Two pore fungi that are very common are the false tinder fungus *(Phellinus tremulae)*, shaped like a hoof, and the sulphur polypore *(Polyporus sulphureus)*, orange-red above and bright yellow below.

A canker disease that almost universally afflicts butternut trees is variously called butternut dieback or walnut canker, caused by a sac fungus *(Melanconis juglandis)*. No actual lesion or canker is formed—the slow-growing fungus works from within—but branches progressively die back, producing the stag-headed appearance of the crown. Black spots like ink drops may sometimes appear on dead branches, and the entire tree declines and slowly dies.

Lore: See this tree while you can, if you can. Once common, butternut trees are rapidly declining throughout their range, primarily because of *Melanconis* canker. Few of those that remain are healthy trees, and skeleton trunks that may stand for years reveal the changing aspect of American forest landscapes.

The nuts, once plentiful in grocery stores, today are rarely seen. Their sweetness and high oil content give them the highest food value of any walnut or hickory nut, but kernels are meager and hard to extract. A favorite old-time use of butternuts was to pickle them in their husks and serve them with meats. American natives ate the nuts raw, cooked, ground into meal, and mixed with venison and bear meat. Crushed, the nuts poisoned fish and brought them to the surface. Iroquois tribes extracted the nut oil and used it not only for cooking but also for hair dressing. They tapped the trees for sweet sap, which they boiled down into syrup.

The root bark was known for its laxative properties. A brownish yellow dye, boiled from twigs and husks, colored homespun clothing, probably the first khaki. These "butternut jeans" became a uniform of sorts for backwoods regiments, thence labeled *butternuts*, during the Civil War.

The light, weak wood with its splendidly figured grain was extensively used for fine interior paneling, notably for carriages, altars, and cabinet work. But because of butternut's increasing rarity, its wood isn't used much and the nut has achieved near-gourmet status.

Today butternut is cultivated on a few plantations, usually by grafting scions on black walnut roots. It's a pity to see this important tree fade from our forests.

Tiny aromatic glands on the white cedar leaf undersides can best be seen with a hand lens. These glands are the source of the resin that produces cedar's characteristic odor.

Cedar, Northern White *(Thuja occidentalis).* Cypress family. Tree, characteristic of cold, alkaline swamps and stream borders, but also growing on dry limestone soils, dunes, uplands. Flattish, aromatic, scalelike leaves and twigs and shreddy, fibrous bark are the identity marks of this conifer. More than fifty varieties have been cultivated for ornamental and landscaping uses.

Other names: Arborvitae, canoewood.

Close relatives: Atlantic white cedar *(Chamaecyparis thyoides)*; junipers *(Juniperus).*

Lifestyle: This tree's two widely differing habitats—swamps and dry, calcareous uplands—have led some botanists to propose two genetic races. In both habitats the trees are biologically similar (evidently correct soil pH is a more important factor than the amount of moisture), but the vastly different habitats result in different ecological associations. We will focus here on the upland cedars.

White cedars hold their leaves for two to five years. Look closely at the undersides and note the tiny resin glands on the center leaf scales, the source of cedar's aroma.

Tiny yellow male and bigger purplish female cones appear on the same tree in spring. Wind pollinates the erect female cones, which ripen by fall, release winged seeds, and hang empty on the tree through winter. Seed production begins at ten to fifteen years, becomes abundant at twenty, and is best after seventy-five. Another method of reproduction, more common in the cedar swamps, occurs when rows of trees sprout from fallen or buried trunks (layering).

This tree thrives best in dense shade but grows very slowly even under optimal conditions; an inch of trunk diameter is typically the work of ten to twenty summers. Even-aged stands following cutting or fire may remain in a state of virtually no growth for many years. This species is considered relatively short-lived, but ages of 250 to 300 years are fairly common.

A row of cedars rising from a fallen trunk illustrates a common method of vegetative reproduction in this tree. Cedars growing in straight lines are often indications that such layering has occurred.

Cedar trunks are often lobed and buttressed at the base, dividing into two or more secondary stems. Trunks may lean or show twisting and distortion, especially near the base. Thin bark makes them highly vulnerable to fire.

Extensive browning and death of branches and foliage may occur in late winter or early spring as a result of sudden thaws accompanied by drying winds. The leaves give off large amounts of water, which cannot be replaced from the roots in still-frozen ground, and parts of the tree thus die from drought. Trees exposed to wind and sun are most vulnerable to this winter drying.

Because white cedar cannot tolerate acid environments, it is a good indicator of pH neutral or basic soils.

Associates: In both upland and lowland habitats, white cedar often occurs in more or less pure stands; one or several older trees are surrounded by numerous smaller offspring, forming fairly dense "family" groupings. Its upland tree associates may include Eastern white pine, Eastern hemlock, and yellow birch. This is the only northeastern conifer that apparently lacks the symbiotic root–fungus association called *mycorrhiza.*

Spring, summer. Dry cedar uplands are good places to look for two orchid species: the striped coralroot *(Corallorhiza striata)* and the calypso orchid *(Calypso bulbosa).*

Arthropod foliage feeders leave fairly conspicuous marks on this tree. Distorted branch tips may indicate the presence of tipdwarf mites *(Calipiterimerus thujae),* which become most active in cool, humid weather. The arborvitae leafminer *(Argyresthia thuiella)* eats the inside of leaves, causing browning and dying of terminal shoots; this is an ermine moth caterpillar, often parasitized by *Pentacnemus bucculatricis,* a tiny wasp. Groups of greenish, caterpillarlike larvae feeding on leaves are probably arborvitae sawflies *(Monoctenus).*

If you notice dead twigs among green foliage, look for holes chewed in twig crotches—signs of the Northern cedar bark beetle *(Phloeosinus canadensis).* Beneath the bark, cedar logs often show this engraver beetle's vertical galleries, from which horizontal galleries of the larval beetles wing out on either side.

Fall, winter. Pendant, spindle-shaped bags of tough silk about two inches long, covered with cedar leaves and twigs, reveal this tree's foremost insect pest, the evergreen bagworm *(Thyridopteryx ephemeraeformis).* This psychid moth caterpillar feeds on the foliage, moving about and gradually enlarging its bag. Males become black, winged moths, but females never leave their bags, mating through an opening at the base of the bag and laying eggs therein. The caterpillars feed throughout spring and summer, but the attached bags containing overwintering eggs are most conspicuous in later seasons, when yellow-bellied sapsuckers and other woodpeckers often feed on them.

The pine siskin is the primary seed feeder. Red squirrels clip off small branches bearing seed cones.

Northern white cedar foliage is important winter food for white-tailed deer. Most browsing occurs in dense cedar swamps, where the deer "yard up" (congregate) during periods of heavy snow cover.

All year. Fungous infections cause much heartwood decay in this species. Two signs of it are prominent on trunks of living trees: bracket-type conks and deep excavations by woodpeckers. Another common excavation in living trees consists of honeycomb galleries that riddle the heartwood, often partially exposed at the trunk base. These galleries are hollowed by black carpenter ants *(Camponotus pennsylvanicus)*, efficient wood destroyers that enter the tree through a wound or rotted area.

Swainson's thrushes and red squirrels often use strips of the stringy bark for their nests.

Pileated woodpeckers make deep, vertically oblong excavations in cedar and other trees infested with heartrot fungi and (consequently) insects. Often only parts of living trees are affected.

Lore: The name *cedar* is actually a stolen misnomer for this tree. Northern white cedar is a cypress, bearing neither relationship to the true cedars *(Cedrus)* of Eurasia nor similarity to the famed cedars of Lebanon *(C. libani)*.

Its other common name—arborvitae, meaning "tree of life"—has more credentials. For this tree (or perhaps black spruce—nobody knows for sure) proved exactly that to the men of Jacques Cartier's Canadian exploring expedition of 1535. Suffering from scurvy, they drank a tea brewed from the leaves of an evergreen tree, and their symptoms disappeared. The Ojibwas drank a similar bitter potion to cure headache, while Menominee women made a tea from the inner bark to promote menstruation. (Oil of white cedar is a camphorlike heart stimulant, toxic in any pure quantity.)

Native Americans used this tree primarily, however, for birchbark canoe frames and ribs. It split easily, didn't shrink or warp, and separated along the annual growth rings when log ends were pounded (a feature known as *ring shake* or *wind shake*, making cedar undesirable for many modern construction purposes). Because of its durability in contact with soil and moisture, cedar proved an ideal wood for posts, shingles, fishing floats and lures, telephone poles, railroad ties . . . and, still, canoes.

Cherry, Black *(Prunus serotina)*. Rose family. Tree in woods, thickets, edges. Mature trees are easily identified by the black, scaly bark. Leaf undersides show a line of downy reddish hairs fringing the midrib base.

Other names: Wild cherry, rum cherry, bird cherry.

Close relatives: Mountain-ashes *(Sorbus)*; roses *(Rosa)*; hawthorns *(Crataegus)*; blackberry and raspberries *(Rubus)*; shadbushes *(Amelanchier)*.

Lifestyle: Of the several North American cherry species, black cherry is the largest (no others rank as forest trees) and is one of our most common wild fruit trees. It is distinctive in any season, highly adaptable to almost any dry or mesic forest habitat, and one of the most valuable trees to wildlife and people.

As a young, fast-growing tree, it thrives in full sunlight, but it is also shade tolerant and thus common in the understory of many forest communities. As it ages and its crown rises into the canopy, it becomes more shade intolerant. A long taproot anchors the young cherry, then gives way to a spreading lateral root system, making older trees quite vulnerable to wind-throw. Fire, cutting, or browsing stimulates new growth from root collars and stumps.

Like quaking aspen (but much less finicky in its habitat requirements), black cherry is opportunistic, colonizing openings and edges, but it lives much longer (150 to 200 years). Black cherry is extremely cold hardy and can even colonize deep woodland "frost pockets" where other trees cannot survive.

The white flowers, appearing in drooping clusters when the leaves are new, are bisexual and insect pollinated. The purple-black ripe cherries, about pea size, each contain a pit and hang in clusters like the flowers. Seeds, abundant at intervals of three to four years, remain viable for two years after falling.

Twigs and leaves contain high levels of hydrocyanic or prussic acid (2,470 parts per million in young leaves, decreasing to 450 ppm during the first six weeks), so the foliage is toxic to livestock and humans. Note the tiny

Mites cause formation of wild cherry pouch galls, commonly seen on black cherry leaves in spring. Leaf galls are common indicators of mite feeding and breeding.

double glands on the leafstalks, characteristic to all cherry species. They secrete nectar, resulting in an important coaction.

Associates: Seldom found in pure stands, black cherry mixes with typical deciduous forest trees including oaks, elms, maples, white ash, and American basswood.

Spring, summer. Although man and cow are poisoned by cherry foliage, a host of mites and insects find it delectable. Insect feeders are mainly the larval forms of various gnats and lepidopterans.

Tiny mites *(Eriophyes padi)* cause formation of wild cherry pouch galls, masses of green or red fingerlike protrusions on the upper side of leaves. Bunchy galls on twig tips, bright red in spring, are produced by the cherry bud gall gnat *(Cecidomyia serotinae).*

Black cherry is a primary food plant for more than two hundred species of butterfly and moth caterpillars. The red-spotted purple *(Limenitis arthemis)* is one of many adult butterflies and their caterpillars found on black

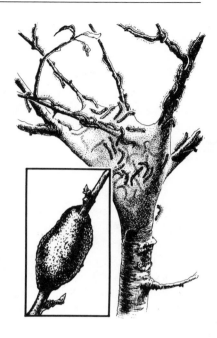

Webbed tents in the crotches of cherry and other trees of the rose family are made by masses of Eastern tent caterpillars. The inset shows the egg mass of the adult moth.

cherry. Its spiny, humped caterpillars consume leaves from the outer sides, leaving the midrib. The coral hairstreak *(Strymon titus)*, a bright green caterpillar with rose coloration at both ends, is often found on young trees (look for ant activity at stem bases, where these caterpillars rest just beneath ground surface in daytime, attended by the ants). The Eastern tiger swallowtail *(Papilio glaucus)*, green, humped caterpillars with a purple eyespot on each side of the thorax, fold sheltering leaf edges over themselves by means of silken threads, often high in the tree.

Moth caterpillars are legion. Some of the most conspicuous include several species of sphinx moth *(Smerinthus, Paonias, Sphinx)*, large green caterpillars with rearing, sphinxlike postures and projecting rear horns. Skeletonized leaves may be signs of the cherry casebearer *(Coleophora pruniella)*. These tiny moth caterpillars construct black, pistol-shaped cases of silk and excrement (frass) in which they live as they move about the plant.

The Eastern tent caterpillar *(Malacosoma americana)* forms grayish, webbed tents in forks or crotches of the tree. These gregarious, hairy, brownish caterpillars often defoliate entire trees in outbreaks that cyclically occur for two or three years in succession at about ten-year intervals. The outbreaks subside when egg parasites radically diminish the population. Birds such as cuckoos and Northern orioles consume the caterpillars. On trees located near ant nests, a competitive interaction sometimes occurs; the ants (often Allegheny mound ants, *Formica exsectoides*), attracted to the leafstalk nectaries, attack any caterpillars they encounter on the tree.

Another cyclical leaf feeder is the cherry leaf beetle *(Pyrrhalta cavicollis)*, a small red beetle whose brownish, spotted larvae may suddenly appear in large numbers and not be seen again for several years.

A "shot-hole" pattern of perforated leaves may indicate presence of a sac fungus called cherry leaf spot *(Coccomyces hiemalis)*, the most common leaf disease of cherry.

Fall, winter. With the ripening fruits come numerous bird foragers. Some seventy bird species are known to feed on black cherries. Game birds such as ruffed grouse and ring-necked pheasant devour many fruits on the ground, while other birds—notably woodpeckers, cedar waxwings, thrushes, and grosbeaks—consume them in the tree. Occasionally birds will become intoxicated on dead-ripe, slightly fermented cherries; a bird of glazed eye and uncertain balance in or near a late-season fruiting tree, you may be sure, has had a few too many. Cherry pits are dispersed by birds in their droppings and by regurgitation of pits after marathon eating sessions. A bird's digestive process improves the seed's germinating capacity.

Mammals also relish the fruit and disperse seeds. Black bears, red foxes, Eastern chipmunks, cottontail rabbits, white-footed mice, and red, gray, and fox squirrels frequently forage on fallen cherries. Bears and raccoons, among others, climb trees for the fruits, sometimes leaving broken branches and torn bark. And the high-cyanide twigs and foliage do not deter the browsing of white-tailed deer and moose. Voles are common winter feeders on the bark at snow level.

On twigs, insect signs are often abundant even in winter. Dead, rolled leaves fastened to twigs with silk may shelter hibernating caterpillars of the red-spotted purple butterfly. A large, baglike cocoon attached lengthwise to a twig is probably that of a cecropia or robin moth *(Hyalophora cecropia)*. Portable cases of the cherry casebearer also remain attached to twigs over winter. Look for shiny, brown-varnished bands of insect eggs encircling twigs near their ends: these are the wintering egg masses of the Eastern tent caterpillar.

All year. Probably the most common and conspicuous fungus seen on cherries is black knot *(Dibotryon morbosum)*, a black, warty, parasitic growth on twigs and small branches. Black knot may infest a tree only spottily or may litter the entire crown with tumorlike masses, which kill branches and eventually the entire tree. Trees infested with this sac fungus are most easily seen in winter when the leaves are gone. A number of small inquiline insects, among them the dogwood borer (see Flowering Dogwood), have adapted to living and breeding in these growths.

Lore: For fine furniture, cabinets, interior paneling, and veneer, black cherry wood is considered second only to black walnut. Hard but easily worked, it holds up under shock and pressure, making it valuable for such uses as tool handles, gunstocks, printers' blocks and backing. The wood's reddish brown color deepens with age.

Cherry bark has been used in the manufacture of prussic acid cough medicines. The smell and taste of broken twigs have the distinctive bitter almond flavor of this acid, the ingredient that makes the tree toxic. Native Americans brewed the inner bark and root bark to make a sedative tea and astringent wash.

Fruits, slightly bitter even when dead ripe, aren't very palatable to humans, but with a little sugar they transform into excellent jelly.

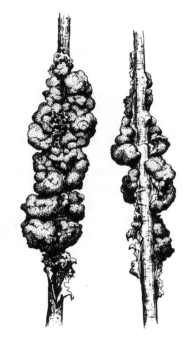

The black knot fungus, very common on black cherry, parasitizes branches, sometimes giving the tree a tumor-infested appearance. Trees may carry these warty growths for years.

Used for flavoring rum and brandy, they also appear in the guise of a liqueur known as cherry bounce.

Chestnut, American *(Castanea dentata)*. Beech family. Tree in dry to mesic deciduous forests, today mainly an understory species. Leaves are beechlike but longer and narrower. The fruit is a large, spiny bur enclosing one to three flattened nuts.

Close relatives: Eastern chinquapin *(C. pumila)*; Chinese chestnut *(C. mollissima)*; American beech *(Fagus grandifolia)*; oaks *(Quercus)*; unrelated to horse chestnut *(Aesculus hippocastanum)*.

Lifestyle: This majestic tree, once a dominant species of the American deciduous forest, was familiar to our great-grandparents. It made up fully twenty-five percent of our eastern woodland. American chestnut, however, has been all but wiped out by an imported blight disease that has swiftly eliminated all but a few isolated stands. Sprouts from old roots survive and may reach twenty feet in height and live long enough to produce one or two seed crops (in a kind of blight-induced puberty) before they too succumb and die. Today the only large chestnut trees are dead ones, durable skeletons that occasionally remain on hillsides and oak–hickory highlands.

Unisexual flowers appear on the same tree in early summer, the male ones in long, stiff, yellow-green catkins. Insect-pollinated female flowers occur at the base of shorter stalks. Nuts were produced in abundance annually.

Farmers once considered chestnut a weed tree; fast growing and intolerant of shade, it sprouted along fencerows and everywhere it wasn't supposed to. It also lived long, with a crown spread often exceeding the tree's height and a taproot that plunged deep. Typical mature chestnut trees stood eighty feet tall with three-foot trunk diameters. The loss of chestnut is a significant reason why many of our deciduous woodlands have a far different aspect than they did only a century ago.

Associates: Tree associates were predominantly oaks—black, white, and red—and pignut and shagbark hickories, along with white ash and black cherry.

Spring, summer. "There is not a chestnut in the wood but some worm has found it out," noted Thoreau of the numerous insect larvae hosted by this tree. Nobody knows how many and to what extent dependent insects declined along with the chestnut, but effects of the ecological gap it left must have rippled throughout the ecosystem. The same insects that feed on beech and oaks might generally be expected on chestnut. But so sparse are the trees today and so beset by the killing fungus that occasional insect foragers probably play a negligible role. The tree no longer lives long enough, or in enough places, to center significant biotic communities.

Important associates included squirrels and Eastern chipmunks (despite the nut's spiny bur, described by one forester as "the most effective antisquirrel device nature has invented"), animals that probably helped distribute the tree by nut burial. White-tailed deer also fed on the nuts. Northern bobwhites and wild turkeys foraged on the ground for nuts, and in the trees fed the now-extinct passenger pigeon.

All year. Cankers of the notorious chestnut blight *(Cryphonectria parasitica)* are easily seen on infected stems. This sac fungus attacks the inner bark, producing reddish or yellowish cankers that swell and split, loosening the bark and girdling the stem. The highly infectious spores are transported to other chestnut trees by wind, birds, and insects.

Lore: It's a dismal story, this spread of the virulent blight that has virtually eliminated one of America's foremost trees. For want of a few dollars in the right place at the right time to quarantine the disease, America lost a splendid tree plus a major timber and wildlife food resource.

The fungus arrived from Japan about 1900 on Asiatic chestnut seedlings. It spread rapidly and, by 1950, had destroyed eighty percent of all American chestnuts. Today, despite the fact that only small, occasional stands remain completely blight-free, the tree refuses to die out entirely. Scientists for decades have been trying to breed a blight-resistant variety or introduce fungus parasites. A hypovirulent (less potent) strain of the fungus that has appeared on the European chestnut *(C. sativa)* significantly weakens the blight effects and permits self-healing of cankers. Despite its complex genetics, this strain, introduced into American chestnuts, may provide the key that will launch a comeback of the tree. The American Chestnut Foundation, located at West Virginia University, was organized in 1983 to support restoration efforts. One of the largest chestnut stands, containing many uninfected mature trees, is located in West Salem, Wisconsin.

There was "no nut in our woods to compare with it as food," wrote Ernest Thompson Seton. A tea made from the tannin-rich leaves was the only medicine ever reported as used by Native Americans for a whooping cough remedy. Today all commercially marketed chestnuts are Chinese chestnuts *(C. mollissima)*, grown in California.

Chestnut wood, softer than oak and durable in both soil and air, was used for almost every construction purpose. The iceboxes that preceded modern refrigerators were often built of chestnut. Today the distressed wood of chestnut, retrieved from old barns and fences, is in great demand for recycling into interior trim and furnishings. Wormy chestnut, also popular for paneling, comes from old forest logs.

Chokecherry *(Prunus virginiana)*. Rose family. Shrub or small tree found in forest edges, thickets, openings, or the understory in wet to dry soils. Egg-shaped leaves and dark, smooth bark combined with long, drooping flower and fruit clusters identify this cherry.

Other name: Bird cherry.

Close relatives: Mountain-ashes *(Sorbus)*; roses *(Rosa)*; hawthorns *(Crataegus)*; blackberry and raspberries *(Rubus)*; shadbushes *(Amelanchier)*.

Lifestyle: Sometimes called a smaller, scraggly version of black cherry, chokecherry is unlike that tree because of its clone-forming habit. It typically grows in colonies of genetically similar stems all sprouted from the same root system. Also distinctive are the two-toned terminal buds, dark brown at the tip, pale brown in the middle. Otherwise, chokecherry shares most of the same flowering and fruiting traits as black cherry.

Though moderately shade tolerant, which enables it to form understory clones in open woods, chokecherry prefers sunny, open sites. The clonal unit is much longer-lived than an individual stem; a fire that destroys all standing plants will stimulate vigorous resprouting.

Epicormic branching, which often results from insect defoliation or other stress, is often seen in chokecherry. It is characterized by profuse budding and crowding of twigs and branches.

The ripe fruit is redder in color than the black cherry drupe and is considerably more astringent.

Chokecherry is one of the most widely distributed native trees on the continent.

Associates: A forest understory resident, chokecherry occupies the oak–hickory and northern hardwood forest communities. Tree associates often include black cherry, sassafras, hop hornbeam, and many others.

Spring, summer. Most insect foragers common to black cherry are equally at home on chokecherry. Especially common to both cherries is the Eastern tent caterpillar (see Black Cherry). *Epicormic branching,* a compensatory budding of new branches, may result from repeated defoliation by this insect; the new branches will look bunchy and distorted. Also appearing in outbreaks of one to two years on both cherries are caterpillars of the Ferguson's or cherry scallopshell moth *(Hydria prunivorata),* which webs leaves together.

A gregarious, leaf-rolling moth caterpillar, variously called the chokecherry tentmaker, uglynest caterpillar, or cherrytree tortrix *(Archips cerasivoranus),* also constructs dense webs. Unlike the webs of *Malacosoma,* however, these enclose the leaves (on which the caterpillars feed) at branch ends. As the caterpillars grow, more leaves and branches are encompassed, until a small tree may be almost entirely sheathed in webbing.

Fruits are dispersed mainly by birds, and typical avian and mammalian foragers are largely the same for this species as for black cherry.

Lore: The fruit, delicious as it looks, is not one you want to sample; if you do, you won't die, but your "pucker power" will be awesome. Chokecherries are strongly astringent (hence the name); ripening reduces the astringency, but only cooking and processing into jelly or pies make them edible to most people.

Native Americans used decoctions of the inner bark for various medicinal purposes. This plant shares the prussic acid chemistry of the entire cherry tribe.

Webs of the chokecherry tentmaker, a tortricid moth caterpillar, grow to encompass entire branches and tops of shrubs. Masses of these caterpillars may defoliate the plant.

Cleavers *(Galium aparine)*. Bedstraw family. Herb in shady moist woods, thickets. Whorls of six or eight leaves surround the square, prickly stem at intervals, and the plant generally sprawls in tangles over other vegetation. Some thirty *Galium* species grow in our area, many in dry woods and edges; most have smooth stems. This species, however, is one of the most common.

Other names: Bedstraw, goosegrass, catchweed, scratchgrass, stickleback, and some sixty others.

Close relatives: Wild licorice *(G. circaezans)*; sweet woodruff *(Asperula odorata)*; blue field madder *(Sherardia arvensis)*; partridgeberry *(Mitchella repens)*; bluets *(Houstonia)*.

Lifestyle: Its scratchy, recurved prickles are like Velcro, just strong enough to adhere to your shirt if pressed—hence the name cleavers. The fasteners seem not to be a plant defense but rather a means of dispersal. The plant, with its burry twin seed heads, lies ready to hitch a ride on any passing pelt or pants; the stem easily breaks off when pulled.

This *Galium* is an annual, reproducing entirely by seed; such an exclusive reliance on seed reproduction is unusual among woodland plants. The small, white, bisexual flowers rise on short stalks from the leaf whorls. Seeds germinate in the fall, gaining the plant a head start for spring growth.

Associates: This is mainly a plant of beech–maple and oak–hickory forests.

Spring, summer. Upper leaves with inrolled edges signify the presence of *Eriophyes galii*, a mite.

A gall gnat called the bedstraw midge *(Dasyneura americana)* may produce aborted flower buds.

Moths to watch for include the drab brown wave *(Lobocleta ossularia)*, the common tan wave *(Pleuroprucha insulsaria)*, and the large lace-border *(Scopula limboundata)*. These are all inchworm or geometer moths whose twiglike caterpillars move by "looping."

Galiums are not important bird or mammal foods.

Lore: If cleavers seem relatively unimportant to wildlife, their simple usefulness to humankind has been known for centuries. To the ancient Greeks, the stems clinging on one's clothing signified this plant's fondness for people; they named it *philanthropon* ("man lover"). As food, the tender young shoots make excellent boiled greens; chilled, they can be added to salads. Ripe seeds, roasted and ground, make a good coffee (commercially grown coffee, *Coffea arabica*, belongs to the same order of plants).

In tea and tonic form, the plant, which contains citric acid, found use by European herbalists as a diuretic. Dried plants were used for mattress stuffing (hence the name bed-straw). The fragrant bedstraw *(G. triflorum)*, common around the world, increases in fragrance as it dries. *Galium* was also said to repel fleas. Legend has it that the Christ child lay on a bed of *Galium*.

An enzyme in these plants causes milk to curdle, and they were once widely used for this purpose in making cheese.

Clubmosses *(Lycopodium* spp.). Clubmoss family. Low evergreen shrubs. Superficially resembling large mosses, these prostrate plants form a dense ground cover on acidic soils. Erect conelike or clublike sporophylls (fertile stalks) produce spores that give rise to tiny gametophytes (sexual forms of the plant), a process called *alternation of generations*. About a dozen species grow in northeastern North America. They occupy a variety of habitats from wet to dry and have varying acidity and shade tolerances. Most, however, prefer moist, shaded woodlands.

Other names: Ground pine, ground cedar, running pine, running moss, snakemoss.

Close relatives: Spikemosses *(Selaginella).*

Lifestyle: Because clubmosses are not seed plants, they occupy (with Wood Ferns) a unique position in this book. The visible plant is only its vegetative form, which sprouts from the tiny bisexual gametophyte produced by a spore. The entire growth span from spore to gametophyte to the vegetative sporophyll requires about twenty years—seven or more from spore to gametophyte, and ten or more from gametophyte to the visible plant.

Dense mats of clubmoss spread by arching or creeping stems (if the latter, either above or below ground), rooting at tips or irregular intervals; all of these characters depend on the species. As growth advances, the old stems of previous years wither and die, but since new growth increases faster than the old growth dies, colonies spread rapidly. The mature plants release enormous quantities of powdery spores in the fall.

Despite the fact that clubmoss leaves bear distinct resemblances to pine or hemlock needles or to cedar sprigs, clubmosses are closely related neither to these plants nor to true mosses. Fossils show that clubmoss ancestors once grew to huge tree size. Botanically, clubmosses (along with the horsetails, *Equisetum*) represent an evolutionary stage between plants that have no conducting tissues (algae, fungi, mosses, liverworts) and the higher plants. Clubmosses have a simple vascular system of food- and water-conducting tissue.

Modifying effects of the environment may be seen even within the same clone of plants; a portion exposed to full sunlight will have a different appearance than a shade-grown portion.

Creeping, horizontal stems of clubmoss give rise to upright branches that often form a dense ground cover. This species has a cedarlike foliage; others have a mossy appearance.

The growth of clubmoss generally indicates a nutrient-poor, relatively acid soil.

Associates: As if mirroring the needle-leaved trees below which they often grow, the coniferlike clubmosses are common though not exclusive to pine and mixed woodlands. Several clubmoss species such as *L. obscurum*, *L. clavatum*, and *L. complanatum* (tree, staghorn, and running pine, respectively) may be found growing together. *Lycopodium* needs thorough investigation into its plant and animal coactions. Detailed observations could reveal much more than we now know about its ecology.

Spring, summer, fall. Spores of some clubmoss species seem to "burrow" deep into the ground. The gametophytes these produce derive nourishment from an association with fungal threads and masses called *mycorrhiza*, a system that is vital to the plant's nourishment.

Little is known about clubmoss insect associates. A fairly common feeder is the European earwig *(Forficula auricularia)*, a reddish-brown, beetlelike insect with pincers protruding from the tail. Scale insects also feed on the plant. Look for smaller insects and ground spiders too.

Slugs and snails are mollusk foliage feeders. Two that may appear on clubmosses are the fern or gray field slug *(Deroceras laeve)* and the brown garden snail *(Helix aspersa)*.

In edge areas where young saplings (especially white birch) are present, Nashville warblers often build ground nests in clumps of clubmoss.

Lore: Clubmosses were once widely uprooted and used for Christmas greens. Today they are protected by law in most places and should be left alone.

One of the plant's most intriguing elements is its spore mass, a yellowish, dustlike cloud composed of almost microscopic grains. The uniformity of the spores' size once made them useful as standards for microscopic measurement. They also have a unique water repellency that made them commercially valuable as pill coatings (called vegetable sulphur) and in wound dressings to stop bleeding. Blackfoot and Potawatomi peoples inhaled the dust to stop nosebleed.

The spores are also highly flammable; they found conspicuous usage in fireworks, in the flash powder once used by photographers, and in stage effects for theatrical performances. In orchard fruit culture, the spores have been mixed with flower pollen as carriers in various artificial pollination techniques.

We find it difficult to imagine that ancestors of these relatively minor members of the plant kingdom once dominated (with horsetails and extinct calamites) the earth's vegetation. Forests of tree-size clubmosses originated during the Devonian period, long before the evolution of dinosaurs or even insects. During the succeeding Carboniferous period, thick beds of this vegetation were buried, compressed, and carbonized into the material we know as coal.

Columbine, Wild *(Aquilegia canadensis).* Buttercup family. Herb in dry or open woodland. Its drooping flower (red on the outside and yellow within) features five upended spurs. The three-lobed leaflets are also distinctive. Cultivated garden columbines are hybrids of this and several other species.

Other names: Red columbine, meeting house, rock bells.

Close relatives: Baneberries *(Actaea)*; buttercups *(Ranunculus)*; anemones *(Anemone)*; hepaticas *(Hepatica)*.

Lifestyle: Its form and color make wild columbine one of our best known and most popular wildflowers, virtually impossible to misidentify. Those long, upturned spurs are nectar repositories; the red tubes are the petals, culminating in the spurs at one end and the flowing, united red sepals at the mouth. The male stamens, maturing before the female pistils, protrude from a central column until all pollen has been discharged; then the pistils elongate. Since individual flowers mature at different rates, this sexual-timing arrangement helps guarantee cross-fertilization; self-fertilization is unlikely anyway, owing to the flower's pendant position.

Plainly these flowers are designed to attract a long tongue and an eye for red. Note how the tubes contract just below their tips, where the nectar is secreted; this is probably a defense against insects without sufficient equipment to tap so deeply. Following pollination, the flower tilts upright, and the dried ovaries become rattle-boxes in the wind, releasing seeds (follicles) as they deteriorate.

This is a perennial plant, rising from a stout rhizome. A basal rosette of leaves that develops in late summer or fall stays green over winter, producing the flowering plant in spring.

Columbine is an indicator of limy or near-neutral soils, preferring dry over moist sites.

Columbine leafminers feed beneath the leaf epidermis, leaving white trails behind. After their larval existence in the leaves, they emerge as adult flies. Leaf mines are characteristic insect signatures.

Associates: *Spring, summer.* A dying plant often indicates the presence of the columbine borer *(Papaipema purpurifascia)*, a salmon-colored, noctuid moth caterpillar that bores into stems and roots.

White, winding trails, very common on columbine leaves, are feeding tunnels of columbine leafminers *(Phytomyza aquilegivora)*, larval flies.

Look for columbine dusky wing butterflies *(Erynnis lucilius)*, purplish-winged skippers, hovering over the plant; the caterpillars, which chew holes in the leaves, are stout and pale greenish yellow with reddish streaks or spots—they hide in rolled-up leaves on the plant.

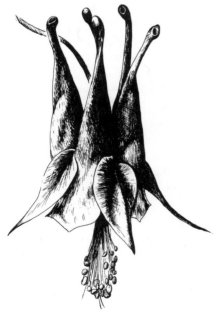

Holes bitten into the nectaries (at top) of columbine flowers show that not all insects gain access to nectar in conventional ways. Pollination is accomplished most efficiently by hummingbirds.

Columbine's nectaries are much too deep for most bees to reach, but honeybees *(Apis mellifera)* and halictid bees *(Halictus)* often collect pollen from the flowers. Large bumblebees *(Bombus)* may sometimes penetrate far enough to reach the nectar, but even long-tongued moths and butterflies cannot easily position themselves on the inverted flower to bend their proboscises upward. Small nectar feeders often nip holes in the nectaries from the outside; such robbery is one hazard of being a long-spurred flower.

But this flower's most efficient pollinators and nectar-feeders are hummingbirds with their needlelike bills and hovering flight. The flower's red color and long spurs indicate an evolved partnership; watch for ruby-throated hummingbirds wherever columbines are in flower.

Lore: Flowers are traditional tokens of love and esteem, but the gift of columbine was a token of war between the sexes, a symbol of cuckoldry and deserted lovers. To a woman, the gift was a stunning insult; to a man, it brought bad luck.

The great scientific namer Linnaeus made some strange analogies. He often affixed Latin names to plants based on their supposed resemblances to birds or mammals (has any vertebrate ever been named for its resemblance to a plant?). Thus *Aquilegia*, meaning eagle, refers to the flower spurs, bent like talons at their tips. The name columbine refers to another bird, the dove; those same bent spurs were said to resemble the heads of pigeons dunking around a water dish. Other botanists have likened the flowers to "jeweled earrings" and "red and yellow petticoats."

Nibble a flower spur for a sweet taste of nectar, but don't chew on the leaves—they contain enough prussic acid to induce an unpleasant narcotic effect on some.

Cottonwood, Eastern *(Populus deltoides)*. Willow family. Tree in rich soils, floodplains, lowland woods. Recognize cottonwood by the triangular leaf shape, the flattened, glandular leafstalks, and the large, gummy end buds in winter.

Other names: Common cottonwood, Carolina poplar, necklace poplar.

Close relatives: Aspens, poplars *(Populus)*; willows *(Salix)*.

Lifestyle: Cottonwood leaf shape has been likened to an Egyptian pyramid, with its coarse teeth as stone steps. Before the leaves emerge come the hairy flower catkins—"necklaces"—with male and female catkins on separate trees. Wind pollinates the female flowers and distributes the densely tufted seeds in early summer. Anyone who lives near a cottonwood stand is familiar with this tree's annual production of cotton; the seed tufts pile up in deep windrows along fences and curbing. For this reason, and because of its shallow, wide-spreading root system that heaves pavements and clogs sewers, cottonwood is considered a messy tree, often outlawed in cities. Seeds readily germinate on bare, moist soil within a few hours of release, but few seedlings survive.

Unlike its close relative quaking aspen, cottonwood does not sprout natural clones. Like willow, it propagates vigorously from twigs or cuttings stuck into the ground. It is shade intolerant, a feature that gives young trees pioneering status and mature ones dominance above the forest canopy. Young cottonwoods grow rapidly, often five feet in a year. Heights of eighty to one hundred feet and trunk diameters of three to five feet are fairly common, making these some of the most massive trees in the eastern and midwestern United States. They often begin deteriorating, however, at age seventy to eighty.

Cottonwood does not thrive in cold climates; warmth, moist soils, and high humidity suit it best. Flooding and silting, which may inundate the tree in its riverine habitats, suit it too. Because cottonwoods don't mind getting their feet wet, they often help form, colonize, and stabilize river islands.

Associates: Cottonwoods may form extensive groves, especially along water courses. Often, though, they associate in mixtures with other lowland trees such as willows, Northern hackberry, sycamore, and box elder. Many of the insect species hosted by this tree are also common to quaking aspen. Cottonwood "specialists" are emphasized here.

Spring, summer. On decaying stumps or logs, look for crown coral mushrooms *(Clavicorona pyxidata)* in dingy yellowish clumps with crownlike branch tips.

Numerous aphids specialize on poplars. The cottonwood leaf beetle *(Chrysomela scripta)*, a black and orange-red insect that skeletonizes leaves, and the cottonwood borer *(Plectrodera scalator)*, a black longhorned beetle with whitish pubescence, are especially prominent. Probably the most serious insect pest of cottonwood, the latter tunnels into trunk bases, weakening the tree until it breaks and falls; sawdust and wood shreds on the ground are signs of its presence.

A related species, the poplar borer *(Saperda calcarata)*, leaves blackened, swollen scars on the bark and feeds on bark of young twigs.

Several underwing moth species *(Catocala)* frequent cottonwood and other poplars. Well camouflaged on tree trunks, adult moths are active at night, as are the caterpillars, which are plump in the middle and taper toward both ends.

Before the leaves emerge, watch for bees collecting resin from the shiny buds.

Almost all the birds and mammals that feed on aspen buds and foliage likewise feed on cottonwood. This is also a favored beaver tree.

All year. A fungus often seen on cottonwood is cytospora canker *(Cytospora chrysosperma)*, causing oval, sunken spots that may enlarge and girdle branches. A more common canker is *Dothichiza populea*, causing elongated, cracked areas on branches and trunks that expose the brown, diseased wood.

Lore: Cottonwood is a fragrant tree. Its leaves and buds give off a sweet aroma when crushed.

The soft, weak wood isn't much in demand as a construction material since it warps badly. It is mainly used for crating, excelsior, plywood, and pulpwood.

Because of cottonwood's fast growth and spreading root system, its major human use is for erosion control plantings along ditches and shorelines and for shelterbelts, windbreaks, and ornament, especially in western plains areas. The cottonwood is the official state tree of Kansas, Nebraska, and Wyoming.

Currants and Gooseberries *(Ribes* spp.). Saxifrage family. Erect or spreading shrubs in moist or dry woods. Maplelike leaves alternate on the stem, and lines descend on twigs from each side of the leaf scars. Gooseberries have spines and prickles on the stems and, in the prickly gooseberry *(R. cynosbati)*, on fruits as well. Currants, except for the wetland species *R. lacustre*, are smooth without bristles or spines. Gooseberries bear flowers and fruits in short clusters; currants bear them in long spreading or drooping clusters. The commonest woodland species encountered are the American black currant *(R. americanum)* and the prickly gooseberry. About a dozen other forest and edge species also exist in our area; several more occupy swamps or wet ground.

Other names: Pasture gooseberry or dogberry *(R. cynosbati).*

Close relatives: Hydrangeas *(Hydrangea)*; sweetspires *(Itea virginica)*; saxifrages *(Saxifraga).*

Lifestyle: Currants and gooseberries include both solitary and cloning plants, which sometimes rise from layered stems that have rooted. They tolerate both shade and sun, doing best in sites that give them moderate amounts of both.

The ball-shaped, insect-pollinated, bisexual flowers are mainly greenish yellow or purplish and rich in nectar. Root germ cells exist in the stem tissues, as in willows, making *Ribes* easily propagated from stem cuttings. The berries are usually black or reddish purple, contain many seeds in a fleshy pulp, and are always tipped with the dried remains of the flower calyx.

Associates: Look for these common, low-understory shrubs in dry to mesic oak forests or in mesic beech–maple woodlands.

Spring, summer. Ribes has a full complement of insect feeders on leaves, stems, and fruits. Look for green, black-striped bugs causing circular depressed spots on terminal leaves; these insects are four-lined plant bugs *(Poecilocapsus lineatus)*, a common pest of *Ribes.*

Caterpillars of the gray comma butterfly *(Polygonia progne)*, an angle wing, are yellowish and spined; when alarmed, these caterpillars raise both ends of their bodies, forming a letter C.

Moth caterpillars include the currant spanworm *(Itame ribearia)*, yellow with many black dots, which may defoliate entire plants. Look for this looper's blue-green egg masses near twig crotches. Another geometer is the orange-barred carpet moth *(Dysstroma hersiliata)*.

The currant borer *(Synanthedon tipuliformis)* is a clearwing moth that looks like a black and yellow wasp. Its yellowish caterpillar bores into the stems; canes with dieback are signs of its presence.

Fruit that turns red and drops prematurely is probably infested with maggots of the currant fruit fly *(Epochra canadensis)*, also called gooseberry maggot. Yellow-bodied adults are about housefly size.

The currant stem girdler *(Janus integer)*, a sawfly, causes the plant tips to wilt and droop. Imported currantworm sawfly larvae *(Nematus ribesii)*, green with black spotting, feed in hordes, devouring leaves and defoliating plants.

Chief pollinators are honeybees *(Apis mellifera)* and bumblebees *(Bombus)*.

Ribes fruits are consumed by numerous songbirds, gamebirds, and small mammals including Eastern chipmunks, ground squirrels, red squirrels, striped skunks, and cottontail rabbits. White-tailed deer eat the foliage and twigs.

Late summer, fall. On leaf undersides, look for small, orange-yellow pustules that resemble a coarse felt. These contain the teliospore stage of the white pine blister rust *(Cronartium ribicola)*, a fungous disease that infects and causes heavy losses in its alternate host, white pine. These spores produce sporidia, distributed by the wind. The aeciospores, produced on pine and infecting *Ribes* plants, may carry for hundreds of miles. The *Ribes*-produced spores, however, usually infect pines within only a few hundred feet, since these spores require free moisture and cool temperatures to grow on pine needle surfaces.

Lore: *Ribes* is, of course, an enemy to the pine grower. Since the early 1900s, currants and gooseberries have been subject to widespread eradication programs because of their role as alternate hosts for white pine blister rust. To protect pine plantations, foresters recommend that all *Ribes* plants within one-half mile be eliminated. In commercial pine-growing areas, laws prohibit the planting of *Ribes*.

The rest of us may enjoy these plants for their sweet or tart fruits, which make excellent jellies, pies, sauce. All species are rich in pectin, and cooking reduces the spines of gooseberry fruits. Black currants have especially high vitamin C content. The nectar-rich flowers are edible too. *Ribes* plants used for commercially grown fruits are mainly European in origin; native American species have never received much attention from plant breeders.

The name currant apparently derives from the berry's so-called resemblance to the

Corinth or currant grape (the dried "currants" we see in supermarkets are not currants at all but grapes of this type). *Gooseberry* comes from a Dutch word meaning "cross-berry."

Dogbane, Spreading *(Apocynum androsaemifolium)*. Dogbane family. Shrubby herb in upland woods, thickets. Its red stems, paired blue-green leaves, nodding, pinkish flowers, and paired seedpods are distinctive.

Other names: Fly-trap dogbane, honey bloom, bitter root.

Close relatives: Periwinkles *(Vinca)*; oleander *(Nerium oleander)*; blue stars *(Amsonia)*; milkweeds *(Asclepias)*.

Lifestyle: The bisexual flowers are traps—not for their proper pollinators, the long-tongued butterflies, but for smaller flies and moths that get caught by their tongues in the flower's V-shaped nectaries. These insects haven't the size and strength to pull out, so they dangle and die. Rose-striped lines inside the flower lead to those sometimes lethal nectaries, which are quite fragrant.

Though adaptable to sunny, open sites, this dogbane thrives best in light-shady edge locations, in which it spreads by perennial, horizontal rootstocks. Another clue to dogbane's identity is its acrid, milky sap, similar to that of milkweeds, which oozes from broken stems.

This species often hybridizes with the closely related Indian hemps *(A. cannabinum, A. sibiricum)*, resulting in many mixed forms that are lumped under the name *A. medium.*

Associates: *Summer.* Almost anywhere this dogbane grows you will find its foremost insect associate, the shiny green and copper-colored dogbane leaf beetle *(Chrysochus auratus)*. Resembling in color, shape, and size the notorious Japanese beetle *(Popilla japonica)*, it feeds gregariously and almost exclusively on dogbane foliage. The beetles quickly roll off the leaves if disturbed. You

Dogbane leaf beetles, which rarely feed on any other plant, may be seen wherever the plant grows in its edge habitats. In form and color, they resemble the destructive Japanese beetle.

may also find their yellowish egg masses on the plant's stems or leaves.

Monarch butterfly caterpillars *(Danaus plexippus)*, though primarily milkweed feeders, also feed and pupate on dogbanes. Look for large, yellow-striped caterpillars and green, gold-dotted pupal cases on the plant.

The snowberry clearwing *(Hemaris diffinis)*, a sphinx moth with projecting rear horn and sphinxlike posture (the adult insect strongly resembles a bumblebee), feeds on dogbane, as does the dogbane tiger moth *(Cycnia tenera)*, also called the delicate cycnia.

Few if any vertebrate animals consume dogbane; it induces vomiting when ingested.

Lore: The milky sap contains cymarin, a cardiac glycoside that is toxic not only to dogs and humans but to livestock and most other mammals. Insects that can synthesize this chemical are themselves toxic, at least in some cases, to creatures that cannot.

Stem fibers, long and stringy, can be twisted into strong, durable cordage to use for emergency laces and fasteners in the woods.

Native Americans found a decoction of the roots useful as a diuretic. Potawatomies and Chippewas also used it as a medication for heart palpitations, and an extract has sometimes been employed as a substitute for digitalis.

Dogwood, Flowering *(Cornus florida)*. Dogwood family. Small tree in under-story of dry to mesic forests. Its opposite, parallel-veined leaves, spectacular white blossoms in spring, alligator-hide bark, and clustered, scarlet fruits in fall are the best field marks. Another woodland species, not as common, is the alternate-leaf dogwood *(C. alternifolia)*.

Close relatives: Bunchberry *(C. canadensis)*; gray dogwood *(C. racemosa)*; gums *(Nyssa)*.

Lifestyle: The bisexual flowers—some twenty in each bloom—are actually the greenish clusters centering the four white, notched bracts that resemble petals. Showy advertisements for insects to come pollinate its flowers, they appear at about the same time as the leaves begin to emerge. The notch that tips each of the bracts is a remnant of their former function as bud scales that protected the flowers through the winter.

This dogwood begins flowering at age six or so, producing an abundant seed crop about every other year. The fleshy, scarlet drupe contains a single seed (in occasional trees, it may be hollow and nonviable), which usually germinates in the spring.

Soil moisture is the crucial factor in seedling survival; this dogwood grows best in rich, well-drained soils and cannot tolerate frequent flooding, high water tables, or prolonged drought. Although flowering dogwood seldom grows in extensive pure stands, you are more likely to see several together rather than a single tree. A cloning species, it sends up stems from the rhizome as well as from layered stems or branches. Fire injury causes it to sprout vigorously from the root collar; cutting also encourages sprout growth.

Any stress in the crown of the tree will often trigger *epicormic branching* (sprouting of new twigs on the trunk). This dogwood's checkered bark, patterned like an alligator's back, covers an often crooked or low-divided trunk that seldom rises higher than forty feet. Slow-growing flowering dogwood thrives in open shady areas of the midlayer between forest shrubs and the tree canopy; heavy shade, however, rapidly eliminates it.

Research has shown that its leaves carry on their most efficient photosynthesis at an intensity one-third of full sunlight. Inspect the leaves for the tiny, whitish, flattened hairs attached at the middle, a distinctive feature helpful to wildlife biologists when they analyze the stomach contents of foliage feeders. Turning bright scarlet in autumn, the leaves are extremely rich in calcium. When they fall, they decompose much faster than most other forest leaves (three times faster than hickories, ten times faster than oaks and sycamore), making these leaves a prime soil builder of a high pH bed, in which dogwood itself best thrives. The leaves also concentrate fluorine.

The scarlet fruits are high in fat content (twenty-four percent by weight), much worth eating by birds. Such high-energy foods combined with brilliant leaf color represent an evolved relationship called *foliar fruit flagging*; the red color attracts birds (many of them autumn migrants), which consume the fruits and disperse the seeds in their droppings, often many miles from the original tree.

Associates: Flowering dogwood is a common resident of oak and beech–maple forests. It is not usually found in coniferous woodlands.

Spring, summer. Recent devastating attacks by the anthracnose fungus *Discula* have resulted in widespread mortality of this tree. Blighted leaves, cankers, and epicormic branching are symptoms of the infection, a cause of increasing concern for dogwood lovers.

Rose-tinted, sluglike caterpillars, much attended by ants for the sweetish fluid they excrete, are larvae of the spring azure butterfly *(Lycaenopsis argiolus)*. These larvae are subject to attack by tiny parasitic flies, against which the ants apparently defend the caterpillars. Look for the small adult blue butterflies ("violets afloat") fluttering around dogwood buds in early spring, sometimes even before the snow disappears.

Moth caterpillars include the dogwood thyatirid *(Euthyatira pudens)*, which feeds in loosely rolled leaves; the northern eudeilinea *(Eudeilinea herminiata)*, a hooktip moth feeding on leaves; and the dogwood probole *(Probole nyssaria)*, an inchworm leaf feeder.

Dogwood sawflies *(Macremphytus tarsatus)*, black, whitish-powdered larvae resembling caterpillars, feed in masses on the foliage, sometimes defoliating trees.

Dogwood calligrapha beetles *(Calligrapha philadelphica)*, spotted and almost circular in shape, also feed on the leaves of this tree.

Inspect the twigs for other insect associates. Swollen, club-shaped galls are caused by dogwood clubgall mites *(Mycodiplosis clavula)*, which feed inside the gall until fall.

A series of closely spaced holes along a twig may indicate the dogwood twig borer *(Oberea tripunctata)*, a longhorned beetle grub that pushes its excreta through the holes from its feeding chamber in the twig center. Twigs may break off as the grub tunnels down toward the trunk.

If you notice wilting or dieback on the tree, look for swollen, cankerlike areas on the trunk, often near the ground line. These are signs of infestation by the moth larvae of dogwood borers *(Synanthedon scitula)*, which feed on the cambium and often girdle limbs or trunk.

Fall. Twig clubgalls may be visible in fall as well as earlier.

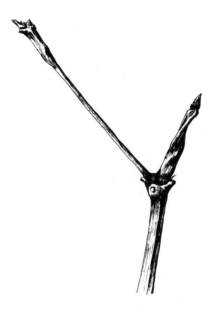

The swollen twig end on the left is the residence of dogwood clubgall mites, common on flowering dogwood. Galls are most visible after the leaves drop in autumn.

Look for twigs with rows of torn, splintered surfaces, where female periodical cicadas have inserted eggs. Larvae drop to the ground after hatching; twigs and leaves above the wound often die, showing conspicuous wilted areas amid surrounding foliage (see Red Oak).

All dogwoods are important wildlife food plants. Probably this species has a somewhat greater usage by songbirds than other dogwoods because of its foliar fruit flagging. Ripe berries seldom remain long on the tree when the fruit feeders arrive. Especially frequent consumers include Northern flickers, red-eyed vireos, Swainson's and wood thrushes, American robins, cedar waxwings, Northern cardinals, and evening and pine grosbeaks.

Common fruit eaters among mammals are cottontail rabbits, fox and gray squirrels, and Eastern chipmunks. White-tailed deer often consume the twigs and foliage.

Lore: These scarlet fruits, unlike the similar fruits of bunchberry, are bitter and unpalatable to humans.

Sources are strangely reticent about how dogwood came to be so named. (My own off-the-wall theory, based on experience in cutting survey lines, is that it originated from the fetid smell of the fresh-cut wood, strongly resembling the odor of dog feces.) Almost all dogwood cut for commercial purposes is utilized in the textile industry, mainly for shuttles in weaving, since this hard, smooth wood has little wearing effect upon thread. Golf club heads are also made of this wood.

Native Americans used the root bark to produce a scarlet dye for blankets, feathers, and belts. They also boiled the inner bark for a diarrhea and fever medicine. Tonics brewed from the astringent bark (containing the glucoside cornin and gallic acid) were also used by our ancestors for treating malarial fevers and as a substitute for quinine during the Civil War (bitter was always considered better).

Many varieties of flowering dogwood, displaying various colors of flower bracts and fruit, have been cloned for ornamental plantings. For deep esthetic pleasure, though, a forest dogwood tree decked in full spring flower or red autumn color is the most splendid sight.

This is the state tree of Missouri, North Carolina, and Virginia.

Dogwood, Gray *(Cornus racemosa)*. Dogwood family. Shrubs forming thickets in dry to wet-mesic sites in open woods and edges. Opposite, grayish-green leaves, erect red pedicels holding the white fruits in autumn, and cloning groups that show mounded profiles are distinctive features. Other shrub dogwoods include roundleaf dogwood *(C. rugosa)*, silky dogwood *(C. amomum)*, and red-osier dogwood *(C. stolonifera)*; the latter two species occupy wetland habitats.

Other names: Gray-stemmed dogwood, red-panicle dogwood, panicled dogwood.

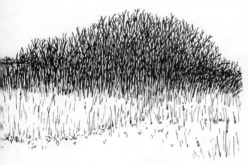

A cloning group of gray dogwood shows the distinctive, mound-shaped profile that results from differential ages of stems in the expanding clone. Sumacs show a similar cloning form.

Close relatives: Flowering dogwood *(C. florida)*; bunchberry *(C. canadensis)*; gums *(Nyssa)*.

Lifestyle: Much less attention-grabbing (at least to humans) than flowering dogwood, gray dogwood is also smaller in size and different in growth habit—altogether more modest than its showy cousin. A person unfamiliar with dogwoods would hardly identify the two as related species, though certain similarities in leaf, flower, and fruit become obvious upon inspection.

Gray dogwood likes the sun. Its cloning

habit is very pronounced; a gray dogwood stem standing by itself is seldom seen (you can recognize these clones from a distance by their rounded, biscuit-shaped forms, with the oldest, tallest stems in the center, the shortest and youngest at the rims).

The whitish, bisexual flowers appear in long, erect, cone-shaped clusters called *racemes*, requiring no specialized pollinators. The white berries are conspicuously red-stemmed. Leaves are quite narrow, and the bark appears smooth and light gray, giving this species its common name. Leaves turn reddish or purplish in autumn, and the red panicles (fruit stems) often linger for weeks after leaves and fruit have fallen. This late-season jolt of bright color is gray dogwood's only real flashiness.

Associates: On drier sites, plant associates may include staghorn sumac and greenbriers; in wetter locales, buttonbush, poison sumac, and other shrub dogwood species are common.

Yellow warblers frequently nest in gray dogwood thickets. The plant's opposite branching provides firm support for such tightly woven nests as this, as well as for looser nest constructions.

Spring, summer. Dogwood-feeding insects are common for most dogwood species, though different habitats may determine which dogwood insects become the most abundant foragers.

The flowers are pollinated by many insects, but beetles seem especially attracted by the odor. Larvae of the dogwood sawfly *(Macremphytus tarsatus)*, resembling powdery, white-bodied caterpillars, gang in masses to skeletonize leaves of this dogwood.

A common gall found only in gray dogwood is that of the dogwood bud gall gnat *(Cecidomyia)*. Look on the tips of upper branches for enlarged, marblelike swellings produced by these fly larvae.

Because the upper twigs form a firm base of support and the surrounding foliage of cloning stems provides dense camouflage, gray dogwood thickets are good places to look for bird nests. Among the most common residents are willow flycatchers, gray catbirds, yellow warblers, and American goldfinches.

Fall, winter. In dried leaves that remain attached by silk to the twigs, you may find deserted, oblong cocoons covered with tan hairs. Small ones, about a half-inch long, are those of the male white-marked tussock moth *(Orgyia leucostigma).* Inch-long or larger cocoons are those of females, and on these you may find a crusty, foamlike mass containing eggs, which will hatch in spring. Since the females are wingless, a female cocoon indicates that the insect probably spent most of its life cycle on this same plant. Though these insects forage on some 140 plants (see American Basswood), gray dogwood is a common host for them.

Brown, papery, spindle-shaped cocoons about three inches long attached lengthwise to twigs belong to the cecropia or robin moth *(Hyalophora cecropia)*; the large green caterpillars also feed on many other trees and shrubs.

Partridge hunters know that gray dogwood thickets shelter ruffed and sharp-tailed grouse, which feed on the berries. Ring-necked pheasants also relish the fruits. Vacated nests of songbirds—perhaps adopted by white-footed mice, which pile soft plant materials atop the nest, creating downy chambers inside—are especially visible after the leaves have fallen.

Lore: Chippewa natives pounded the astringent inner bark to use as a rectal treatment for hemorrhoids. The fruits are not edible to humans.

Highlighted by their red stems in the fall, the fruits present a colorful aspect that contrasts nicely with the coral-white berries and darker-hued foliage. One year, when I decided to make my own greeting cards, I collected a quantity of these scarlet panicles. Attaching them on blank cards with odd twists of grapevine tendril and miscellaneous buds, catkins, and curled grass leaves, I created various designs and scripts from nature that were, at least, highly original. Perhaps these panicles serve somewhat the same function for fruit dispersal by birds as the red foliar flagging of flowering dogwood.

Dutchman's Breeches *(Dicentra cucullaria).* Poppy family. Herb in rich woods. The distinctive flowers of these spring ephemerals are white, yellow-tipped, and double-spurred like upside-down leggings. The feathery, gray-green leaves are finely cut and many-lobed.

Other names: White hearts, soldier's caps, ear-drops.

Close relatives: Squirrel corn *(D. canadensis)*; wild bleeding heart *(D. eximia)*; allegheny vine *(Adlumia fungosa)*; corydalises *(Corydalis)*; fumitory *(Fumaria officinalis).*

Lifestyle: Two of the four petals are united to form the two-spurred bisexual flower, with the other two petals inside and projecting liplike over the stamens. The two horns or "breeches" contain the nectaries. These are not quite so difficult for insect access as the similarly upended wild columbine, but they still require long, specialized mouth parts. Flower clusters, rising on separate stems directly from the root, last for about eleven days.

Presence of this woodland perennial, which often grows gregariously from clustered, grainlike tubers just below the surface, indicates a neutral to slightly acid soil rich in humus.

Associates: Early spring flowers commonly associated with this species include spring beauty, trout lily, and bellworts. The closely related squirrel corn, which prefers a somewhat moister habitat, may also be found nearby.

Spring. Besides bees, not many insects can successfully manage the pendulous flower structure. Most insects are much better at working down than climbing up to nectaries.

Early-ranging bumblebees *(Bombus)* are the main nectar feeders and pollinators. Their eight-millimeter-long tongues reach just far enough to secure a drop or two from each "legging," and in so doing, the insects brush against stamens and stigmas. The honeybee *(Apis mellifera)*, with only a six-millimeter tongue, can't plunge this deeply, but it does collect pollen from the flower. Bumblebees occasionally nip holes through the spurs from outside, thus bypassing the conventional route.

The long seedpods, which mature in late spring, open lengthwise. The seeds are widely dispersed by ants.

The pine mouse is an occasional consumer of the small root tubers.

Lore: This plant is named for its supposed resemblance to the old-fashioned legwear of a Netherlands native. Name as we will, however, the business of flowers is always and essentially sex, a fact that not many popular names of plants convey.

Leaves of Dutchman's breeches should not be nibbled or used in salads—they contain an alkaloid that can produce a narcotic effect known as *blue staggers*, and have been known to kill cattle.

Elderberry, Red *(Sambucus pubens).* Honeysuckle family. Shrub in moist woods, forest openings. Opposite compound leaves, stout warty twigs, pyramidal flower and fruit clusters, leaf scars connected by ridges, and brilliant red fruits mark this species. Its close relative, the common elderberry *(S. canadensis),* generally grows in wetter habitats and has purple-black fruits.

Other names: Red-berried elder, mountain elder.

Close relatives: Viburnums *(Viburnum)*; honeysuckles *(Lonicera)*; twinflower *(Linnaea borealis)*; unrelated to box elder *(Acer negundo).*

Lifestyle: This shrub, woodier than the more familiar elderberry of ditches and swamps, prefers drier sites in thickets, edges, and the forest understory. Slow growing in

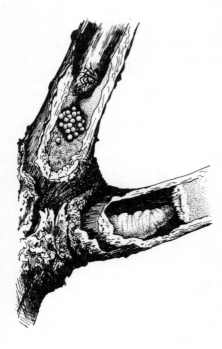

shade, it rises quickly in full sunlight, producing yellowish-white, insect-pollinated flowers in domed clusters early in the spring. It fruits in early summer (much earlier than common elderberry), displaying its small, scarlet, berrylike drupes at about the time that *S. canadensis* is flowering.

Red elderberry also has much less tendency to reproduce by cloning than the wetland species.

Associates: Red elderberry usually appears as solitary stems in mixtures with other edge or forest shrubs, mainly in beech–maple forests.

Spring, summer. A blue and yellow beetle on the foliage, eating notches in the leaves, is the elder borer *(Desmocerus palliatus)*, whose larvae bore into stem bases and cause dieback of branches.

Inspect broken twigs from which the soft, brownish pith has been hollowed for nest chambers of small carpenter bees *(Ceratina)* or of spider and potter wasps (Pompilidae, Vespidae), which stock their larval cells with insects or spiders and make mud partitions.

Cutaway branches of red elderberry show (at left) unhatched insect eggs and a dead spider stocked by a wasp, and (at right) a wasp larva. Small carpenter bees also nest in the hollowed-out stems.

Except in areas where beech–maple forest has been cut over, these shrubs are hardly abundant enough at any single site for the fruits to provide significant amounts of wildlife food, but many birds, especially red-eyed vireos, woodland thrushes, gray catbirds, and brown thrashers, relish them.

Lore: The fruits, like those of common elderberry, are hardly edible to humans when raw because of their unpleasant taste and smell. Cooked, mixed, dried, or processed, however, they make excellent jelly, pie, and wine, and they are extremely rich in vitamin C. Steeped to make a tea, they can also relieve stomach upsets.

Don't eat any other part of this plant, though. *Sambucus* leaves, stems, and roots can cause severe nausea and diarrhea.

Elm, American *(Ulmus americana).* Elm family. Tree in floodplains, bottomlands, and mixed deciduous forests, also colonizing disturbed sites and once widely planted for landscaping in cities and parks. Its characteristic vase-shaped form and its saw-toothed, feather-veined leaves lopsided at the base are good identity marks.

Other names: White elm, water elm, soft elm.

Close relatives: Slippery elm *(U. rubra)*; water-elm *(Planera aquatica)*; hackberries *(Celtis).*

Lifestyle: Most people have probably encountered these trees in city parks or along residential avenues (where many of the trees are dead or dying because of Dutch elm disease). Though thriving best in full sunlight, this elm's moderate shade tolerance, fast growth, and adaptability to both wet and dry sites make it one of the most opportunistic trees in North America.

Elms are also among the earliest flowering trees in spring. The greenish, clustered, bisexual flowers emerge before the leaves, are wind pollinated, and develop into winged fruits called *samaras* before the leaves are fully grown.

Seeds require moist ground to germinate; most of them dry out rapidly and die. Root systems are usually shallow and wide-spreading. Sometimes natural grafts occur between roots of separate trees, one way in which viral and fungous diseases are transmitted. Forest elm trunks diverge at taller heights (thirty to sixty feet) than open-grown trees (ten to twenty feet) owing to the greater competition for light in woodland conditions.

Inspect the buds, tipped slightly off-center above the leaf scar, which looks like a sleepy face wearing a dunce cap at a rakish angle. This asymmetrical pattern is repeated in the lopsided leaf base and in the zigzag twigs, which elongate from the bent buds.

The leaves turn golden in autumn, heralding the tree's second annual leaf fall; the first occurs as the bud scales (which are modified leaves) shed profusely from the expanding flowers in early spring. Autumn leaves are high in calcium and potassium, yielding rich humus.

Because their vulnerability to disease increases with age, old elms are becoming uncommon sights. The species itself, however, appears in no danger of extinction.

Associates: American elm's preferred sites are on the rich alluvial soils favored by box elder, Eastern cottonwood, and sycamore, among others. On upland or drier sites, it mixes with American beech, sugar maple, American basswood, and other deciduous trees.

Spring, summer. Two fatal vascular diseases—one caused by a virus, the other by a fungus—have combined to wipe out large numbers of American elms. The fault lies partly with past landscaping practices of lining streets or parks with this single species, thereby

Larval tunnels of the European bark beetle, foremost transmitter of Dutch elm disease, radiate outward from the vertical gallery tunneled beneath elm bark by the adult female beetle.

providing the means for rapid spread of disease. Both diseases are transmitted by specific insects.

Elm phloem necrosis, caused by the virus *Morus ulmi*, infects and discolors the sapwood just beneath the bark and cambium layers in the food-conducting tissue called *phloem*. Roots are stricken first. The bark loosens and falls away, and wilting and defoliation may proceed rapidly. An odor of wintergreen pervades the diseased wood. The virus carrier is the whitebanded elm leafhopper *(Scaphoideus luteolus)*, which hatches from eggs on the bark, feeds on the leaves, and moves from diseased to healthy trees.

The sac fungus *Ceratocystis ulmi*, cause of the notorious Dutch elm disease, probably originated in Asia but is so named because it was first investigated in the Netherlands. This disease afflicts all native elms. After its first appearance in Ohio in 1930, it spread rapidly in this country, often following traffic routes. Symptoms may include rapid or summer-long wilting and defoliation of branches or late, stunted leafing-out in spring. The fungus, which lives in cracks and beetle galleries under the bark, kills the tree by secreting toxins that clog the water-conducting tissues *(xylem)*. Most trees die in the same season that infection occurs, though a few may linger for one or two years. The fungous spores are introduced into healthy trees by two bark beetle species. The beetles feed only on healthy wood, usually within two hundred feet of their original tree, but they breed in already dead or dying elm trees with bark still intact, sometimes flying long distances to find them.

The most common carrier of these fungous spores is the smaller European elm bark beetle *(Scolytus multistriatus)*. First reported in New England in 1919, this dark, two-toned, shiny beetle bores into the bark and tunnels a vertical brood gallery. Larvae that hatch along this tunnel also make tunnels that radiate horizontally from the parent tunnel. The adult beetles emerge from the bark, leaving numerous shothole exits, then proceed to feed on wood in the crotches of young twigs. The native elm bark beetle *(Hylurgopinus rufipes)* is more uniformly gray-brown in color and makes parent tunnels transverse to the grain; larval tunnels create a butterfly-shaped pattern. The European species prefers elm trees in open, urban locations, while the native beetle often selects shaded habitats and forest elms. Sometimes both species occur on the same tree, with the European bark beetle inhabiting the sunnier portions. You can often see the engraved tunnels of bark beetles on the wood surface of dead trunks or on the back surface of shed bark. Small holes peppering the bark of dead elms and wounds in twig crotches of living trees are common signs of the beetle.

In the wake of these beetles may follow other fungi. Common and thick-footed morel mushrooms *(Morchella esculenta, M. crassipes)* often appear on the ground near dead elms.

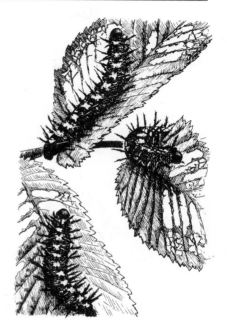

Masses of spiny black and red caterpillars industriously defoliating entire branches are mourning cloak butterfly larvae. The adult insect is one of our earliest spring butterflies.

Other insects abound on elms. Elm cockscomb gall aphids *(Colopha ulmicola)* produce green, red-tipped, comblike galls between leaf veins. The winged aphids migrate to grass roots in summer, then return to elms in autumn.

Larvae of *Fenusa ulmi*, a small black sawfly you may see flying near the trees in spring, create blotch mines between the lateral veins. Similar mines are created by larvae of the elm casebearer moth *(Coleophora ulmifoliella)*.

Elm lace bugs *(Corythucha ulmi)*, sap feeders found wherever American elms grow, cover leaf undersides with brown specks of excrement.

Mourning cloak butterfly caterpillars *(Nymphalis antiopa)*, spiny black with red spots, feed in masses on leaves and twigs, sometimes attracting black-billed and yellow-billed cuckoos, which feed on them. Other butterfly caterpillars include angle wings, notably the question mark *(Polygonia interrogationis)*, spiny and reddish brown, and the hop merchant or comma *(P. comma)*, also spiny.

Many moth caterpillars are frequently found on elm: The elm or four-horned sphinx *(Ceratomia amyntor)* is white striped with four projecting horns behind the head. Several

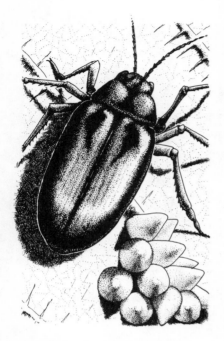

The elm leaf beetle skeletonizes leaves. Its cone-shaped eggs (at lower right) are laid in clusters on leaf undersides. Both larval and adult beetles feed on the leaves.

dagger moth species *(Acronicta)*, hairy with long pencillike tufts, feed on elm, and the double-toothed prominent or elm leaf caterpillar *(Nerice bidentata)*, with its jagged, saw-toothed back, is well camouflaged on elm leaves. Spring cankerworms *(Paleocrita vernata)*, fall cankerworms *(Alsophila pometaria)*, and elm spanworms (*Ennomos subsignarius*, see American Basswood) are inchworm caterpillars that sometimes dangle from the tree on a silk thread.

Other foliage feeders include the elm leaf beetle *(Pyrrhalta luteola)*, a serious pest that may defoliate entire trees. Look for olive-green beetles on leaf undersides, which the yellowish, sluglike larvae skeletonize to lace. Adult beetles chew small circular holes in the leaves and often crawl into houses in late summer. This insect is a favored morsel of cedar waxwings collecting high-protein food for nestlings.

Elm calligrapha beetles *(Calligrapha scalaris)*, oval with dots and colorful cryptic markings, also feed on leaves.

The elm or giant American sawfly *(Cimbex americana)* feeds with its rear body curled around a twig.

American elm is not as valuable a food tree for vertebrate wildlife as many of its tree associates. Nevertheless, it attracts many seed eaters in summer. Wood ducks, rose-breasted grosbeaks, and purple finches are among the more frequent. Fox and red squirrels also relish the seeds.

Northern (formerly Baltimore) orioles often suspend their nests high in the thick foliage of drooping outer boughs.

Once a dead elm loses its bark, it no longer provides a haven for Dutch elm disease carriers, and removal of barkless trees is not always advisable from a wildlife interest. Red-headed woodpeckers, especially, excavate nest holes in dead elms. And the climbing wild grapes and Virginia creeper that often use these dead trees as trellises provide important wildlife foods.

Fall. Clusters of buff-colored gilled mushrooms with off-center stems growing from knotholes or wounds on the trunks (often high in the tree) may be elm mushrooms, also called elm tree pleurotus *(Pleurotus ulmarius).*

Look for native elm bark beetles, some of which may emerge from the bark of dead elms at this time and fly to healthy elms, where they overwinter.

All year. Overlapped clusters of sticky, orange-brown mushrooms commonly seen along scars on dead or dying elms are probably *Flammulina velutipes*, the velvet shank or winter mushroom.

Decaying, mineral-rich elm leaves produce a soil highly preferred by earthworms.

Lore: The Iroquois tribes used elm, not birch, for their bark canoes. They felled a tree (often by burning the base), then poured boiling water on it to loosen the bark so that it would strip off in large sheets. The resulting craft, though considerably heavier than a birch canoe, was sturdier. Instead of pitch, smaller strips of elm bark were used to seal leaks. These natives also twisted the inner bark fibers to make rope.

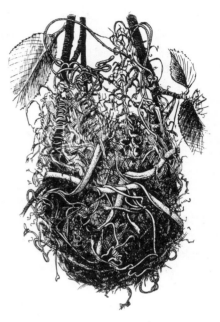

The baglike nest of the Northern oriole, suspended from an outer bough, is a marvel of construction. These birds often select the drooping end of an American elm branch as a nest site.

Elm wood, hard and tough, is difficult to split. It warps easily and is not durable in contact with soil. Its main commercial uses have been for the construction of farm implements, wagon wheels, barrels and crates, and truck flooring.

Despite this elm's stately mature appearance, commercial foresters have long considered it a weed tree of little value except for urban landscaping. Isolated trees show some resistance to the deadly Dutch elm fungus. Experimental remedies, ranging from insecticide sprays to beetle parasites to tree inoculations, have had little success in controlling the disease. The long-term hope is that elms will develop their own immunity to the fungus.

Elm, Slippery *(Ulmus rubra).* Elm family. Tree in moist woods, bottomlands. This is a ragged elm, not as symmetrical or regular in shape as American elm; its trunk often divides in a U-shaped crotch and spreads irregular ascending and horizontal branches.

Though this is the smallest native elm, it has the largest leaves (up to nine inches long), with upper leaf surfaces extremely rough and sandpapery. Unlike most other elms, it also has reddish-hairy twigs and buds.

Other names: Red elm, moose elm.

Close relatives: American elm *(U. americana)*; water-elm *(Planera aquatica)*; hackberries *(Celtis)*.

Lifestyle: Slippery elm grows faster than American elm but is not so opportunistic. This tree prefers moderately shaded woodlands. In drier upland forests, its presence indicates soils of high lime content. It sprouts vigorously when cut and may produce clones.

Most aspects of flowering are similar to those of the American elm, but the samara containing the seed may be almost an inch broader.

It has a more southerly distribution, reaching its northern limits in the northeastern states and southern Canada.

Associates: Slippery elm never grows in pure stands; scattered individuals mix with other deciduous species including white oak, sugar maple, American basswood, and others.

Spring, summer. Most plant and animal associates common to American elm—including the disease organisms causing phloem necrosis and Dutch elm disease—also frequent other native elms. Several insects, however, seem somewhat partial to slippery elm.

Serpentine feeding trails beneath the leaf epidermis are signs of elm leafminers, which develop into tiny adult flies. As with many leaf mines, its distinctive shape identifies the insect that produced it.

Spindle-shaped, hollow pouch galls on the leaves are produced by *Gobaishia ulmifusus*, the slippery elm gall aphid. The slippery elm midge *(Dasyneura ulmi)* produces swollen, bunchy growths, deforming leaf clusters.

An interesting long blotchlike mine is produced on upper leaf surfaces by the fly larva of the elm leafminer *(Agromyza aristata)*.

Look for blackish or orange-brown moths with white irregular lines on the forewings. These are white-lined bomolochas *(Bomolocha abalienalis)*, whose caterpillars feed on the leaves.

Twig browsers include cottontail rabbits and white-tailed deer. One of the tree's common names, moose elm, derives from the moose's reputed fondness for the young shoots, but the tree is uncommon in moose range. Porcupines relish the inner bark.

Lore: This tree is mainly noted for its mucilaginous inner bark, a slimy, fibrous layer resembling licorice in taste. It has high food and medicinal value. In the spring, Native Americans peeled it from the tree in long strips, dried it, and ground it into pulp for use as a nutritious flour, a wound dressing, and a soothing tea for sore throat. A piece of this material also quenches thirst when chewed. Slippery elm inner bark was once popular as a pleasant "chew" and home remedy. It is still commercially available in lozenge or tonic form as a mild relief for raw throats. Pioneers used this fibrous layer for making tough thongs and lacings.

The freshly cut wood itself has a faint licorice odor. Though much heavier than American elm wood, this lumber is used for many of the same purposes (all elm wood is marketed as "soft elm").

Ferns, Wood (*Dryopteris* spp.). Polypody family. Herbs in moist to dry woodlands. Their deeply cut leaves, kidney-shaped fruit covers *(indusia)*, fruitdots *(sori)* attached or adjacent to veins on leaflet undersides, scaly stalks, and basketlike, clustered growth form are characteristic. Though this genus includes several wetland and dry cliff species, typical forest species are the marginal wood fern *(D. marginalis)*, the spinulose or toothed wood fern *(D. spinulosa)*, the male fern *(D. filix-mas)*, and Goldie's fern *(D. goldiana)*, the largest. Many other fern genera also inhabit woodlands and edges, but wood ferns are among the most common.

Other names: Shield ferns, evergreen ferns; varieties of *D. spinulosa*, especially, have many vernacular names.

Close relatives: All ferns in the polypody family.

Lifestyle: These species all hybridize widely, their combined characters often making precise field identification difficult even for experts.

The basic reproductive scheme of these spore-bearing plants is an alternation of generations similar to that of clubmosses. Gametophytes, the actual sex forms of the plants, are so tiny and inconspicuous in the soil that they are seldom seen. The visible plant is the asexual sporophyte, or spore-producing, generation.

Though the four woodland species mentioned have somewhat different microhabitat preferences, all thrive in conditions of full or partial shade, all are perennial plants, and all are at least semievergreen.

D. marginalis, conspicuously green in winter, has a partially exposed rhizome resembling the trunk of a small palm tree, also suggesting a tree fern. Its large, marginal fruitdots are also distinctive, and the plant often shows a two-tone green contrast between older and younger fronds.

The many varieties of *D. spinulosa* are found in many habitats, but probably the most

common woodland variety is the evergreen wood fern *(D. s. intermedia),* which prefers limy or neutral soil; the laciness of the leaves is a good field mark.

D. filix-mas inhabits rocky northern woodlands, also on limy ground. The green-bronze tint and large leaf size of *D. goldiana* provide good identity clues to this neutral-soil species.

Millions of spores empty from the dried spore cases *(sporangia)* in the fall and are wind dispersed. Spreading rhizomes, however—one end dying as the other advances—produce most of the visible sporophyte plants.

Associates: Many wood fern species grow in close proximity to each other, accounting for the numerous hybrid forms. This is especially true in oak woodlands that contain contiguous damp and dry areas.

Spring, summer. Much more is known about insect foragers on cultivated and greenhouse ferns than on wild-growing plants. Dur-

Spore cases are variously sited and shaped, depending on the fern species. This wood fern shows kidney-shaped sporangia on the underside margins of spore-bearing leaflets.

ing years of forest tent caterpillar irruptions (see Quaking Aspen), I have frequently found its white cocoons enmeshed in fern leaflets. This insect cocoons anyplace that offers minimal shelter, though; it is not particularly partial to ferns.

A small pyralid moth caterpillar *(Phlyctaenia theseusalis)* webs and rolls the tips of fern leaves.

Fall, winter. Evergreen fronds provide an important winter food for spruce and ruffed grouse. White-tailed deer also eat wood fern foliage. Wood ferns are not, however, major wildlife food plants.

Lore: Fern botanists have defined, revised, and redefined the proper relationships of wood ferns for decades. This uncertain genus, with its many hybrid forms, seems to mock most of the conventional rules by which botanists determine species.

Some ferns are edible to humans, but wood ferns are not. The male fern, with bitter, astringent stems and rhizomes, is the source of filix-mas or aspidia, a drug for expelling tapeworms. This fern, common in Europe, was said to confer invisibility if carried or worn.

All wood ferns, with their wide-spreading roots and rhizomes, make excellent soil and slope stabilizers.

Geranium, Wild *(Geranium maculatum)*. Geranium family. Herb in woodlands. Five-parted hairy leaves and five rose-purple petals on a long stylar beak or "crane's bill" distinguish this spring wildflower, the most common of some fifteen *Geranium* species in the northeast.

Other names: Spotted geranium, spotted cranesbill, alum-root, shameface, rock weed.

Close relatives: Herb Robert *(G. robertianum)*; garden geranium *(Pelargonium)*; storksbill or alfilaria *(Erodium cicutarium)*.

Lifestyle: The flower, like many bisexual flowers, actually goes through male and female unisexual phases in succession, thus preventing self-fertilization. By the time the long, beaklike pistil is ready to receive pollen, the male anthers have withered or dropped off. An individual flower generally lasts from one to three days. Depending on weather, it may be a male flower for most of that time; on a warm, sunny day, it may convert to its female form within hours. Occasional flowers with blue anthers are known as blue-eyed geraniums. Nectar guides, those lines on the petals that direct insects to the white-woolly petal bases, show darker purple and translucent.

After insect pollination, the petals drop off and the long, beaklike pistil lengthens to an inch or more. This "crane's bill" is actually a sort of elongated tent, with its sidebands connected at the tip and held by tension at the bottom, where five seed containers are attached. As the seeds ripen, the sidebands dry and become taut. Suddenly they spring loose and curl up the central "tent-pole," flinging out the seeds. These symmetrical, curled-up catapults make identification of this plant easy in fall or winter.

The curled-up bands of the seed capsule, marking an explosive seed release, are distinctive fall and winter features of wild geranium. This geranium is a typical edge dweller, preferring light shade.

A perennial, geranium grows from winter buds on thick underground rhizomes rich in tannin. As the leaves age in summer, some become white-spotted.

This species prefers the light shade of open woods and thickets, thriving neither in dense shade nor full sunlight.

Associates: *Spring, summer.* Geranium's common wildflower associates include bellworts and jack-in-the-pulpit.

Feeding in masses on leaf and stem sap is the wild geranium aphid *(Amphorophora geranii)*, yellowish green with black markings.

Various butterfly species visit the flower for nectar—the common sulphur *(Colias philodice)* is a frequent one—but pollination is accomplished mainly by the larger bees.

This plant, among many others, attracts Japanese beetles (see Wild Grapes). The essence of its fragrance was once used as a bait in beetle traps for this destructive pest.

Geranium seed feeders include mourning doves and Eastern and least chipmunks.

Lore: Geranium's thick, tannic rhizome provided an astringent medication for Native Americans. The Chippewas dried and powdered it, serving the bitter tea to their children for toothache, sore mouth, and intestinal upsets. It was also used as a coagulant to stop bleeding.

This plant's near relative, the European geranium *(G. sylvaticum)*, is important in the history of science. Observing it in 1787, the German botanist Christian Sprengel figured out the mutualistic relationship between flowers and pollinating insects. The significance of cross-fertilization itself had to await the mind of Charles Darwin.

Ginger, Wild *(Asarum canadense)*. Birthwort family. Low herb in rich, moist woods. Two broad, heart-shaped leaves on hairy stalks surmount and shelter the solitary three-lobed flower, which is purplish-brown.

Other names: Canada snakeroot, asarabacca.

Close relatives: Birthwort *(A. clematitis)*; pipe-vine *(Aristolochia tomentosa)*; Dutchman's pipe *(Aristolochia durior)*; Virginia snakeroot *(Aristolochia serpentaria)*; heart-leaf *(Hexastylis)*.

Lifestyle: An insect-pollinated flower must flaunt itself like the sexual creature that it is. To human eyes, however, ginger does not flaunt. Its single flower per plant seems rather to crouch beneath a broad roof of leaves; its color is not a "turn-on" either. Clearly this flower, so low that it often lies partly buried in leaf humus, occupies a special niche of the forest ecosystem, resembling trailing arbutus in this respect.

The key to wild ginger's lifestyle lies in its early flowering, in April when the ground has barely warmed. Most active insects at this time consist of small flies and gnats. For these the cup-shaped flower provides abundant pollen for food and deep shelter from chill winds. In fact, this flower's structure shows a tendency toward the type of insect trap seen in its close relative, Dutchman's pipe.

In a reverse sequence of the unisexual flowering seen in wild geranium, the female pistil matures first, its lobes sticky; when it withers, a sex change occurs and twelve male stamens, loaded with pollen, arise. Cross-fertilization is also assured by the fact that only one plant grows from a perennial rhizome. As the seeds mature, the leathery capsule replacing the flower inverts, opens, and releases them.

Wild ginger grows in small or large colonies, sometimes covering many square feet in dense carpets. The leaves are evergreen with new ones replacing the old in spring.

Associates: *Spring.* Wild ginger patches are good places to look for the showy orchis *(Orchis spectabilis)*, one of the most spectacular wild orchids.

Ginger flower's color, resembling the liver hues of skunk cabbage and red trillium, seems to attract flesh-eating flies such as blow flies (Calliphoridae) and flesh flies (Sarcophagidae). Watch too for other pollinating flies, which may include March flies (Bibionidae), fungus gnats (Mycetophilidae), and syrphid flies (Syrphidae).

Purplish-brown, tentacled caterpillars feeding side by side on a ginger leaf may be larvae of the pipe-vine swallowtail butterfly *(Papilio philenor)*. The large adult butterflies, appearing in early spring, are brownish black with green iridescence on the hindwings.

Seeds, bearing small, oily portions called *elaiosomes*, are collected and dispersed by ants.

Lore: Though the rhizome's odor and peppery taste closely resemble the spice used for flavorings, this is not the commercially marketed ginger; that spice comes from the root of the unrelated tropical ginger plant *Zingiber officinale*, grown in Indonesia and Jamaica. The dried rhizomes can, however, be substituted for commercial ginger, and an interesting candy can be made by boiling the rootstocks, then simmering them in a sugar syrup.

Native Americans used the powdered rhizomes as a seasoning. Ginger tea was also used as a carminative medicine (to relieve gas) and for indigestion, heart palpitations, and earache.

Gooseberries. See Currants and Gooseberries.

Grapes, Wild (*Vitis* spp.). Grape family. High-climbing vines in woods and thickets. Recognize wild grapes by their broad, toothed, frequently lobed leaves, their shreddy vine bark, their twining, forked tendrils, and, of course, their purple-black fruits in autumn. About thirty species, which frequently hybridize, occupy North America.

Close relatives: American ampelopsis *(Ampelopsis cordata)*; pepper vine *(A. arborea)*; Virginia creeper *(Parthenocissus quinquefolia)*; Boston ivy *(P. tricuspidata)*.

Lifestyle: "By their fruits ye shall know them." Such identity marks apply to grapes along with most other plants that bear fruits eaten by humans, and we tend to ignore the flowers that produce the fruits (pollinating insects, of course, do otherwise). Grape flowers, though fragrant, are generally greenish and inconspicuous, but look at them closely. Though bisexual in structure, some are functionally unisexual, with either the stamens or pistil rudimentary and sterile. Thus a flower cluster, while having all the right parts, may actually be fertile only as one sex—and so not all grape flowers produce grapes. To complicate matters, some grape flowers are truly bisexual in function as well as form. These plants mix it up in almost every possible way.

The fruit itself—the grape—is a berry; that is, the seeds (four or less) are embedded in the fleshy pulp. Fruit taste and tartness vary widely, even within a single species, as does the annual yield of fruit. Some years there is hardly a berry to be found, while other years yield a superabundance. Fruits can ferment on the vine; when they wither, they lose their tartness and become raisins.

The tendrils are modified flower stalks. Depending upon the species, a tendril grows opposite almost every leaf or every third leaf. Tendrils occasionally betray their origins by bearing flowers and even fruit.

Wild grapes, though manifesting wide shade and moisture tolerances, are essentially sun-loving plants. In good habitat, a vine may be long-lived, growing to a diameter of several inches and often swinging free of (or breaking) its tree support when it becomes weighty. Big gnarled vines hang like ropes from the forest canopy.

Associates: Aside from providing food for wildlife, grapevines benefit forest environments in other ways. They open up the canopy by felling trees or branches with their weight, thus permitting sunlight to penetrate to the ground. They opportunistically use standing dead timber, such as disease-killed American elm, as supports for vine growth and fruit production.

Spring, summer. A widespread sac fungus causes diamond-shaped cankers on vines, resulting in dead branches; *Cryptosporella viticola* is called dead-arm disease or branch necrosis. Small angular spots with yellowish margins on leaves are early symptoms.

Insects that forage on grape are legion, and many of them also feed on its close relative, Virginia creeper.

Most conspicuous on leaves are insect galls of various kinds. Fleshy, pea-shaped galls on leaf undersides with openings on the upper leaf surface indicate presence of the yellow-ish-green grape phylloxera *(Phylloxera vitifoliae)*, this plant's most injurious aphid. The most damage occurs when one of every three or so aphid generations migrates down to the roots, where they feed and form nodules, frequently killing the vine. Green or red conical galls that look like dunce caps on upper leaf surfaces are the work of *Cecidomyia viticola*, the grape gall or tube midge. The grapevine tomato gall midge *(Lasioptera vitis)* makes green or reddish pea-size swellings on leaf veins and tendrils.

The many moth caterpillar feeders include several sphinx species. These large, rear-horned caterpillars, some of which make squeaking sounds, are easily recognized. The patterns of adult wood-nymph moths *(Eudryas)* resemble bird droppings.

The eight-spotted forester *(Alypia octomaculata)*, a bluish-white caterpillar banded with orange, sometimes defoliates vines.

Grapevine loopers *(Eulithis)* are slender, pale green inchworms that pupate in loose

Colorful Japanese beetles, the scourge of lawns and gardens, attack hundreds of wild plants too. Grape is one of their favorites. Tattered leaves are signs of their presence.

webs on the foliage. *Dyspteris aborivaria*, another inchworm known as the badwing geometer, rolls grape leaves, as does the grape plume moth *(Geina periscelidactyla)*.

Grape leaffolders *(Desmia funeralis)*, yellow-green pyralid moth caterpillars, fold and fasten leaf portions by strands of silk.

The grapeleaf skeletonizer *(Harrisina americana)*, a smoky moth caterpillar with black spots and spines, feeds in orderly rows on upper leaf surfaces, consuming everything except the veins.

Roundish, white, clear-winged moth caterpillars may be grape root borers *(Vitacea polistiformis)*, which drop to the ground and bore into the roots. The adults resemble paper wasps, even mimicking their behavior.

Orange blotch mines in the leaves indicate the larvae of *Antispila viticordifoliella*, a tiny shield bearer moth. Look for oval holes cut in the leaves; the insects use these cut shields for their cocoons.

Several common beetle species also forage on the leaves. The notorious Japanese beetle *(Popillia japonica)* is known to feed on almost three hundred plant species, but grape is one of its favorites, and it is a major pest of the plant. These gregarious, metallic green and copper-colored insects skeletonize leaves down to lacy tatters.

Earlier in spring, when the leaves are new, the grape flea beetle *(Altica chalybea)* chews industriously. It is small and dark metallic blue in color.

In summer, an inch-long tan beetle with black spots on each side, the spotted grapevine beetle *(Pelidnota punctata)*, is conspicuous. It draws leaves together for shelter.

Chains of small holes in leaves signify the feeding of hairy brown beetles, adults of the grape rootworm *(Fidia vitacida)*. The grubs attack the roots, causing plants to lose vigor and die back.

The grape curculio *(Craponius inaequalis)*, a small dark beetle, lays eggs and feeds first on the leaves. The larvae then feed beneath the green berry skin.

The grape leafhopper *(Erythroneura elegantula)* is yellow and red. It feeds on developing leaves in spring.

Several songbirds collect shreddy grapevine bark as a favorite material for nests, most notably the red-eyed vireo, gray catbird, Northern mockingbird, brown thrasher, and Northern cardinal. These birds, plus yellow-breasted chats, also build nests in low, densely foliaged vines.

Red squirrels construct spherical nests of leaves, grasses, and bark strips in grapevines; deer mice and white-footed mice build smaller round nests of finer fibrous materials.

Fall. Interesting fungal patterns can sometimes be seen on the inner surfaces of shed vine bark, notably the mycelial fans of shoestring root rot, *Armillaria* (see White Oak).

A globular mass of leaves and other plant material in a high-hanging grapevine is probably the summer nest of a red squirrel. Winter nests are usually built in tree cavities.

Among the insects to be observed on fruits are caterpillars of the grape berry moth *(Paralobesia viteana)*, which web several ripe berries together or to leaves, making a hole in each berry. Then the caterpillar folds over a leaf and pupates inside the fold. These folded leaves may remain on the vine into winter.

Grapevine looper caterpillars may also be seen in the fall.

The large Virginia creeper sphinx moth, also called hog sphinx *(Darapsa myron)*, visits the decaying or fermented fruit to feed. Bees and wasps puncture ripe fruits too.

Game birds that relish the fruit include ruffed grouse, ring-necked pheasant, Northern bobwhite, and wild turkey. Among songbirds, the most common feeders are pileated and red-bellied woodpeckers, American rob-

This "landscape scene" growing on the dead inner bark of a grapevine is a mycelial fan, probably of an Armillaria. *At night, the fungus sometimes casts a faint luminescent glow.*

ins, all of the woodland thrushes, cedar waxwings, gray catbirds, and Northern cardinals. During their southward migration, flocks of Tennessee warblers sometimes descend on grapevines to feed.

Although birds disperse many seeds, grape's primary seed distributors are probably mammals, which are attracted to the fruit by odor. Inspecting mammal scats in the fall will often reveal pear-shaped grape seeds in abundance. Raccoons often deposit scats at bases of trees; grapevines sprouting there will find support close at hand. Other main feeders include black bears, opossums, striped skunks, and fox squirrels. Nests become more visible in the fall after the leaves are gone.

Lore: If not the oldest profession, viticulture surely ranks beside it, for wine has accompanied civilization from the Bronze Age. Wine is almost the universal drink of humankind. Entire economic and trade systems have been built around it, and its use in religious, cultural, and ceremonial activities continues to this day. Grape is the first cultivated plant mentioned in the Bible; entire rosters of Old Testament rules applied to viticulture, which produced fruit and vinegar as well as wine. This fruit was the old-world grape, *V. vinifera*, which probably originated in the Caspian–Black Sea region. Transplanted to America, it flourished only in the southwest, where it was grafted with native American vines and now produces most of our raisins, domestic wines, and table grapes.

The earliest Norse explorers found native grapes growing so abundantly on the East Coast that they named the country Vinland. Native Americans ate the fruits raw (the Chippewas mainly used *V. vulpina*, the frost or forest grape), but they also made a decoction of the roots, which they used as an internal medicine for rheumatism and diabetes.

In Massachusetts, Ephraim Bull developed the Concord grape in 1852 from the native fox grape *(V. labrusca)*; Muscadine and Scuppernong varieties were derived from *V. rotundifolia*. These domestic grapes now produce most of the juice, jelly, and jam market brands. Not only hardier than the old-world grape, they are also more resistant to the grape phylloxera aphid, which all but devastated European vineyards when it was accidentally introduced there. The grafted rootstocks of both continents support today's wine industry.

Though not as sweet, wild grapes can, of course, be used for the same food or wine purposes as vineyard stock. Unripe fruits are rich in pectin. In addition, young leaves make a fine cooked green by themselves or for baking with rice or meat.

Woodsmen know that thick old grapevines can also provide emergency water. A six-foot section, cut first above, then below, will yield about a pint of clear, watery sap.

Greenbrier, Common *(Smilax rotundifolia)*. Lily family. Thorny climbing vine in open woods, thickets. Identify this greenbrier by its green, prickly stem, broadly rounded leaves with parallel veins, and paired tendrils attached to leafstalk bases.

Other names: Catbrier, horsebrier, hellfetter, blasphemy vine, stretchberry, tramps' troubles. The decorative plant sold by commercial florists as "Smilax" is the so-called asparagus fern *(Asparagus plumosus)*, related to greenbrier but neither a *Smilax* nor a fern.

Close relatives: Trilliums *(Trillium)*; Solomon's seals *(Polygonatum)*; bellworts *(Uvularia)*; Canada mayflower *(Maianthemum canadense)*; trout lilies *(Erythronium)*; lilies *(Lilium)*; onions *(Allium)*.

Lifestyle: Woodland greenbriers are the only woody vines of the northeastern United States that have both thorns and tendrils. This species may climb high but often does not. Waist- or shoulder-high cloning thickets form almost impenetrable barriers—flexible rolls of vegetative barbed-wire. In some woods, greenbrier is the dominant understory plant. Seas of sprawling vines and snagging thorns make such places almost inaccessible to human walkers.

Yet this plant offers much of interest aside from its considerable value to wildlife. The greenish flowers are unisexual, borne in clusters on separate plants. A few southern members of the genus have evergreen leaves; most others, although not evergreen, retain the leafstalk bases where the tendrils are attached. Notice the tendrils. Spirals at either end of paired tendrils twist in opposite directions, with a straight section between, the same form seen in tendrils of wild grapes.

Common greenbrier bears two or three seeds enclosed in elastic membranes inside each black berry. These rubbery packages can be pulled and stretched, accounting for the name stretchberry.

Greenbrier likes sunlight but is moderately shade tolerant, thus making it an edge resident. Because it cannot survive in dense-canopied woodlands, its presence gradually decreases as maturing forest growth shades it out.

Associates: *Spring, summer.* Female flowers are pollinated mainly by small flies.

Foliage feeders include two owlet moth caterpillars, the turbulent phosphila *(Phosphila turbulenta)* and the spotted phosphila *(P. miselioides).*

Blotch mines on leaves may indicate the feeding larvae of *Proleucoptera smilaciella,* a leaf-mining moth.

Black greenbrier fruits contain low fat and nutritional content compared with many other wild fruits. Yet they are extensively foraged by birds, especially by early spring migrants, which consume berries remaining from the previous fall. Ruffed grouse, gray catbirds, and hermit thrushes are among the main fruit feeders.

Birds and mammals frequently inhabit the dense, thorny cover. Gray catbirds and brown thrashers are common nesters, as are yellow-breasted chats. Cottontail rabbits take cover, bear their young, and feed in greenbrier patches. White-tailed deer relish the twigs and foliage. Such cropping elicits new sprouting of stems and branches, making the thickets even thicker.

The best way to know greenbrier is to become a thicket creature yourself. Place your eye at ground level beside a greenbrier thicket; you may see mazes of small trails. Drop to the trail level, snake your way in, and wear tough fabrics. The vines will fight you; these patches are havens for the hunted.

Even in winter snow, greenbrier thickets are favored bedding places for white-tailed deer. Melted spots show where they have lain protected by the thorny shrubs.

The warty bark of Northern hackberry instantly reveals this tree's identity. Look for these trees in lowland habitats, where they provide food for many insects, birds, and mammals.

Fall, winter. Nests of the previous spring become more obvious when the leaves fall, as do mammal trails networking the thickets. Evidence of deer cropping, too, is plainly seen now.

Lore: Young shoots, leaves, and tendrils are not only edible but tasty, either fresh or steamed like asparagus. Crushed, washed, and strained, the rootstocks yield a red powder that produces a gelatin, useful as a soup thickener or added to teas or cold beverages. This gelatin can also be used or mixed with tannic acid as a soothing salve for minor burns, bites, and abrasions. Berries have been used in the manufacture of blue dyes.

Hackberry, Northern *(Celtis occidentalis).* Elm family. Tree in moist bottomlands and lime-rich upland soils. On open sites, its vaselike form resembles that of American elm; forest-grown trees show taller, undivided trunks. Its elmlike, lopsided leaves also resemble the leaves of nettles *(Urtica)* in their lacy vein networks. The distinctive bark shows corky, knobby warts, an instant identity mark.

Other names: Sugarberry, hack tree, nettle tree.

Close relatives: Elms *(Ulmus)*; water-elm *(Planera aquatica).*

Lifestyle: This tree (one of my personal favorites) is mainly southern in distribution, approaching its northern limits in the Lakes states and southern Canada.

Small, greenish, unisexual flowers appear on the same tree soon after the leaves emerge in spring—male flowers in clusters at the base of the annual shoot, wind-pollinated female flowers solitary at bases of the shoot's upper leaves. The pea-size, purple, berrylike drupe, which eventually dries to resemble a tiny prune, contains a single wrinkled seed—a dangling fruit entirely unlike the winged samaras of the closely related elms.

The zigzag meshwork of twigs results from the fact that these twigs have false end buds; they sprout from the side instead of the tip. Though not a cloning tree, hackberry sprouts readily from stumps or its shallow, fibrous roots following fire or cutting. Moderately shade tolerant, it grows relatively fast and lives fairly long (150 to 200 years). The leaves turn light yellow in autumn.

Associates: Although hackberry does not grow in pure stands, several often grow in close proximity. Look for them in floodplain forest mixtures of sycamore, Eastern cottonwood, box elder, and others. Upland tree associates may include American basswood, American elm, white ash, and red maple.

Spring, summer. Hackberry leaves record a variety of insect feeders. Small, nipplelike galls on leaf undersides are produced by psyllids, often called jumping plant lice—in this case, the hackberry nipplegall maker *(Pachypsylla celtidismamma).* Several other psyllids of this genus create similar galls on leaves and twigs.

Butterfly caterpillars or adult butterflies on hackberry may include the question mark (see American Elm) and two *Asterocampa*: the tawny emperor *(A. clyton)* and the gray emperor or hackberry butterfly *(A. celtis).* The latter two caterpillars, yellowish green and striped with curiously antlered heads, feed gregariously. Look for the adult butterflies on the trunks, where they often alight (they also sometimes alight on people looking for them).

A dark green, humped caterpillar is probably that of the snout butterfly *(Libytheana bachmannii),* so named from the adult's projecting, beaklike mouth parts. Fossils of snout butterflies have been found in Pleistocene deposits that also held ancient hackberry leaves.

Common moths include the ruddy dagger *(Acronicta rubricoma)* and the thin-lined owlet *(Isogona tenuis).*

Fall. Foliage that turns prematurely yellow or brown in early fall may be infested with hackberry lace bugs *(Corythucha celtidis),* gauzy-winged insects that suck sap.

Hackberry seeds are relished and dispersed by many birds, especially Northern flickers, yellow-bellied sapsuckers, American robins, and cedar waxwings. Squirrels,

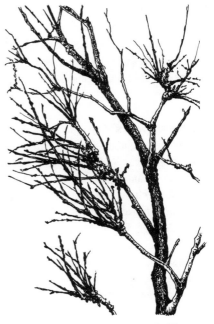

Witches' brooms are dense, twiggy growths. The common one on hackberry originates from a fungus–mite coaction that stimulates abnormal and distorted branching.

especially the nocturnal flying squirrel, are among the mammal feeders.

All year. A distinctive mark of many hackberry trees is a thickly profuse tufting of twigs at ends of branches in the crown; this is best seen after the leaves drop but is present in all seasons. These dense twig clusters, called witches' brooms, result from the combined activities of a fungus (the powdery mildew *Sphaerotheca phytoptophila*) and the hackberry witchesbroom gall mite *(Eriophyes)*. These unsightly growths do little harm to the tree, which may carry them throughout its life.

Lore: In some states hackberry has been widely planted for shelterbelts and windbreaks. Its tolerance of city air pollution also makes it a popular tree for streets and parks, though its witches' brooms reduce its esthetic value.

The ripe fruit, consisting of only a thin flesh surrounding the seed, tastes sweet and datelike. Immense quantities would be required to make jam or jelly, so we seldom get more than an appetizing taste before the birds and squirrels harvest them.

The famed "lotus" of Homeric antiquity, noted for its irresistible fruit, which made travelers forget about going home, was supposedly a hackberry (specifically the European nettle tree, *C. australis*). Archaeologists in China discovered hackberry seeds they dated at about 500,000 years, making them the oldest known remains of human plant food.

Hackberry is not an important timber tree. The wood resembles elm, is marketed with it when sold at all, and is difficult to work.

Hawthorns *(Crataegus* spp.). Rose family. Thorny shrubs and small trees, densely thicket-forming in open woods, edges, overgrown pastures. Their long, sharp thorns, stiff, zigzag branching, variably shaped leaves, and small, applelike fruits identify this group.

Other names: Thornapple, thorn, haw, May bush.

Close relatives: Mountain-ashes *(Sorbus)*; shadbushes *(Amelanchier)*; cherries *(Prunus)*; roses *(Rosa)*; blackberry and raspberries *(Rubus)*.

Lifestyle: The hawthorn genus is an exceedingly troublesome one. Unless you're a botanist specializing in these plants, you won't even try to key them down to proper species. Even such specialists widely disagree on how many North American hawthorn species exist; "splitters" say more than a thousand, "lumpers" claim less than a hundred.

Many botanists believe that the huge variations seen in *Crataegus* may have resulted from clearing and disruption of the original forests in eastern North America as pioneers settled the country. This opening-up of the landscape gave hawthorn species the chance to hybridize and colonize on a scale previously unavailable to them, thus enlarging the gene pool.

In any case, these plants show many individual variations, especially in leaf shape, and they also frequently hybridize. Such blurred distinctions generally indicate that a group is undergoing active if not explosive evolutionary change. For this reason alone, the variable hawthorns are interesting to know and watch.

The flowers, appearing with or after the leaves, are spectacular white or pinkish, apple-blossomlike, bisexual, and insect pollinated. They're not very fragrant; indeed, some are malodorous. Ripe fruits (thornapples) may vary in color from yellow to red to black; their fat content is low (one to two percent by weight). One to five seeds in each fruit may require as long as two years to germinate because of their hard seed coats.

Hawthorns are shade intolerant, needing full sunlight and generous space for both their spreading crowns (which sometimes exceed the tree's height) and their root systems. Space

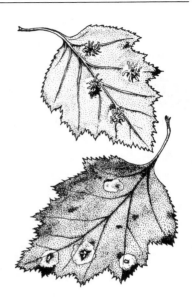

The undersurface of a hawthorn leaf (at top) shows the hairlike spore-producing organs of a Gymnosporangium rust. The upper surface (at bottom) shows characteristic spots of this fungus in its early stages.

competition is usually intraspecies, and a hawthorn thicket generally consists of even-aged trees.

To human would-be intruders, a mature hawthorn thicket presents one of the most formidable barriers of the entire plant kingdom; sharp, spearlike thorns like meshed poniards arm these thickets. The more hawthorns growing together, of course, the more secure becomes each plant. Thus although their competition for sunlight shades out younger hawthorns, it also provides a defense against browsing herbivores.

Associates: *Spring, summer.* Hawthorn leaves are frequently invaded by several fungi. Yellow or orange spots on upper leaf surfaces, with raised orange or brown spots centered by hairlike growths on the undersurface, probably indicate cedar-hawthorn rust *(Gymnosporangium globosum).* During late summer, the spores produced by the hairlike appendages are carried by wind and may produce galls on the fungus's alternate host, red cedar *(Juniperus virginiana).* The two trees must usually be located within a mile of each other for this fungus to exist.

A leaf blight fungus *(Fabraea maculata)* produces angular, reddish-brown spots on upper

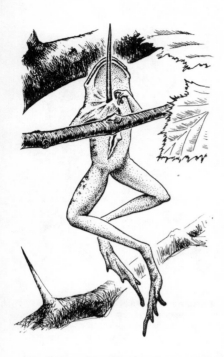

leaf surfaces, each containing a black, pimple-like fruiting body. Spots may enlarge to kill the entire leaf and in severe cases defoliate much of the tree.

Insect feeders on hawthorn foliage are numerous. Curled or crinkled leaves are generally signs of aphid feeding. Stippled and speckled leaves indicate hawthorn lace bugs (Corythucha cydoniae), dark, gauzy-winged insects; their spiny nymphs may also be present. The gall gnat Cecidomyia bedeguar produces a tufted, roundish gall on leaf midribs. Another gnat, Trishormomyia crataegifolia, makes a cockscomb gall on the leaves.

Moth caterpillars that feed principally on hawthorn include the hummingbird clearwing (Hemaris thysbe), a sphinx moth. The large adult, with transparent wing windows, is a daytime flier. The Eastern tent caterpillar creates large webs in forks of trees (see Black Cherry), and several underwing species (Catocala), plump caterpillars tapering at both ends, are also common.

Bees, flies, and beetles pollinate the flowers.

This impaled frog is only one type of creature often stored on thorns for later consumption by shrikes. Other prey may include large grasshoppers, earthworms, or small birds and mammals.

An old-field hawthorn savanna, often an overgrown pasture, provides excellent habitat (as do smaller hawthorn islands) for wildlife; it provides a semiopen yet effective cover for concealment and nesting. Among the most common nesters are mourning doves, black-billed and yellow-billed cuckoos, willow flycatchers, gray catbirds, brown thrashers, yellow warblers, yellow-breasted chats, and Northern cardinals. Look too for nests of loggerhead shrikes. Any insects, amphibians, or small birds or mammals that you find impaled on a thorn are signs of shrike presence. Unlike hawks, these birds have no grasping talons and must lodge their prey on a thorn or wedge it in a tree crotch to feed upon it. The birds also store their prey on thorns or barbed wire as territorial displays and may not ever eat it.

Fall, winter. Wormy fruits may indicate infestation by codling moth caterpillars (Carpo-

capsa pomonella), also called apple worms, probably the most serious pest of apple orchards.

Hawthorn fruits, perhaps owing to their low food-energy value, are not used by wildlife to the extent that one might think. Though many birds and mammals are known to eat them, only a few species consume them to any large degree. These include ruffed and sharp-tailed grouse, cedar waxwings, and fox sparrows. Birds occasionally become intoxicated on fermented fruits when feeding during a warm, wet fall. In winter, when many preferred fruits are unavailable, the fruits are more appreciated.

Lore: If you've sampled many thornapples, you know they vary widely in both taste and texture. Some are dry, mealy, or bland, while others are succulent, sweet, "just right." Most make a good apple jelly, and they contain plenty of pectin. Steeping the fruit also makes a decent tea.

Native Americans squeezed the raw, ripe fruits, then dried and stored them as small fruitcakes for winter cooking. A decoction of the root was given for menstrual pains, and the thorns were used as awls. During the last century, extracts of the fruit were found beneficial for treatment of certain heart and rheumatic disorders.

The immensely tough wood has no commercial value, since the trees are so small, though it is excellent material for homemade tool handles or other small items. Many ornamental hawthorn varieties, with great differences in showy flowers, attractive fruits, and colorful foliage, have been developed for planting in parks and gardens.

Hawthorn is the state flower of Missouri.

Hazelnut, American *(Corylus americana).* Birch family. Shrub in edges, fencerows, thickets. Identify this nut-bearing shrub by its catkins, hairy twigs, double-

The tiny, female flowers of American hazelnut are flaring red, but why is a mystery, since they are wind pollinated and do not need to attract insects. Male flowers are drooping catkins, formed in the fall.

toothed leaves, and ragged husks on the nuts. The beaked hazelnut *(C. cornuta)*, with bristly, beaklike husks, has a more northern distribution.

Other name: Filbert.

Close relatives: American hornbeam *(Carpinus caroliniana)*; hop hornbeam *(Ostrya virginiana)*; birches *(Betula)*; alders *(Alnus)*; unrelated to witch hazel *(Hamamelis virginiana)*.

Lifestyle: This shade-intolerant shrub sends up numerous clones from the roots, thus forming small, bushy groups rather than solitary stems.

Just before the snow disappears in early spring, look for tiny, bright red, budlike clusters near the twig ends. These are the female flowers. The male flowers are the drooping catkins, which first appear in the fall as compact, tightly sealed fingers, opening up to release pollen (about four million grains per catkin) in early spring. As in all birch family members, both unisexual flowers occur on the same plant.

The small, hard-shelled nut that results is exceedingly nutritious, consisting of twenty-five percent protein, sixty percent fat, and the rest carbohydrate. Fruiting begins at about age six and may continue for forty years or so, the lifetime of a shrub.

Associates: *Spring, summer.* This shrub typically grows in oak savanna habitat.

Although many insects feed on *Corylus*, a smaller number of species have a decided preference for it.

A greenish butterfly caterpillar with salmon or orange sides may be Juvenal's dusky wing *(Erynnis juvenalis)*. These caterpillars fold leaves, tying the fold together with golden silk strands, for shelter.

In curved, silken tubes between leaves, look for larvae of *Acrobasis rubrifasciella*, a leaf-crumpler moth.

Narrow, winding mines on leaves are made by larvae of a nepticulid moth *(Nepticula corylifoliella)*.

A compact, thimblelike leaf roll indicates the presence of *Attelabus rhois*, a snout beetle larva.

Galls on male catkins are caused by a gall gnat larva, *Cecidomyia squamicula*.

Fall, winter. Early-falling nuts may be infested by hazelnut weevils *(Curculio neocorylus)*, which leave small holes in the shell.

A casebearing moth larva *(Coleophora corylifoliella)* constructs tiny, flattened cases often found on stems in winter.

Ruffed grouse relish the catkins, and beavers and snowshoe hares feed on the bark. Blue jays, fox and gray squirrels, and Eastern chipmunks harvest the nuts. Check beneath the shrub for nut litter, the usual signs of mammal feeding.

Lore: Commercial filbert production relies mainly on the imported giant filbert

(C. maxima), native to Europe. Crossbred varieties of this and American hazelnut are also cultivated by nut growers.

Hazelnut figured high in Celtic mythology. The ancient Irish, particularly, regarded it as a tree of knowledge, repository of spiritual favors and good luck.

Native Americans used green hazelnut burs (the developing nuts) as ingredients for making a black dye, and the Chippewas fashioned the wood for ceremonial drumsticks. Nuts, of course, were collected for food (though many people seem allergic to them).

"Water witchers" have prescribed hazelnut branches as ideal divining rods. More reliable uses, perhaps, are found for the nut oil, which forms a base for perfumes, and for the wood, which makes a fine drawing charcoal for artists.

Hemlock, Eastern *(Tsuga canadensis)*. Pine family. Coniferous tree in cool, moist woodlands. Identify hemlock by its short, flat needles that appear in two-ranked, flattened sprays, by its wide, ragged crown and stout branches, and by its small cones.

Close relatives: Spruces *(Picea)*; tamaracks *(Larix)*; pines *(Pinus)*; balsam fir *(Abies balsamea)*.

Lifestyle: Both hemlock and balsam fir carry their flat needles in sprays, and needles of both species are white-lined below. Hemlock needles are shorter, however, and unlike fir needles are stalked. Notice that the two-ranked appearance on the twig is deceptive; the needles are actually arranged spirally but lie flat. Some of them lie upside-down on the shoot, white lines up. Needles remain on the tree about three years.

Both pollen and seed cones appear on the same tree at about age twenty. The latter ripen in the fall, drop seeds during the winter, and fall off the next spring. Produced abundantly every two to three years, seeds need moist ground and shade for germination. The shade of parent hemlock, however, is usually too dark for them and the big tree roots take up most of the available soil moisture, so seedlings do better away from their parent tree (the main reason why hemlock infrequently grows in pure stands).

Hemlock, indeed, casts some of the densest shade of any forest tree, not only because its foliage is thick but also because conifer canopies tend to filter out light across the entire spectrum. They therefore cast "blue shade" (in contrast to the "green shade" of broadleaf trees, which reflect the green portion of the spectrum). Young trees shoot up rapidly in the full sunlight of a forest opening, but they can also survive many years of slow growth in dense green shade. They usually live to 150 to 200 years, though much older hemlocks exist.

A shallow, sensitive root system makes this imposing tree highly vulnerable to ground fires, drought, wind-throw, and human intrusion (such as nearby roads, footpaths, or digging). Dead branches may persist on the tree for many years; the trunk forms hard, flintlike knots as the new wood closes around old branch scars. Hemlock bark is thick and ridged, sometimes comprising up to twenty percent of a tree's cubic volume.

Notice the drooping twig ends, which may tell you the direction of prevailing winds— they often curve away from it.

Associates: A big hemlock creates its own microenvironment on the ground beneath. The soil will be fairly dry and highly acidic because of the accumulated needle litter. These features plus its dense shadow allow relatively few plants to survive beneath the tree.

Because hemlock itself often germinates on the rotting logs or mossy rocks of green-shaded forests, its main tree associates are mixtures of northern hardwoods. These include yellow birch (a foremost associate), sugar maple, red maple, and American beech. Hemlock groves may occasionally be seen on lakeshores, north-facing slopes, and other sites, but typically the tree grows singly and scattered in mixed forest growth.

Spring, summer. Two uncommon orchids worth watching for in acid hemlock litter are rattlesnake plantains *(Goodyera)* and the magnificent showy orchid *(Orchis spectabilis)*. Look too for common wood sorrel *(Oxalis montana)*, a frequent associate.

Hemlock's insect foragers are numerous and in some cases destructive. Yellowing foliage and twisted needle tips in spring indicate feeding of hemlock mites *(Nalepella tsugifoliae)*.

Mottled greenish-yellow caterpillars that drop and hang on silken threads may be hemlock loopers or spanworms *(Lambdina fiscellaria)*. This geometrid moth is probably hemlock's most serious defoliator, typically feeding on needles from the top of the tree downward. Two other spanworms, the false hemlock looper *(Nepytia canosaria)* and the hemlock angle *(Semiothisa fissinotata)*, also devour needles.

Dieback of the upper crown and yellowing of twig tips—especially when associated with loosened bark and the presence of woodpecker holes or *Armillaria* root rot—probably signifies a dying tree infested with larvae of the hemlock borer *(Melanophila fulvoguttata)*, a buprestid beetle. These borers attack drought-stricken or otherwise weakened trees and kill many.

Nesting birds in hemlock groves may include golden-crowned kinglets, veeries, black-throated blue warblers, black-throated green warblers, magnolia warblers, Blackburnian warblers, dark-eyed juncos, and pine siskins. Yellow-bellied sapsuckers often drill rows of holes in the trunk, where they periodically feed (see White Birch).

Late summer, fall. These are mushroom seasons, especially on dead or dying hemlocks. A brown-capped pore fungus on the ground near rotting stumps may be the bitter bolete *(Tylopilus felleus)*. Closely related is the purplish-pink yellow foot *(T. chromapes)*, so named because of its yellow stalk.

Clumps of honey-yellow to brownish mushrooms growing at the base of trees or on decayed trunk portions are probably honey mushrooms *(Armillaria mellea)*, also called shoestring root rot. Honey mushrooms are the fruiting bodies of this rot-causing fungus with its stringlike "roots"; infected wood often glows in the dark. Also look for associated signs of wood borers and bark beetles.

A white, fan-shaped, clustered fungus growing densely from the wood may be angel wings *(Pleurotus porrigens)*.

Prominent seed foragers on the cones include black-capped chickadees, dark-eyed juncos, crossbills, and pine siskins.

Winter. Because hemlock foliage holds much snow, snow depth beneath the trees is significantly reduced. Thus white-tailed deer, which begin to flounder in snow deeper than twenty inches, often yard up in hemlock groves during periods of heavy snowfall. Deer also consume foliage and twigs of hemlock as high as they can reach.

Another bark and twig feeder, often settling itself high in the tree for days on end, is the porcupine. Foliage sprays and twig tips littering the snow beneath a tree are sure signs of a feeding porcupine, as are irregular patches gnawed down to the wood on upper trunks or branches. The chewed twig ends show diagonal cuts.

Lore: Native Americans found a variety of uses for this tree. They steeped young needles in water for a tea rich in vitamin C (obviously not the suicidal potion that Socrates drank—that tea came from the unrelated poison hemlock, *Conium maculatum,* an herb in the parsley family). The dried and ground inner bark provided a nourishing flour and thickener and was also applied to wounds and abrasions to stop bleeding. As a mouthwash it eased sore gums, and bark tea was a remedy for diarrhea.

An old hunter's trick for reducing human odor when stalking animals is to apply hemlock bark to the body. The bark also produces

Hemlock twigs littering the snow are signs of porcupine feeding in the tree. The animals nip off branch tips, holding them in their paws to eat the needles, but many fall to the ground.

a mahogany dye. Peeled off in rectangular sheets in spring when it loosens easily, the bark was sought by the leather industry for tanning hides. It remains the chief source of natural tannin for that industry.

The value of hemlock lumber—much inferior to pine for building purposes because of its brittleness, lack of durability, and blade-chipping knots—has increased owing to the rising prices of better lumber. Its only satisfactory uses, however, are for railroad ties (it holds nails and spikes well), crating, lath, and paper pulp. Hemlock ranks poor as a fuel wood (it throws sparks) and also as a Christmas tree (it sheds needles). Landscapers, though, have found young hemlocks useful for shady border plantings.

Hemlock is Pennsylvania's state tree.

Hepatica's densely hairy flower stalks are obstacle courses for climbing insects, such as ants, that would raid the nectaries without pollinating the flower.

Hepaticas *(Hepatica* spp.). Buttercup family. Low herbs of early spring in woods. Hepaticas have three-lobed leaves, hairy stalks, and white to pink, lavender, or blue flowers. Identify the two species—round-lobed hepatica *(H. americana)* and sharp-lobed hepatica *(H. acutiloba)*—by the angularity of their lobe tips. Round-lobed prefers somewhat acidic soil; sharp-lobed is more common on limy soil. Both species often occur in the same woods, however, and the two may hybridize.

Other names: Liverwort, liver-leaf, squirrel cup, snow trillium, mayflower, blue anemone, kidneywort.

Close relatives: Anemones *(Anemone)*; buttercups *(Ranunculus)*; columbines *(Aquilegia)*; baneberries *(Actaea)*.

Lifestyle: The flowers—some fragrant, some not—show generally the same structure as those of wood anemone; six to twelve lustrous sepals substitute for absent petals. Leaves are evergreen, lasting for a year, and new ones replace the old purplish ones soon after the flower wilts. Flowers close at night and may remain closed during cloudy days. Along with marsh marigold and spring beauty, hepaticas are among the earliest flowers of spring, sometimes appearing before all the snow has melted. Fruits are achenes.

Associates: Sharp-lobed hepatica is chiefly a resident of beech–maple woodlands.

Spring, summer. Hepaticas depend on insects not only for flower pollination but for seed dispersal as well. Early-flying bees and flies are the main pollinators. And the one-seeded achenes are collected and stored by ants. Earlier in the season, however, hepatica's new, densely hairy stems may keep small crawlers, such as ants, off the plant before the seed has set.

Lore: In a simpler age plant shapes and other features were believed to signal, by their resemblances to human body parts, their medicinal uses. This was the so-called doctrine of signatures. It seemed unthinkable that hepatica's liver-shaped leaf, for example, could have no use for liver ailments. At best, some remedies based on this idea may have been good placebos; at worst, they added toxic trauma to the original illness. Although hepatica leaves have probably never killed anyone, neither have they cured any livers.

The Chippewas used a mildly astringent decoction of the roots to treat convulsions in children. They also placed hepatica roots on or near their traps for fur-bearing mammals as charms to aid success.

Hickories (*Carya* spp.). Walnut family. Trees in moist or dry woods. Identify hickories by their feather-compound leaves, large buds, and nuts enclosed in four-parted husks. Two species, the shagbark *(C. ovata)* and shellbark or kingnut *(C. laciniosa),* have loose, shaggy bark separating from the trunk in long strips like warped shingles. The latter species plus pecan *(C. illinoensis)* prefer rich, bottomland soils; most other hickories, including bitternut hickory *(C. cordiformis),* occupy mesic or drier habitats.

Close relatives: Butternut *(Juglans cinerea)*; black walnut *(J. nigra).*

"Shagbark hickory trunks," remarked one observer, "look like they have been out in the rain too long." Warped, shinglelike strips of bark, often loose at both ends, are distinctive features of this tree.

Lifestyle: Most hickories begin flowering at about age twenty, and they start bearing heavy nut crops at about age forty. Thereafter they produce abundantly at about three-year intervals, so a meager crop in any given year is not unusual.

The male catkins and the small, wind-pollinated, female spikes appear on the same tree shortly after the leaves unfold. Leaves turn gold in autumn.

Hickories have deep taproots, making them stand firm in the wind. Their big buds and five to seventeen leaflets (depending on species) are often pungently fragrant when crushed. Like other nut trees, the leaf scars below the buds bear eccentric faces by which you may identify the various species in winter. A twig in cross section shows the pith in five-pointed star form.

Hickories grow slowly and live two hundred to three hundred years. These trees are moderately shade tolerant. Though they may produce stump sprouts after cutting or fire, they don't actually clone. Shagbark and bitternut species produce the allelopathic toxin juglone, though to a lesser extent than black walnut.

Associates: With oaks, hickories formed one of the dominant climax forest types of eastern North America. Wherever upland hickories grow, look for black, red, or white oaks. Hickories also share many animal associations with oaks, butternut, and black walnut.

Spring, summer. Prominent insect feeders on leaves include several butterfly and moth caterpillars. The banded hairstreak butterfly larva *(Strymon falacer)* is green or brown and sluglike. Of moth caterpillars, look for several underwing species, plump in the middle and tapering toward both ends. A tufted, gregarious species is the hickory tussock or tiger moth *(Halisidota caryae)*. The hickory leafroller *(Argyrotaenia juglandana)*, pale green-translucent, feeds inside the leaf rolls it makes. The elm spanworm (see American Basswood) can defoliate hickories.

Leaf and petiole galls are fairly numerous, most of them created by *Phylloxera* aphids and *Caryomyia* gall gnats. They may be pouchlike, cone shaped, warty, or pleated along leaf veins. A common twig gall, caused by the aphid *Phylloxera caryaecaulis*, looks like a partially opened hickory nut.

A tree that loses its leaves in early summer, showing dead tops and branches, may be infested with hickory bark beetles *(Scolytus quadrispinosus)*. The dark brown beetles, hickory's most injurious insect pests, bore into leafstalks, buds, and green nuts, then lay eggs beneath the bark, where larvae tunnel at right angles to the female's egg gallery. This butterfly-shaped series of tunnels is easily seen on dead, barkless trunks. The larvae, which sometimes girdle the tree, emerge through perforations in the bark.

Twig girdlers and twig pruners are common trimmers of hickory (see Red Oak).

Inspect green nuts that drop early; if the shells have circular cavities, they probably contain larvae of the hickorynut curculio *(Conotrachelus affinis)*, reddish-brown and gray beetles with beaks. A tree often jettisons injured nuts, as if to reduce further energy investment in them.

Masses of white wool on leaf undersides are the filaments of green larvae resembling caterpillars, the butternut woollyworm *(Blennocampa caryae)*, a sawfly. The larvae eat inward from the sides of leaves.

Flower catkins are relished by rose-breasted grosbeaks, among other songbirds.

Fall. The largest, most conspicuous caterpillar on hickory is the hickory horned devil *(Citheronia regalis)*, a five-inch-long green and spined creature of intimidating appearance. This larva of the regal or royal walnut moth is America's largest native caterpillar, appearing in late summer or early fall.

Periodical cicada egg scars are commonly seen on twigs in the fall (see Red Oak).

Nuts are devoured by wood ducks, wild turkeys, Eastern chipmunks, and fox, gray,

Can you detect its head end? It's where the longest horns protrude. Of fearsome aspect and dimension, the hickory horned devil is our largest native caterpillar.

red, and flying squirrels. Red squirrels gnaw open the nuts from the end; flying squirrels usually open them only on one side. By burying nuts, squirrels are the principal agents of this tree's dispersal. In certain areas, squirrel activity beneath hickories may encourage pine germination (see Eastern White Pine).

Lore: For both utility and food, few American trees rival the genus *Carya*. Hickory wood is exceptionally hard, strong, and elastic. It finds a wide market in sporting equipment, tool handles, ladders, gunstocks, and furniture. The best lumber comes from shagbark hickory, which also produces most of the hickory nuts sold (excluding the commercially grown pecan). Shellbark nuts are larger and sweeter; those of bitternut and sometimes pignut *(C. glabra)* are inedible. A hybrid cross between pecan and hickory produces "hicans," which look like large hickory nuts.

For smoking meats, bitternut wood is said to produce the best hickory-smoked flavor. Hickory wood is also unexcelled as firewood, burning cleanly and producing the most heat value per cord of any eastern hardwood. A cord gives the btu equivalent of 1.12 tons of coal, 175 gallons of fuel oil, or 24,000 cubic feet of natural gas. Hickory also produces a high-grade charcoal.

Almost exclusively native to North America, hickories covered Europe and Mediterranean lands in preglacial periods (the shellbark has been reintroduced there). Hickory's very name is thoroughly American, deriving from the Algonquin word *pohickery*. Native peoples ground and cooked the nuts with cornmeal, then baked the mixture into small cakes. Crushed green shells were thrown into pools to stun fish for food. The Chippewas burned small shoots and inhaled the fumes for headache and used hickory wood for their bows.

In early spring hickories can be tapped like sugar maple, producing relatively small quantities of sap for a tasty syrup.

Honeysuckles *(Lonicera* spp.). Honeysuckle family. Shrubs and climbing and trailing vines in woods, thickets, swamps. Both shrub and vine honeysuckles have opposite, untoothed leaves, papery bark, and transverse lines connecting the opposing leaf scars. Depending on the species, the tubular, flaring flowers are white, yellow, orange, pink, purple, or red; berries are orange, red, blue, or black. Forest and edge shrub species include the Tartarian *(L. tatarica)*, fly or four-lined *(L. involucrata)*, American fly or Canada *(L. canadensis)*, and Northern fly *(L. villosa)*; vines include the Japanese *(L. japonica)*, the wild or mountain *(L. dioica)*, the wild or rock *(L. prolifera)*, and the trumpet *(L. sempervirens)*. The alien Tartarian and Japanese honeysuckles have escaped cultivation to become the most common and widespread species.

Other name: Woodbine (actually vine honeysuckle *L. periclymenum*; also a name applied to the unrelated Virginia creeper).

Close relatives: Bush honeysuckle *(Diervilla lonicera)*; elders *(Sambucus)*; viburnums *(Viburnum)*; coralberry *(Symphoricarpos orbiculatus)*; feverworts *(Triosteum)*; twinflower *(Linnaea borealis)*.

Lifestyle: During the mild days of earliest spring, the first shrubs you are likely to see leafing out are honeysuckles. The green mist of their unfolding leaves in the still-bare woods and thickets is one of spring's first bold announcements. Honeysuckles also flower and fruit early, displaying colorful berries when most wild fruits are still green and immature.

Early timing is not characteristic of all honeysuckles, however; members of the genus show wide variation.

Twenty or so species of *Lonicera* inhabit eastern North America. The most distinctive mark of the entire group, perhaps, is the arrangement of leaves, flowers, and fruits. The spectacular bisexual flowers, teeming with insect activity, supply much nectar, but some species (and individual plants within a species) have more fragrance than others. *Lonicera* flowers have two distinct forms of petal lobes at the outer rim; no species displays both types. In one type (vine and a few shrub honeysuckles), the petal lobes are arranged unevenly, the bottom one tonguelike, bent down. Most shrub honeysuckles have the petal lobes evenly spaced. (The long, tubular forms of trumpet and four-lined honeysuckles are exceptional cases.) Some vine honeysuckles also have united upper leaves, giving an oblong or circular shape to this terminal foliage.

A unique feature of honeysuckle budding, though not always present, is the occurrence of several buds superposed one above another on the stem or twig. The largest and lowest is usually the bud that opens and develops, but one of the others may replace it if for some reason the first one fails.

Superposed buds of honeysuckles provide backup shoots if a spring frost, for example, should kill the lowermost shoots. The line connecting the opposite leafstalks is another mark of honeysuckles.

Most shrub species grow best in full sunlight, but some of the vines prefer moderate shade. Honeysuckle vines climb by twining stems alone without the aid of tendrils or holdfasts.

Occasionally you may see a Japanese honeysuckle flowering again in the fall, when day length corresponds to the spring flowering period. Foliage of this species is also semievergreen.

Associates: *Spring, summer.* The tubular flowers attract long-tongued insects. Japanese honeysuckle flowers and other white-flowered species are good places to watch for large, hovering sphinx or hummingbird moths (Sphingidae), which are major pollinators of these plants. Day-flying sphinx moths include the hummingbird clearwing *(Hemaris thysbe)* and snowberry clearwing *(H. diffinis)*, the latter resembling a bumblebee. Caterpillars of these species, greenish and rear horned, feed on honeysuckle foliage.

Other moth caterpillars commonly seen on honeysuckle include those of the brown-winged sallow *(Homohadena badistriga)* and the gray scoopwing *(Callizzia amorata).*

Tiny moth larvae of *Lithocolletis fragilella* make blotch mines on leaf undersides. On Tartarian honeysuckle, look for rolled and ragged leaves or white, pointed cocoons fastened to leaves. These are signs of the European honeysuckle leafroller *(Harpipteryx xylostella),* yet another moth.

Massed caterpillarlike larvae of the honeysuckle sawfly *(Zaraea inflata),* yellow striped and black spotted, may defoliate entire vines or shrubs.

The red-flowered, vaselike, and scentless trumpet honeysuckle is a hummingbird flower, adapted for pollination by ruby-throated and other hummingbirds.

Thick-foliaged honeysuckles attract several songbirds for cover and nesting, chiefly gray catbirds, American robins, Northern cardinals, and red-winged blackbirds (typically wetland nesters, these blackbirds often move to upland fields and thickets when high populations crowd the wetter habitats).

Late summer, fall. Despite honeysuckle's usually profuse fruiting and its frequent use for wildlife plantings, the colorful berries are not preferred wildlife foods, though they are a readily available supplement. Purple finches rank among the most frequent consumers. Occasionally birds that devour fermented berries become rather comically disoriented. Recent research shows cedar waxwings that feed on Tartarian honeysuckle fruit develop red patches in normally yellow feathers, the result of fruit pigments.

Lore: Japanese honeysuckle, introduced about 1806, is so dense and aggressive a plant—often smothering growth and overwhelming trees—that it has come to be considered a pest. Many foresters and landscapers advise its eradication. Several Eurasian shrub honeysuckles, however, are widely used for ornamental and garden plantings. Even Japanese honeysuckle shows some promise as a potential source of medicine.

Berries of most honeysuckles won't hurt you, but they are virtually tasteless. An exception is the blue fruit of the Northern fly honeysuckle, which is sweet, tasty, and can be prepared like blueberries for pies or jelly.

Native Americans apparently had even less use for honeysuckles than most wildlife. A root decoction, combined with other ingredients, was a Chippewa treatment for lung congestion.

Despite the label, honeysuckle perfume is a synthetic combination of oils. And the plants are not commercially important in the production of honey.

Against these negatives stands my vision of mountain honeysuckle. Sprawling in the shade of small pines, its top "dish" of leaves frames a flower head resembling a pair of intricate blue jewels—a surprise as vivid and refreshing as a sudden cool gust in the midday heat.

Hornbeam, American *(Carpinus caroliniana)*. Birch family. Small tree or large shrub in moist woods, bottomlands. Recognize this hornbeam by its smooth, fluted, musclelike trunk and bluish gray, beechlike bark.

Other names: Blue beech, water beech, musclewood, ironwood (a confusing name since ironwood more commonly designates hop hornbeam).

Close relatives: Hop hornbeam *(Ostrya virginiana)*; birches *(Betula)*; hazelnuts *(Corylus)*; alders *(Alnus)*.

Lifestyle: The trunk of this distinctive member of the deciduous forest understory resembles a hard, sinewy arm with biceps flexing along its length. Hornbeams are the hardest woods of the birch family, harder even than hickories, as you know if you've ever tried to cut one down (the axe bounces back at you).

American hornbeam is highly shade tolerant, slow growing, shallow rooted, and relatively short-lived. Greenish unisexual flowers appear on the same tree along with the birchlike leaves. The male catkin dangles at the base of the erect female catkin, which is wind pollinated. A small, ribbed nutlet develops at the base of a three-lobed leafy bract that somewhat resembles a narrow maple leaf. The bracts form loose terminal clusters that

Fluted, muscular ridges identify the hard, smooth trunk of American hornbeam. Often leaning and seldom very big, this tree prefers moist, shady lowland habitats.

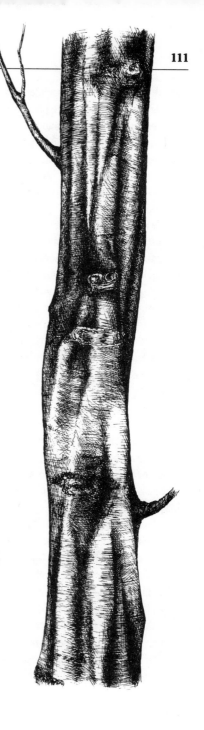

often remain on the tree into winter. When the nut finally falls, this bract functions like a sail, winging the seed away on the prevailing wind (see illustration with Hop Hornbeam).

The leaves turn scarlet and orange in autumn. Shaded beneath the forest canopy, this tree leans and zigzags, forming a wiry, flat-topped crown.

Associates: Look for this tree in mesic and lowland forest mixtures of American elm, box elder, red maple, yellow birch, and American beech, among others.

Spring Summer. This tree seems relatively free of major insect foragers. Catkins are eaten occasionally by ruffed grouse, ring-necked pheasants, and Northern bobwhites. Dead trees provide favored nest-cavity sites for black-capped and Carolina chickadees.

Fall, winter. Hornbeams rank second in importance as wildlife food plants. Nutlets are consumed by the aforementioned game birds, by yellow-rumped warblers, and by fox and gray squirrels. Beavers cut down the trees for food and lodge materials (a tribute to the strength of beaver incisors), and white-tailed deer often crop twigs and foliage.

Lore: American hornbeam wood is superb material for tool handles and wedges, but the tree is so slender, offering so little wood for the effort required to cut it, that its use for these purposes is limited. Since it decays rapidly upon contact with soil, it doesn't make good fence posts. It does make a good seasoned firewood, and its charcoal was once used in gunpowder.

Native Americans apparently made little use of the tree.

Hornbeam, Hop *(Ostrya virginiana).* Birch family. Tree in upland deciduous woods. Shreddy, scaly bark, birchlike leaves, catkin flowers, and clusters of papery sacs, each containing a single nutlet, identify this tree.

Other names: Ironwood, leverwood, beetle-wood, hard-tack.

Close relatives: American hornbeam *(Carpinus caroliniana)*; birches *(Betula)*; hazelnuts *(Corylus)*; alders *(Alnus).*

Lifestyle: Its inflated fruit clusters resembling hops give this tree its name (the name *hornbeam* refers to the wood's onetime major use for ox yokes). This hornbeam—the only true hornbeam, some would say—occupies mesic habitats similar to those of American hornbeam, and the two may overlap. Hop hornbeam is a larger, straighter tree, though it too is a shade-tolerant subdominant that thrives beneath the high canopies of climax hardwoods. It also grows along woodland edges and even in the open.

Both male and female flowers—male catkins usually in threes, female catkins paired on the same shoot—appear along with the emerging leaves, which will turn dull yellow in the fall. The saclike bract enclosing the wind-pollinated female flower swells as the season advances and turns from green to brown. When mature, these papery seed bags hang in conelike clusters, making hop hornbeam impossible to mistake at such a time. The trees do not fruit abundantly every year, however.

Unlike American hornbeam, *Ostrya* has a deep taproot (and therefore is not easily tipped over by wind) and is fairly long-lived. The lumber is moderately durable in contact with soil. Like *Carpinus*, however, it is slow growing and its wood is equally hard. The bark is rich in tannin.

Associates: Look for this tree scattered in the understory of oak–hickory forests, also to a lesser extent in beech–maple woodlands.

Spring, summer. Fungous and insect associates are generally the same as those found on yellow birch and sugar maple.

A few moths that specialize on this tree include the eyed and sleeping baileyas *(Baileya ophthalmica, B. dormitans)*, noctuids. Larvae of the casebearer moth *Coleophora ostryae* make flat, reddish brown cases on leaves and twigs. Broad, linear mines in leaves may indicate feeding of tiny *Nepticula ostryaefoliella* larvae, nepticulid moths.

A comparison of hornbeam fruit clusters: Hop hornbeam (above) produces papery, overlapping seed bracts, while American hornbeam (below) has looser, three-lobed bracts.

Fall, winter. The mustard sallow *(Pyreferra hesperidago)* feeds on hop hornbeam as a caterpillar and is frequently active as a yellowish adult noctuid moth in fall and even in winter around the tree.

The male catkins provide an occasional food source for grouse in the fall and winter. Yet the seeds and foliage of this tree appear even less commonly in wildlife diets than American hornbeam, perhaps because of this tree's scattered occurrence in habitats where the best food is usually oak or beech mast.

Lore: Hop hornbeam wood has relatively little commercial value. American pioneers nevertheless found many uses for it: tool handles, rakes, levers, sled runners, wooden dishes, and various items of wagon gear. Fiendishly difficult to work because of its hardness and strength, the wood required lots of time and uncommon skills. Once finished, however, these items proved virtually indestructible. Metals have largely replaced this wood in products for which it was formerly used.

Native Americans used the wood for bows. The heartwood of branches was chopped and boiled into a decoction taken internally for kidney pain and, with other ingredients, for coughs and lung ailments.

Although this is an attractive tree for yard and park plantings, its deep root makes it hard to transplant. And because it cannot tolerate salt, winter salting of roads and subsequent soil leaching make this a tree that is seldom seen from a car window.

Indian Pipe *(Monotropa uniflora)*. Heath family. Herb in rich, shady woods. No part of this plant is green; waxy-white, translucent stems, scalelike leaves, and a solitary, nodding white or pinkish flower identify it.

Other names: Corpse plant, ice plant, ghost flower, bird's nest.

Close relatives; Pinesap *(M. hypopithys)*; pipsissewa *(Chimaphila umbellata)*; laurels *(Kalmia)*; trailing arbutus *(Epigaea repens)*; wintergreen *(Gaultheria procumbens)*; blueberries *(Vaccinium)*.

Lifestyle: Botanists of an earlier generation, convinced that nature had made a bad mistake, deplored this strange little perennial for its "degenerate morals." How dare a seed plant give up being green and become a parasite! Today, botanists call Indian pipe an *epiparasite*, for it feeds indirectly from the roots of green plants. Its source of nourishment is subsurface mycorrhizal fungi, which interconnect with the roots of nearby plants and derive nourishment from them. The fungi act as a middleman that processes food delivery to Indian pipe from its green neighbors.

Indian pipe has the basic bisexual flower parts, though its leaves are vestigial, since they carry on no photosynthesis. The terminal waxy flower nods until it is pollinated by an insect. Then it bends erect, forming a dry fruit capsule. The stalk turns black and may last, tough and dry, through winter. Germinating

Indian pipe often remains standing, black and withered, over winter. Waxy-white in flower (inset), it looks funguslike. Like some fungi, it derives all its nourishment from other plants.

seeds form immediate mycorrhizal bonds, and several stems usually rise together in hooded "ghostly array" from a parent mycorrhizal mat. The plant always grows in shade, never in open sunlight.

Associates: *Summer.* Indian pipe's key associates, necessary to its survival, are the subsurface fungi by means of which it obtains nourishment.

Look for Indian pipe in densely shaded pine and deciduous woodlands.

Identity of the foremost pollinating insects remains largely unknown, though the flower's habitat, drooping position, and pale hue might give us some clues about certain insect types to look for.

Lore: One would think that such a plant, given its appearance, must have a vivid folklore history. Instead it has probably often been mistaken for a strange mushroom.

Its common name derives from the plant's supposed resemblance, when in flower, to a peace pipe. To some Native Americans, the clear sap was an eye medicine, believed to be capable of sharpening vision; whether this use was mainly medicinal or ceremonial (often a false distinction in tribal cultures) remains unclear.

Jack-in-the-Pulpit *(Arisaema triphyllum).* Arum family. Herb in damp woods, swamps, bogs. The woodland variety, one of three, is sometimes considered a separate species *(A. atrorubens)*; the other two varieties or species occupy wetter habitats. Its three-parted leaf, a striped floral leaf (spathe) forming a hooded canopy over the enclosed clublike spadix ("Jack"), and a cluster of scarlet berries in the fall are identifying marks.

Other name: Indian turnip.

Close relatives: Green dragon *(A. dracontium)*; skunk cabbage *(Symplocarpus foetidus)*; philodendron *(Philodendron)*; breadfruit *(Artocarpus communis)*; golden club *(Orontium aquaticum)*; calla lily *(Zantedeschia aethiopica).*

What sex is this flower? Unless you pry open the flap, you won't be able to say for sure. The jack-in-the-pulpit that rises here next year may be of the opposite sex.

Bright red fruit clusters make jack-in-the-pulpit even more conspicuous in autumn than in spring. By this time the leaves have withered or entirely disappeared.

Lifestyle: Sometimes a spadix develops flowers of both sexes, but more often the flowers are unisexual on each plant. They are located at the base of the spadix deep inside the pulpit. Thus you must gently pry open the enclosure to tell whether the plant is male or female. Female flowers look like tiny green berries surrounding the column base; male ones resemble threads, shedding pollen.

While Jack is not technically an insect-trapping plant, the design of the flower often results in the entrapment of insects in its lowermost chamber, which contains the sex organs. The ledge just above this chamber (an enlargement of the spadix) permits easy ingress but not so easy egress because of the slippery walls. In male plants, a gap where the spathe folds together provides escape—but even some insects that find this opening are too large to squeeze through it. Thus many plants gradually assemble a corpse litter.

Jack rises from a perennial underground stem called a *corm*, a food-storage organ to which the roots attach and that may produce additional corms. The corm may be labeled bisexual, for from it may arise either a male- or a female-flowering plant in any given year. Which sex will arise depends on the amount of food accumulated by fall in the corm. If food is ample, a female flower with two leaves arises in spring. If less ample, a male flower with one leaf results. And if the corm is starved, only a leaf emerges. This marvelous flexibility accommodates the varying energy needs of the two sexes and the storage status of the corm itself as determined by seasonal environmental conditions. Over a period of years, each corm generally puts up male and female flowers in about equal numbers.

Associates: *Spring, summer.* Jack's woodland flower associates may include bellworts, wild geranium, and violets. Pollinating and sometimes entrapped insects often include fungus gnats (Mycetophilidae), possibly attracted by a funguslike odor (the plant has no nectaries). By gentle probing, you can inspect the "prison chamber" without destroying it.

Because of its chemical defenses, this plant has few insect foliage feeders.

Fall. Scarlet berries on the plant are often attractive to birds. Yet field studies have found only a very few bird species that regularly consume Jack's berries. Ring-necked pheasants are probably the chief feeders, and wood thrushes eat them to some extent.

Lore: "Female botanizing classes pounce upon it as they would upon a pious young clergyman," reported one teacher of my grandmother's generation, but he didn't say why. Beyond the intrinsic interest of its flower and its unusual biology, Jack offers little to involve us. There is no tonic or throat soothe here. Acrid sap prevents foliage consumption by humans as well as most insects and other creatures. Calcium oxalate is the chemical that produces the burning taste.

The corm also contains this substance (it can even irritate bare hands), but dried corms can be eaten or ground into flour, as Native Americans did (drying them destroys the blistering poison). The Chippewas used a decoction of the corm as an external wash for sore eyes, and some tribes apparently boiled the berries for food.

Lady's Slippers *(Cypripedium* spp.). Orchid family. Herbs in damp to dry woods or thickets, swamps, bogs. The most common woodland species are the pink lady's slipper or moccasin flower *(C. acaule)*, the yellow lady's slipper *(C. calceolus)*, and the showy lady's slipper *(C. reginae)*. The first two occupy either damp or dry habitats; the less common showy generally inhabits wetter areas. All show a large, vividly hued, inflated sac or pouch (actually a fused petal) terminating a stem that rises separately from the oval, parallel-veined leaves.

Other names: Squirrel shoes, stemless lady's slipper, American valerian (all *C. acaule*), yellow moccasin flower, whippoorwill's shoe (both *C. calceolus*).

Close relatives: Orchids *(Orchis, Habenaria)*; twayblades *(Listera, Liparis)*; ladies' tresses *(Spiranthes)*; coralroots *(Corallorhiza)*.

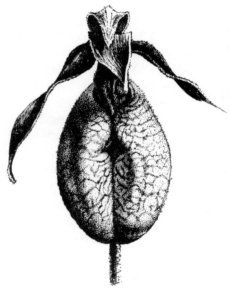

The moccasin flower evokes sexual analogies (sex is, of course, what flowers are all about). The cleft in the flower pouch allows an insect to enter but not leave. Exit is through a "back door" near the top.

Lifestyle: The insect–flower symbiosis reaches its peak of development in the orchids, whose sometimes bizarre flower anatomies attract insect pollinators and all but prevent self-fertilization. Lady's slippers enclose their bisexual flower parts within saclike balloons projecting from the base of two smaller petals. The insect enters from a tonguelike sterile stamen at the top (or, in the case of *C. acaule*, through the infolded cleft in the pouch). Fine, slanting, nectar-bearing hairs on the smooth-walled inner surface nudge the insect toward the sticky, overhanging receptacle (stigma) at the stem end, a constricted passage from which it cannot backtrack. The only way out is by squeezing through the passage and so brushing against the anthers, which smear the insect with pollen for the next sac it enters. The exit is smaller than the entrance, so sometimes these sacs become traps for the larger bees.

Elongated fruit capsules split to release hundreds of thousands of powdery, wind-dispersed seeds—among the smallest seeds of any flower. Only a very few of these seeds ever find the right combination of habitat, microclimate, and symbiotic fungus to thrive. These seeds contain no food tissue for the seedling plant. When a seed germinates, it produces a mass of cells called a *protocorm*, which must be joined by a mycorrhizal fungus *(Rhizoctonia)* before it can absorb soil nutrition. This pregrowth process may require two years or more, and the growing perennial may then take another few years to produce a flower. Often a plant will produce leaves but no flower in any given year. Seeds may remain viable for eight years or longer in a cool microenvironment.

The tough, dried flower stalk may remain over winter, marking the spot to look for new shoots rising from a spreading system of spaghettilike roots and ball-shaped tubers in spring. (These roots, perhaps reflecting the doctrine of signatures discussed under Hepaticas, have been widely regarded as aphrodisiacs.) Orchids generally indicate an environment in a state of flux, a transient stage of plant succession. Orchid species are notoriously finicky about where and when they will germinate and flower. The yellow lady's slipper, for example, thrives best in limestone areas. Orchids' specific soil and moisture requirements appear fully as intricate as their pollination devices. Picking them is illegal in several states.

Associates: *Spring, summer.* The fungus and insect symbionts mentioned are absolutely vital to the growth and survival of these plants. Both small and large bees invade the flower sacs, but the most effective pollinators are the midsize, ground-nesting andrenid and halictid bees, honeybees *(Apis mellifera)*, and smaller bumblebees *(Bombus)*. Charles Darwin, who placed various insects in the flower sacs of yellow lady's slippers, concluded that the flower was best adapted to pollination by *Andrena*, a solitary bee. Large bumblebees that get trapped may sometimes bite their way free, leaving a mutilated sac.

Large, oval holes in the leaves may indicate slug feeding, which can defoliate the plant.

Foliage of the yellow lady's slipper suffers from damage by several spider mite species. Their relative infrequency makes the orchids insignificant as food plants for birds and mammals. White-tailed deer, however, apparently play an important role in the germination of showy orchids. Colonies of this species often develop in old winter deer yards in white cedar lowlands; milling deer trample the seeds into soil loosened and aerated by their hoofs.

Lore: Such a slipper, wrote one grouchy botanist unimpressed by orchid to-do, is "fit only for very gouty old toes."

If you develop rashes easily, handle these plants with care; *Cypripedium* can produce an irritating contact dermatitis (another good reason not to pick them). The active compounds include a volatile oil and the resinoid cypripedin.

Native Americans dried and powdered the roots of yellow lady's slippers and applied the moistened powder for toothache.

Laurel, Mountain *(Kalmia latifolia).* Heath family. Gnarled shrub or small tree often forming dense evergreen thickets in acidic sandy or rocky woods. Its thick, leathery leaves, spectacular flowers, and rounded seed capsules identify it.

Other names: American laurel, calico bush, spoonwood, calmoun, mountain ivy, broad-backed kalmia.

Close relatives: Rhododendrons *(Rhododendron)*; trailing arbutus *(Epigaea repens)*; wintergreen *(Gaultheria procumbens)*; Indian pipe *(Monotropa uniflora)*; blueberries *(Vaccinium)*.

Lifestyle: Masses of rose-pink, star-shaped flowers decorate this plant in spring, but *Kalmia* flowers don't just passively barter nectar for sexual transactions. They are spring-loaded and actively bombard an alighting insect with pollen. You can test this mechanism yourself with a pin or grass blade. The slightest touch against one of the ten bent-over stamens, held under tension at the petal base, will release it. A tiny, sticky "string" of pollen is flung upward, normally to coat the furry body of a bee. Pollen may be thrown a foot or more, perhaps landing on another laurel flower without insect aid at all.

Fruits are rounded capsules that release wind-dispersed seeds. Germination is best on shady patches of moss.

This is a cloning, shade-tolerant plant. It may also reproduce by layering when a lower branch becomes buried in leaf litter.

Associates: A forest understory species, mountain laurel primarily occupies southern and mountain hardwood areas—especially the Alleghenies—extending north only to Indiana and southern Canada.

Spring, summer. The flower's main pollinators are bumblebees *(Bombus)* and honeybees *(Apis mellifera).*

Gray stippling that mottles leaf undersides may indicate rhododendron lace bugs *(Stephanitis rhododendri).*

Dying stem tips or sawdust from holes near the ground are signs of the azalea stem borer *(Oberea myops)*, a longhorned beetle that girdles twigs in two places about half an inch apart.

Black-throated blue, worm-eating, and hooded warblers frequently nest in mountain laurel shrubs.

Fall, winter. Look for white-fringed black dots on the undersides of the evergreen leaves. These are eggs of scale insects, covered by the waxy shells of their dead parents, a favorite food of chickadees and kinglets.

Seeds are consumed by Northern flickers, Carolina chickadees, and (along with buds) ruffed grouse. White-tailed deer eat foliage and twigs.

This shrub's evergreen foliage provides dense cover for shelter, roosting, or escape.

Lore: Foliage of mountain laurel is toxic to humans and most livestock—even ruffed grouse that feed on the leaves are sometimes killed by the resinoid poison. The flower nectar doesn't harm bees but the honey from this plant is potentially fatal to humans, so wild honey found in the vicinity of these shrubs should be avoided. Suicidal Native Americans were known to drink a decoction of the leaves.

Despite its name, this plant is unrelated to the true laurels (Lauraceae), which crowned ancient poets and heroes. The name *Kalmia* was Linnaeus's tribute to his friend Peter Kalm, the Swedish botanist who traveled in America from 1748 to 1751 and thought this flower the most beautiful he had seen. He introduced the shrub to Europe, where it achieved wide popularity (as in America) for ornamental landscape plantings.

The hard wood has little commercial value, but pioneers found it useful for numerous items, including wooden spoons.

Mountain laurel is the state flower of Connecticut and Pennsylvania.

Leek, Wild *(Allium tricoccum).* Lily family. Herb in rich woods. Its lilylike, onionscented leaves and bulb and its spokelike umbel of white flowers identify this wild onion. Most other wild onions have grasslike leaves.

Other name: Ramp.

Close relatives: Garden onion *(A. cepa)*; garlic *(A. sativum)*; trout lilies *(Erythronium)*;

Canada mayflower *(Maianthemum canadense)*; bellworts *(Uvularia)*; Solomon's seals *(Polygonatum)*; trilliums *(Trillium)*; greenbriers *(Smilax)*.

Lifestyle: Colonies of wild leek indicate a damp, humus soil.

Most green plants conduct their energy building and reproductive activities simultaneously. In this species, leaves and flowers operate on separate timetables. By the time flowers appear, the leaves have withered and died.

The strong onion-flavored bulbs remain, either single or clustered on a rhizome. Bulbs are actually swollen stem bases composed of colorless leaves in multiple layers.

Associates: Wild leek beds favor moist beech–maple forests.

Spring. Look for black or narrowhead morel mushrooms *(Morchella angusticeps)* in wild leek habitat, one of many places in which these morels grow (see White Ash).

Probably the only significant insect feeder on leaves is the widely distributed onion thrips *(Thrips tabaci)*. Barely visible because of their tiny size, they leave signs on the leaves: whitish blotches, crinkled distortions, and browning tips. The foliage is apparently not much eaten by mammals.

Lore: In certain Appalachian and Amish communities, people collect wild leek bulbs for annual ramp festivals and celebrate the coming of spring with steaming caldrons of wild leek soup. For less intimidating soups or stews, a bulb or two in the pot will suffice for flavor; a leaf may add interest to a sandwich. Before the plant flowers, say leek gourmets, is the best time to collect leaves and bulbs.

Native Americans used the plant for food and flavoring but also used the crushed bulbs as a skin remedy for insect bites and stings. The Chippewas made a decoction from the bulb to use as an emetic ("quick in its effect," they said). Leeks are rich in phosphorus and sulphur plus vitamins A and C and are relatively high in protein.

This plant and its close relatives also have a place in history. Welsh defenders wore the plants on their headgear in 640 A.D. when the Saxons invaded Wales. Leek *(A. porrum)* thus became the Welsh national emblem. In our own country, the Menominee tribe identified a shoreline plain on southern Lake Michigan as *shika'ko* ("skunk place"), where leeks grew in abundance. "Skunk place" is now Chicago.

Lily, Trout *(Erythronium americanum)*. Lily family. Herb in moist deciduous woods. Leaves mottled purplish or brown and a solitary yellow flower with reflexed petallike sepals identify this early-blooming spring ephemeral.

Other names: Adder's tongue, dogtooth violet, fawn lily.

Close relatives: Lilies *(Lilium)*; Canada mayflower *(Maianthemum canadense)*; bellworts *(Uvularia)*; Solomon's seals *(Polygonatum)*; Trilliums *(Trillium)*; greenbriers *(Smilax)*.

Lifestyle: Large colonies of this glossy-leaved little plant carpet the woodlands before the tree canopy shades the ground. Try to analyze from the leaf patterns which plants belong to separate colonies and how widely each colony spreads; the purple-brown "trout" patterns of separate colonies are never identical, but those within a single colony may be closely similar.

This plant's various common names point to other characteristics: its appearance during trout-fishing season; its sharp, tonguelike shape as the shoot first emerges from the soil; and its two leaves standing erect like the ears of a fawn.

Trout lily reproduces more by vegetative than by sexual means. Colonies result from the prolific budding of new perennial corms from previous ones. In a mature woodland, such colonies may be a century or more old, older than many of the surrounding trees. Many individual plants produce only one leaf and no flower; these far outnumber the occasional flower and two-leaved plants that rise among them. By the time May flowers bloom, erect green seed capsules have capped the stalks and the leaves have turned darker green, losing much of their mottled patterns. Then the plants are gone, retreating underground until next spring. Their long annual dormancy, however, belies their importance as a link in the woodland nutrient cycle. The roots retrieve molecules of the trace mineral phosphorus from the runoff of spring rains, transferring them to the leaves, which ultimately enrich the forest soil. Trout lilies have been called living phosphorus sinks.

The bell-shaped, bisexual flower, slightly fragrant, attracts long-tongued insects, for its nectaries are deep. But this flower is not so pendant that it can't self-fertilize if a cool spring makes early insects scarce. A true sun-follower, it turns on its stalk.

Associates: *Spring.* Trout lily flowers appear at about the same time, and in much the same habitats, as bloodroot, spring beauty, toothworts, large-flowered trillium, and the early violets, among others.

The mottled color of the leaves attracts many flies. Chief pollinators are blowflies (Calliphoridae), the mining bee *Andrena erythronii*, and queen bumblebees *(Bombus)*. Other insect visitors include butterflies, often the small sulphurs *(Eurema)* and whites *(Pieris)*. Crickets (Gryllidae) and carabid beetles feed on the seed caruncles, helping disperse the plant. The plant is relatively free of pests; few insects feed on or deface the leaves.

White-tailed deer nip off the seed capsules, and black bears dig up the corms to eat.

Lore: Young leaves and corms, though edible when boiled, may be slightly emetic to sensitive stomachs. A tea made of the leaves was said to be a sure cure for hiccups (but what isn't?).

The name dogtooth violet, a misnomer that has stuck, comes from a Eurasian variety with violet flower and toothlike roots. Naturalist John Burroughs originated the name trout lily.

Locust, Black *(Robinia pseudoacacia)*. Pea family. Tree in woods, fields, fencerows.

Identify black locust by its feather-compound leaves, its short, paired spines flanking the leaf scars, its deeply furrowed bark, its white, showy flowers in spring, and its short, flat seedpods in fall.

Other names: Yellow locust, false acacia.

Close relatives: Wisterias *(Wisteria)*; vetches *(Vicia)*; peanut *(Arachis hypogaea)*; tick trefoils *(Desmodium)*; clovers *(Trifolium)*; beans *(Phaseolus)*; garden pea *(Pisum sativum)*; honey locust *(Gleditsia triacanthos)*; redbud *(Cercis canadensis)*.

Lifestyle: Weeks after most trees have begun to leaf out, this tree stands like a black skeleton. Leaves finally emerge from the almost invisible buds sunken in the leaf scars.

After the tree is well foliaged, the abundant, extremely fragrant flowers resembling pea blossoms appear in drooping clusters. Bisexual and insect pollinated, they produce the short, brown pods that often hang on the tree until the following spring. Heavy seed crops are produced at one- to two-year intervals, but seedlings of this tree are rarely seen. Hard, impermeable seed coats permit germination only infrequently; reproduction occurs mainly by cloning.

Black locust is shade intolerant and sprouts quickly to colonize old fields or disturbed sites. Adaptable to just about any soil if not excessively wet or dry, it thrives best in limestone areas. Its spreading root system and cloning habit make it useful for erosion control. Bacteria *(Rhizobium)* in its nitrogen-fixing root nodules, as in other legumes, fertilize and enrich the soil. One study showed that a four-year-old stand of black locust fixed thirty kilograms of nitrogen per hectare per year. In southern Ohio strip-mined lands, these trees were planted by the acre in areas entirely bereft of topsoil. They gradually turned the ruined landscape to impassable jungle thickets.

Sheltering young, more shade-tolerant species, black locust quickly declines when these species rise to overshadow them. The zigzag twigs are brittle, breaking easily in the wind and accounting for the ragged, snaggy appearance of old locusts. Trees begin flowering at about age ten to twelve and seldom live more than one hundred years.

Note the behavior of the leaves on rainy days and at dusk: the leaflets fold while the leaf itself droops, a habit of the related true acacias. Black locust, native to the Appalachian and Ozark regions, has been planted in every state and thrives in many. Introduced to France in

The locust underwing, a fat-bodied brownish moth caterpillar, is a common feeder on black locust leaves. This is only one of many caterpillar species that commonly specialize on locust.

the early seventeenth century, it has become one of the commonest American trees in Europe.

Goldenrods are allelopathic to black locust, so you'll seldom see the tree very near these yellow summer flowers. New plantings, indeed, tolerate little root competition from any other plant species. Even grass growth causes many to fail.

Associates: Its cloning habit causes black locust to sprout thickly around parent trees, often forming dense groves. Tree associates include deciduous species such as oaks, black walnut, black cherry, and tulip tree.

Spring, summer. Locust hosts many insect feeders. On foliage, look for smooth, yellow-green caterpillars with brownish heads marked with two orange-red eyespots. These are silver-spotted skippers *(Epargyreus clarus)*, one of the largest and showiest skipper butterflies. The caterpillars feed at night, resting during the day in two or more leaflets webbed together to make a case.

Among the more common moth caterpillars are one-lined zales *(Zale unilineata)*, locust underwings *(Euparthenos nubilis)*, common springs *(Heliomata cycladata)*, orange wings *(Mellilla xanthometata)*, faint-spotted angles *(Semiothisa ocellinata)*, and honest peros *(Pero honestaria)*. Look for the adult moths too.

Larvae of several leafmining moths and beetles make characteristic mines on leaflets. Soon after the leaves emerge in spring, you may see circular mines of *Xenochalepus dorsalis*, the locust leafminer or locust leaf beetle, a defoliating insect. Later in the season, look for digitate blotch mines covering leaflet midveins on the upper side. On the underside, this moth larva *(Parectopa robiniella)* makes another small mine in which it deposits its waste material.

The locust leafroller *(Nephopteryx subcaesiella)*, another moth caterpillar, rolls several leaflets together and feeds inside.

Elongate galls on the black locust twigs indicate larval feeding of the locust twig borer

(Ecdytolopha insiticiana), a tortricid moth.

Bees are the major flower pollinators.

Fall, winter. Although locust seeds are rich in fat and protein, their use as food by birds and mammals is relatively low. Northern bobwhites, ring-necked pheasants, mourning doves, cottontail rabbits, snowshoe hares, fox squirrels, and white-tailed deer are the main seed consumers.

All year. Signs of black locust's most destructive insect pest, which kills many trees, are evident at any season. This is the locust borer *(Megacyllene robiniae)*, a black, yellow-lined longhorned beetle. Larvae burrow into the inner bark and sapwood, leaving long, winding tunnels. They weaken the tree, deform it, and create an entrance for wood-rotting fungi (especially *Phellinus rimosus*, a bracket fungus). Look for swollen, cracked areas on the trunk, wet areas on the bark in spring and fall, and larval holes in the trunk with masses of sawdust at tree bases. Adult beetles emerge from the trees in late summer

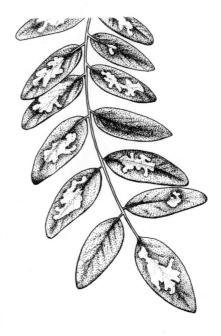

Amoeba-shaped blotch mines covering the leaflet centers characterize the presence of digitate locust miners. On the leaflet underside, look for the insect's waste-deposit mine.

and feed, curiously, upon the pollen of goldenrod, a plant that retards the growth of black locust. Locust borers may indirectly benefit locust stands, however, by stimulating growth of new sprouts as less vigorous trees are killed.

Dense clones provide year-round protective cover for small game.

Lore: Hard and durable, locust wood is valued for fence posts, railroad ties, tool handles, and insulator pins on utility poles. As firewood, locust is hard to cut and start, but it burns cleanly with a blue flame.

Cultivated locust varieties are planted as ornamentals, especially in Europe, where trees are free of the locust borer. Plantings in North America are now mainly for erosion control and wasteland reclamation.

Except for the flowers, all parts of this tree contain the compounds robin, a phytotoxin, and robitin, a glycoside, poisonous to humans and sometimes to livestock. The tree has recently been discovered to produce a fungicide useful for treating wood. Locust honey is commercially produced in Italy and considered a gourmet delicacy. Native Americans ate the seeds after boiling them, and the flower clusters make good fritters.

The last continental glaciation almost wiped this tree out, sequestering it in a small area of the southern Appalachians. All black locusts we see are progeny of that survival.

Bright red spots with halos on the leaves are flat galls of the maple leafspot midge, a larval fly. These common galls may be seen wherever red maples grow.

Maple, Red *(Acer rubrum)*. Maple family. Tree in lowland and upland forests, swamps. Recognize red maple by its smooth, light gray branches and beechlike bark on young trunks, opposite leaves that are whitish below, red twigs and buds, and bright red foliage in the fall.

Other names: Scarlet maple, swamp maple, soft maple.

Close relatives: Sugar maple *(A. saccharum)*; box elder *(A. negundo)*.

Lifestyle: Here is a tree named well, for it has red flowers and new leaves in spring, red twigs and leafstalks in summer, red leaves in the fall, and red buds in the winter.

Though it prefers moist habitats, this tree adapts to a broad range of light and moisture conditions, often colonizing the drier slopes above its primary swampy locales. Young trees often appear in clumps with several stems growing from old stumps or roots.

Gauzy-red flowers appear long before the leaves emerge in spring (about the same time as pussy willows). Male flowers are orange, female flowers are red; flowers of both sexes and bisexual flowers may appear on separate trees or all on the same tree (often on separate branches) and are pollinated by both wind and insects. The winged keys, or samaras, fall in late spring and germinate quickly.

Red maple, less shade tolerant than sugar maple, is also shorter-lived than that species, achieving maturity at seventy to eighty years.

This tree provides one of the most dazzling displays of autumn foliage. In addition to weather and day length, the tree's degree of redness relates to the degree of soil acidity—the more acid the soil, the deeper the red. Most trees that turn red in autumn are males; females tend to turn yellow-orange.

Roots are shallow and spreading, sending up vigorous sprouts after fire, cutting, or browsing. Wounds are slow to heal, since a large area of cambium surrounding an injury dies back before new growth begins. Branches break easily from wind and ice, so red maple, though more adaptable than sugar maple, is generally less hardy.

Associates: Red maple grows in mixed stands. In lowland forest areas, it associates with American elm and yellow birch, among other trees. On uplands, it may be found with oaks, hickories, and black cherry. Northern hardwood associates include sugar maple, American beech, American basswood, and Eastern hemlock.

Few plant and animal associates of red maple are exclusive to this tree. Some, however, seem more common to this species.

Spring, summer. The silky sheath *(Volvariella bombycina),* a white, hairy, bell-shaped mushroom, grows on dead or living trunks singly or in clusters.

On leaves, look for flat, circular galls with cherry-red margins. These are larval dwellings of the maple leafspot midge *(Cecidomyia ocel-laris).* Red or green bladderlike galls on upper leaf surfaces are caused by maple bladdergall mites *(Vasates quadripedes),* and crimson patches (erineum gall) on the leaves indicate *Eriophyes* mites.

Scores of moth species feed as caterpillars on the foliage (see Sugar Maple). Flowers are often bee pollinated.

Young red maples (three to six feet high) in brushy edge areas are favored nest sites for prairie warblers.

Fall, winter. Red maple is a preferred food for white-tailed deer; twigs, foliage, and sprouts may suffer considerable browsing damage.

A group of red maple saplings that show long, vertical strips of bark peeled away is a familiar sight in elk or moose country. Strips still attached to the tree are usually loose at the bottom, since the animals scrape upward with the lower incisors. These marks of feeding often appear high on the trees because the snow was deep.

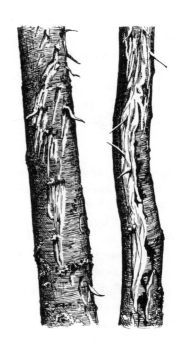

Torn bark scraped upward on sapling-size trees is a mark of elk or moose feeding in winter. Red maple is one of their favorite bark foods. Because of snow level, feeding marks may be quite high.

Other bark and seed feeders are generally the same as for sugar maple.
Watch in the fall for egg laying tree crickets on the trunks.

All year. A canker fungus that often infects red maple is *Cryptosporiopsis*, often originating from tiny wounds caused by autumn egg laying of the narrow-winged tree cricket *(Oecanthus angustipennis)*. The canker is vertical on the trunk, usually less than twenty centimeters long, and eventually appears as larger, notchlike, sunken areas surrounded by infolding callus growth, which may cover the canker within a year. Often, however, secondary cankers *(Valsa ambiens)* may colonize the original one and severely injure or kill the tree.

The most injurious wood fungus, however, is probably *Phellinus tremulae*, the hoof-shaped false tinder fungus (see Quaking Aspen).

Lore: Along with silver maple *(A. saccharinum)*, red maple is classed as a soft maple by the timber industry. The wood is fairly hard but brittle and less strong than sugar maple. Red maple may be tapped in early spring but often produces a much more sugar-dilute sap than sugar maple. It is said that pioneers made ink and dye from bark extracts. The foliage is apparently toxic to horses and perhaps other livestock.

Thoreau wrote admiringly of red maple in one of his last essays, "Autumnal Tints." He wondered about the Puritans' reaction "when the maples blaze out in scarlet." He slyly suggested that they erected meeting houses to avoid worshipping under red maple's indecent "high colors and exuberance."

Red maple is Rhode Island's state tree.

Maple, Sugar *(Acer saccharum)*. Maple family. Tree in mature upland forests. Recognize this most common maple by its opposite, five-lobed leaves, its glossy, reddish twigs, and its paired, winged seeds. Closely similar species include the Norway maple *(A. platanoides)*, with many reddish-leaved cultivated forms, and black maple *(A. nigrum)*, with dark green, three-lobed leaves.

Other names: Hard maple, sugar tree, rock maple.

Close relatives: Red maple *(A. rubrum)*; box elder *(A. negundo)*.

Lifestyle: Highly tolerant of shade and long-lived (three hundred years), sugar maples can survive years of suppressed growth in dense shade before reaching the sun-exposed canopy. With American beech, this tree forms one of the dominant climax types of the eastern deciduous forest.

Unisexual flowers, usually on the same tree, appear along with the leaves, but male flowers outnumber females, sometimes by the vast ratio of fifty to one. Flowers are mostly insect pollinated, and the tree produces abundant seed crops at two- to five-year intervals. Seeds usually germinate the following spring, and their roots easily penetrate the forest litter to reach underlying soil.

The calcium-rich leaf litter helps maintain the limy soil in which this tree best thrives. Despite its shallow, spreading root system, this tree stands relatively firm in the wind but sprouts less prolifically than red maple from stumps. It is not, however, tolerant of air pollution; for city plantings, the Norway maple does much better.

In summer, scan the broad leaves for signs of life. Without a microscope, you probably won't notice the tough sheaths that enclose the leaf veins or the tiny sparkles of glasslike crystals scattered throughout the leaf. These mechanical features plus tannic compounds are probably defenses that give the leaf a fighting chance to survive its many feeders. The leaves usually turn blinding yellow or orange-yellow in the fall, a brilliant explosion of carotene pigments unmasked by the shut-

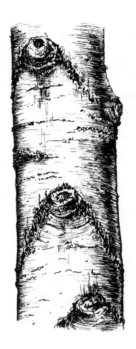

Similar to the "thunderbirds" on white birch, sugar maple's dark chevrons become most visible on mature trunks. Very young trees and older mature ones may not show them.

down of leaf factories and the subsequent decay of green chlorophyll.

Familiar marks in winter are the black chevrons on the trunk, descending like inverted Vs from either side of branches or branch scars. Although other trees may show them, such marks seem much more prevalent on this species.

Associates: In beech–maple woods, sugar maple is the codominant tree with American beech. At any given time, however, one of them is frequently more abundant than the other because of a natural tree rotation (see American Beech). Additional tree associates in mixed stands often include red maple, yellow birch, Eastern hemlock, and American basswood.

Goldenrods are allelopathic to maples.

Spring, summer. Two small spiders are frequent on maple leaves: *Chiracanthium inclusum* rolls under a leaf edge as a retreat, and *Araniella displicata* makes a small orb web on leaf undersides.

A complete list of known insects that are more or less specialized feeders on maple leaves would be very lengthy. Aphids and scale insects abound, often attended by ants, and many are specific to these trees.

One of sugar maple's most destructive pests is the pear thrips *(Taeniothrips inconsequens)*, a narrow-bodied, flea-sized insect that feeds on the leaf buds. The leaves become atrophied and appear tattered and discolored. Increasingly, large acreages of northeastern sugar maples are defoliated by these insects.

Moth caterpillars commonly found on the leaves include the spring cankerworm *(Paleocrita vernata)* and fall cankerworm *(Alsophila pometaria)*, both inchworm-type caterpillars that often drop on silken threads in front of your face and feed (sometimes audibly) in masses.

The green-striped mapleworm, larva of the rosy maple moth *(Dryocampa rubicunda)*, is spiny and yellowish green.

The fiery searcher beetle is one of sugar maple's insect benefactors. A caterpillar hunter, it captures and devours many of the most injurious foliage feeders.

Another gregarious leaf feeder is the forest tent caterpillar (see Quaking Aspen); look for one of its chief predators, the fiery searcher *(Calosoma scrutator)*, a black carabid beetle often seen on maple trunks devouring caterpillars or scurrying along the ground. This and other *Calosoma* species are among maple's most beneficial insects.

The saddled prominent or antlered maple is yet another common moth caterpillar (see American Beech).

Oval sections cut from leaves are signs of the maple leafcutter or casebearer *(Paraclemensia acerifoliella)*, which forms a turtlelike case for itself from the cut pieces.

Leaf stems are the specialty of maple petiole borers *(Caulocampus acericaulis)*, sawfly larvae that tunnel inside the leafstalks, causing leaves to droop and drop.

In early spring, maple sap flows from bark wounds, from drill pits of yellow-bellied sapsuckers (see White Birch), and from human tapping of the tree. Numerous insects are attracted to the sweetish taste, most commonly snow fleas (Entomobryidae), wood gnats (Anisopodidae), and aulacigastrid flies. These, in turn, may bring insect-feeding birds to the flow.

V-shaped wounds on branches or gnawed, saucer-shaped cavities on upper sides of a branch may indicate sap feeding of red squirrels. The squirrels bite into the woody xylem, creating a regular sap flow that evaporates on the bark. The squirrels then make the rounds of these flows, licking up the sweet deposits.

Maple leaves and buds provide some of the earliest green food of the year for nutrient-starved porcupines.

Northern flickers frequently nest in trunk cavities, often renovating a previous nest.

Fall, winter. The fallen leaves (about two percent calcium by volume) provide a nutritious bed for earthworms.

Folded, skeletonized leaves, appearing from late summer through fall, indicate feeding of the maple trumpet skeletonizer *(Epinotia aceriella),* a moth caterpillar that constructs a webbed, trumpetlike tube inside the fold.

In the fall, crumpled, partially skeletonized maple leaves containing a silken tube and a caterpillar are the work of the maple trumpet skeletonizer, a moth. The leaf provides both food and shelter.

Fallen branches are one sign of the maple borer *(Xiphydria maculata),* a wood-boring wasp that tunnels egg galleries into the branches, weakening them.

Maple seeds are extensively eaten by wildlife, predominantly songbirds (red-breasted nuthatches, purple finches, grosbeaks), squirrels (including Eastern chipmunks), and white-footed and deer mice. Porcupines, cottontails, and mice leave gnawed patches from bark feeding in winter. Size of tooth marks and locations on the trunk will usually tell you which animal has fed.

All year. One of sugar maple's most common trunk cankers is *Eutypella parasitica,* causing elliptical or elongate depressions or flattened areas.

Cracked bark and scars extending partway around forest-edge trunks may be signs of the sugar maple borer *(Glycobius speciosus),* a longhorned beetle.

Fox and gray squirrels are known to strip bark from living trees to gnaw the cambium;

young trees are sometimes completely girdled by the foraging of these animals.

Lore: Trees tapped for maple syrup are known as a sugar bush. Some 200 to 250 gallons of sap rise through a mature tree each spring day. Sunny days and freezing nights act as a sort of pump for lifting the stored sucrose made by last year's leaves from the roots. Sugar content ranges between two and three percent in a good year, and at least thirty-two gallons of sap (often more) are required to make one gallon of syrup or eight pounds of sugar. This percentage of sugar to water may seem scanty, but sugar maple offers the greatest concentration of sugar of any tree. The first sap flow of the year is usually the best.

Tapping a maple may remove as much as fifteen percent of the tree's carbohydrate reserves, so any environmental influence that further stresses the tree is of great concern in the sugar bush. Collectively, sugar maples are, in fact, undergoing a long-term decline across the northeastern United States. Multiple causes include regional air pollution, frequent insect irruptions, a warming climate, and other forces.

This tree was especially important and sacred to the Iroquois nations, which celebrated an annual thanksgiving ceremony in early spring. The sap rise signaled a renewed survival covenant for another year. Maple was considered a special gift of the Creator for its syrup and sugar, which these peoples boiled down in small quantities by putting hot rocks into the sap containers. The Chippewas made and stored various grades of syrup and sugar, using birchbark utensils. Other tribes boiled maple seeds for food and also ate fresh or dried seedlings.

There is a faster, easier way of making syrup than boiling—freezing. Modern freezers make it possible to put the sap in overnight, remove the ice the next day, and pour off the unfrozen liquid, which will be syrup.

As one of the most commercially valuable hardwoods, maple uses include furniture, flooring, cabinets, veneer, musical instruments, and recreational items. A distorted grain in sugar maple is bird's eye or curly maple, highly prized in furniture making.

Sugar maple is the state tree of New York, Vermont, West Virginia, and Wisconsin. Its leaf is the emblem in Canada's national flag.

Mayapple *(Podophyllum peltatum)*. Barberry family. Herb in moist woods, openings. Its two deeply lobed, umbrellalike leaves, the single white flower in the crotch beneath them, and the large, lemonlike berry in midsummer are identifying features.

Other names: Mandrake, hog apple, wild lemon, umbrella leaf.

Close relatives: Twinleaf *(Jeffersonia diphylla)*; blue cohosh *(Caulophyllum thalictroides)*; barberries *(Berberis)*; unrelated to the Eurasian mandrake *(Mandragora officinarum)* of ancient lore.

Lifestyle: The description given above refers to this plant's second-year appearance; the first year it raises from a spreading perennial rhizome only a single lobed leaf. The bisexual flower nods beneath the large leaves, hidden from above, and contains no nectar. It is probably often self-fertilized. Number of petals varies from six to nine; leaf lobes are usually seven.

Mayapple often produces almost circular colonies from a single plant that germinated years before. An average-size clone is probably about forty-five years old. The plant thrives best in at least partial sunlight. It emerges furled from the ground, then gradually raises its canopy above the flower bud.

By midsummer, when the yellowish fruit appears, mayapple leaves are looking somewhat worn. Spots on these leaves are caused by leafmining insects, which feed beneath the leaf epidermis.

Associates: *Spring, summer.* Solitary bees and bumblebees *(Bombus)* are probably the chief pollinators; they collect no nectar but abundant pollen for food.

Caterpillars that feed on the leaves include *Clepsis melaleucana,* a tortricid moth, and the variegated fritillary butterfly *(Euptoieta claudia),* orange-red with dark stripes.

Eastern box turtles, which relish the fruits, are probably among the main seed dispersers; turtle-ingested seeds germinate more successfully than seeds directly from the plant. Other fruit consumers include common grackles, white-footed mice, and gray squirrels.

Lore: The ripe, fleshy fruit is edible, though somewhat insipidly sweet. Fruits can be eaten raw, squeezed for juice, or cooked to make jelly or marmalade. All other parts of the plant are highly toxic and should not be consumed. Even handling the stem and rhizome may produce a skin rash in allergic individuals.

Some Native American tribes used a root decoction as a drastic purgative. The Menominees boiled mayapple and splashed the liquid on their potato plants as an insecticide. Drying and roasting the root, then boiling it as a treatment for liver ailments, rheumatism, and constipation apparently reduced the toxic effects.

Podophyllum, the toxic substance, has been found extremely useful in treating skin cancers and venereal warts. This chemical inhibits cell growth, apparently affecting RNA and DNA synthesis directly. Mayapple, its only known source, is not now cultivated for this purpose; as ecologist Richard Brewer points out, the likelihood of finding and developing suitable strains for commercial cultivation "is decreased every time the gene pool of May-apple is diminished through the loss of another forest."

Mayflower, Canada *(Maianthemum canadense).* Lily family. Low herb in moist, shaded woods. One to three alternate, heart-shaped stem leaves, a short terminal cluster of white flowers, and pale red, speckled berries in autumn identify this delicate little plant.

Other names: Wild (or false) lily of the valley, two-leaved Solomon's seal, bead ruby.

Close relatives: Bellworts *(Uvularia)*; Solomon's seals *(Polygonatum)*; trout lilies *(Erythronium)*; trilliums *(Trillium)*; onions *(Allium)*; greenbriers *(Smilax)*.

Lifestyle: Mayflower is a cloning herb rising from perennial rhizomes and underground extensions. Shade and moderate moisture are the only consistent requirements for this species, which often forms a lush, matlike ground cover in rich woods.

Leaves are not invariably two—some individual plants may have only one, others three—but one-leaved plants seldom produce flowers (for reasons previously discussed; see Bunchberry, Wood Anemone). In most colonies, the one-leaved, sterile plants outnumber the flowering ones, probably diverting energy to them through the subsurface connections. The four-pointed, bisexual flowers are extremely fragrant.

Though related and somewhat similar to the true lily of the valley *(Convallaria majalis)* and to three-leaved false Solomon's seal *(Smilacina trifolia)*, mayflower is the only member of its genus found in east-central North America.

Associates: *Spring, summer.* These plants grow profusely on and around the rotting stumps of Eastern white pine. Favorite microhabitats are the hollow gaps beneath the stump.

Its mistlike, sweet-smelling flower cluster surmounts one or more shiny green leaves. To see Canada mayflower this closely, you must drop to ground level, for this plant rises only a few inches.

Probably the foremost insect pollinators are bees.

Slugs sometimes eat holes in the leaves,

and snowshoe hares have also been known to consume the leaves to some extent.

Fall. Though not a major wildlife food, the translucent red berries are eaten by ruffed grouse, Eastern chipmunks, and white-footed mice.

Lore: The bittersweet berries, although not poisonous, are not very palatable.

Mountain-Ash, American *(Sorbus americana).* Rose family. Shrub or small tree in cool, moist woods openings. Its alternate compound leaves with eleven to seventeen leaflets, gummy red buds, flattish sprays of white flowers, and fleshy, orange-red fruits identify the American mountain ash. The northern or showy mountain-ash *(S. decora)* is more common northward, while the European mountain-ash *(S. aucuparia)* is the prevalent ornamental species.

Other name: Rowan tree *(S. aucuparia).*

Close relatives: Apple *(Pyrus malus)*; hawthorns *(Crataegus)*; cherries *(Prunus)*; shadbushes *(Amelanchier)*; roses *(Rosa)*; blackberry and raspberries *(Rubus)*; unrelated to white ash or Northern prickly-ash.

Lifestyle: Mountain-ash rivals flowering dogwood as one of the most beautiful flowering forest trees in spring. It grows in acid habitats—coniferous and northern hardwood forests, bogs, rocky hillsides. Unlike the dogwood, it is mainly a short-lived edge species rather than a forest understory resident, though it is moderately shade tolerant and slow growing.

The small bisexual flowers in flat-topped clusters are insect pollinated. They develop into small, berrylike pomes (like apples) that often remain over winter.

Not a cloning plant, mountain-ash typically grows solitarily and scattered among other northern edge and wetland species. It occasionally hybridizes with chokeberry *(Aronia).*

Associates: In its upland habitats, mountain-ash may associate with balsam fir, white spruce, yellow birch, and maples. It also favors plum thickets *(Prunus).*

Spring, summer. Leaves and flowers that suddenly wilt and appear scorched as if by heat may be infected by fire blight *(Erwinia amylovora)*, a bacterial disease that also produces cracked, scaly cankers on twigs and branches, sometimes girdling the trunk and killing the tree.

Mountain-ash shares with apple and hawthorns many foliage, fruit, and wood insect foragers (see Hawthorns). Skeletonized leaves, especially on upper portions of the tree, may indicate mass feeding of mountain-ash sawflies *(Pristiphora geniculata)*, black-dotted green larvae resembling moth caterpillars.

Yellow-bellied sapsuckers often drill into the bark (see White Birch).

Fall, winter. A common fruit-boring caterpillar is the apple fruit moth *(Argyresthia conjugella).*

Though the pomes, with their low fat content, are not prime wildlife foods, their winter availability often attracts ruffed and sharp-tailed grouse, yellow-bellied flycatchers, cedar waxwings, thrushes, and evening and pine grosbeaks. Fermented fruit can occasionally give feeding birds a "buzz."

Moose relish foliage and twigs of mountain-ash.

Lore: The fragrant inner bark has astringent and antiseptic properties but was apparently little used by Native Americans. They did use the fruits, rich in ascorbic acid, as a tea for preventing or curing scurvy and as a rectal wash for hemorrhoids (the number of native remedies for this condition reveal it as a common ailment even in less stressful times).

The fruit (high in pectin) makes good jelly but is best picked when dead ripe, after repeated freezings have cut its bitter astringency.

Variations in leaf shape characterize mulberry foliage. Many different lobed and unlobed forms are often found on the same tree, but lobed leaves seem predominant on younger trees.

Mulberry, Red *(Morus rubra).* Mulberry family. Tree in rich woods, bottomlands, edges. Its shiny, heart-shaped, sandpaper-textured leaves that are often lobed, milky sap, red-brown trunk, and blackberrylike fruits identify this tree. The similar white mulberry *(M. alba),* an introduced species, has whitish fruits.

Close relatives: Osage orange *(Maclura pomifera);* hops *(Humulus);* hemp *(Cannabis sativa);* fig *(Ficus carica);* breadfruit *(Artocarpus communis);* rubber tree *(Hevea brasiliensis).*

Lifestyle: Botanically the mulberry family stands between the elms and the nettles (Urticaceae), showing certain similarities to each. Lobed leaves are typical on young trees and sprout shoots. Unlobed leaves, which suggest those of American basswood, occur mainly in the tree crown. The somewhat flaky bark resembles hop hornbeam.

Unisexual, wind-pollinated, catkinate flowers appear at leaf emergence in late spring, each sex on a different tree (this explains why many mulberry trees never bear fruit). The fruits—at first red, then turning purple-black in midsummer—are, like blackberry, clusters of drupes. But whereas the blackberry cluster is an aggregate fruit developing from a single flower, the mulberry cluster is a product of many flowers on a single catkin. In other words, each drupe in the cluster develops from a single flower.

This moderately shade-tolerant tree reproduces easily and quickly from seed and from cuttings. Though usually a small, short-trunked tree, red mulberry may reach eighty feet tall in optimal habitat. The tree is mainly southern in distribution, extending only to southern New England, Ontario, and South Dakota.

Associates: Mulberry usually grows scattered among other deciduous bottomland or moist woodland trees including American elm, Northern hackberry, and tulip tree. In edge habitats, I often find it growing in association with box elder.

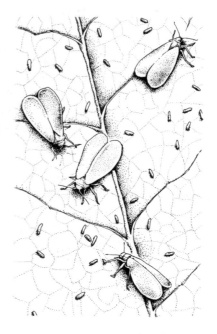

Whiteflies, common feeders on mulberry leaves, are actually sucking bugs that resemble small white-winged moths. Tiny larval whiteflies surround the adult insects in this hand-lens view.

Summer. Jet-black, white-fringed, oval larvae of the mulberry whitefly *(Tetraleurodes mori)*, a sucking bug, mass on leaves. The waxy-winged adults, resembling tiny white moths, fly out in clouds if leaves are disturbed.

Dead branches and cambium mines on the trunk may indicate the mulberry borer *(Dorcaschema wildii)*, a longhorned beetle larva, severely destructive to mulberries in the South.

Seeds are primarily dispersed by birds and mammals. The highly nutritious fruits, even before fully ripened, attract many birds. Frequent feeders include red-headed and red-bellied woodpeckers, American crows, wood thrushes, gray catbirds, Northern mockingbirds, brown thrashers, cedar waxwings, European starlings, Northern cardinals, and Northern and orchard orioles. Gorging birds sometimes become intoxicated on overripe fruits.

Gray and fox squirrels are the top mammal consumers. I have also observed woodchucks feeding on the fruits of low branches.

All year. Clusters of dead and living twigs near branch ends ("witches' brooms") result from repeated twig dieback caused by the coral spot canker fungus *(Nectria cinnabarina)*.

Look for the coral spot cankers at bases of dead mulberry buds and twigs.

Lore: Farmers' wisdom advises that frost danger is past when mulberry leaves appear. The wind gives these leaves sounds of crowd activity. The Old Testament records God's instructions to King David to use these mulberry sounds as camouflage for an attack.

High hopes for an American silkworm industry, using the imported *M. alba* and *M. multicaulis*, collapsed in 1840 with high labor costs and failure of the mulberry plantations.

Sweet red mulberries have never achieved wide popularity in the American diet, mainly because they are easily damaged during shipment (though they freeze well). Unripe fruit, containing hallucinogens (as do the bark and raw shoots), should not be eaten; nervous agitation and extreme digestive upset can result. The new leafless shoots make a good cooked vegetable when boiled. Native Americans used a shredded root and bark decoction as a laxative, and the milky latex from the leaves was a scalp treatment for ringworm.

In urban areas, mulberry is frequently considered a nuisance; its abundant fruit litters and stains sidewalks, cars, and shoe soles. People who wish to attract summer birds to their yards, however, can do no better than to plant a (female) mulberry tree.

Nannyberry. See Viburnums.

Nightshade *(Solanum dulcamara)*. Nightshade family. Low, vinelike shrub in moist thickets, edges. Five violet (sometimes white) reflexed petals with a yellow, beaklike center, leaves with (usually) two small lobes at the base, and drooping clusters of bright red berries identify this plant. The black or common nightshade *(S. nigrum)* has a similar flower that is white, and it produces black berries.

Other names: Bittersweet, bitter nightshade, blue bindweed, climbing nightshade, poisonflower, woody nightshade.

Close relatives: Potato *(S. tuberosum)*; eggplant *(S. melongena)*; tomato *(Lycopersicon esculentum)*; jimson weed *(Datura stramonium)*; tobacco *(Nicotiana tabacum)*; petunias *(Petunia)*; not related to enchanter's nightshades *(Circaea)*.

Lifestyle: Shade-tolerant nightshade, though viny, doesn't really climb; it has no tendrils or pronounced twining habit. Instead, it loops and sprawls across convenient supports, mostly other plants.

The attractive bisexual flower thrusts forward its yellow beak consisting of fused anthers as if aggressively flagging insects, but it offers no nectar. This Eurasian transplant, however, doesn't need elaborate schemes in order to reproduce. Flowers are probably as often self-pollinated as insect pollinated, and they appear continuously from spring through early fall.

Leaves vary somewhat in shape; they may or may not show basal lobes. Fruits often remain on the plant from summer through the following spring.

Associates: *Spring, summer.* Flowers are pollinated mainly by honeybees *(Apis mellifera)* and pollen-feeding beelike flies.

Many of the foliage-feeding insects that feed upon potato are common on nightshade. The three-lined potato beetle *(Lema trilineata)* is reddish yellow with black stripes. The Colorado potato beetle *(Leptinotarsa decemlineata),* yellow with ten longitudinal lines on the back, lays bright, orange-yellow eggs on leaf undersides; look for the red, humpbacked larvae. The potato flea beetle *(Epitrix cucumeris),* tiny and black, appears in masses and riddles leaves. The four-lined plant bug (see Currants and Gooseberries) is another common feeder.

Summer, fall, winter. At least thirty-one bird species are known to consume the berries, and twelve mammal species eat the fruit or leaves. Wood ducks, ruffed grouse, ring-necked pheasants, and wild turkeys are among the game-bird feeders, and many songbirds also eat the berries. The seeds are mainly dispersed via bird droppings.

Striped skunks also devour the fruits, and cottontail rabbits browse on the stems.

Lore: Just how poisonous the red fruits of this species are to humans is undetermined. Recent consensus is that ripe berries are bitter and unpalatable, but not highly toxic. It took Thomas Jefferson to convince us that the closely related tomato wasn't a deadly fruit. Still, few (including this author) have ever tested their theories by eating nightshade berries.

Livestock are sometimes poisoned by eating the foliage. The toxic compound is solanine, an alkaloid. A popular folk remedy for rheumatism used a daily infusion of the dried plant, which presumably was harmless in that condition.

Pliny recommended the juice as "good for those that have fallen from high places" (a nudge toward suicide?), and medieval folk ascribed magical and witch-proofing attributes to the plant. Native Americans, of course, weren't familiar with it, since it didn't appear on these shores until European settlement.

This plant is the true bittersweet (so named from the berry taste), a label mistakenly attached in this country to an unrelated climbing vine (see American Bittersweet).

Oak, Red *(Quercus rubra).* Beech family. Tree in mesic, mainly deciduous forests. Its dull green upper-leaf surfaces, bristle-tipped leaf lobes, flattened bark ridges, and flat, saucer-shaped acorn cups are good field identification marks to look for. This tree is the prototype of the red or black oak group (as distinct from the white oaks), which includes scarlet oak

(Q. coccinea), Northern pin oak *(Q. ellipsoides)*, and black oak *(Q. velutina)*.

Other name: Northern red oak.

Close relatives: White oaks *(Quercus)*; American chestnut *(Castanea dentata)*; American beech *(Fagus grandifolia)*.

Lifestyle: Any oak with pointed, bristle-tipped leaf lobes belongs to the red oak group, sharing most of the biological characters (and associates) of *Quercus rubra*. All oaks of this group produce acorns that require two years to mature.

Wind-pollinated flowers appear in late spring when the leaves are half-grown, the male flowers in slender, dangling catkins, the greenish female flowers solitary and inconspicuous. The catkins often veil the crown portion; the pistillate blooms occur lower on the same tree. Members of the red oak group often hybridize, producing trees with variably shaped leaves and acorns, which defy easy identification.

Red oak is the fastest growing of all oaks and, in optimal habitats, is among the largest and longest lived (two hundred to three hundred years). The tree's profile generally reflects the light conditions in which it grew, regardless of the present site density. (This is true of most trees, but the profile differences are especially pronounced in oaks.) If it grew in the open, the tree has a short, thick trunk and wide-spreading crown; forest-grown trees, on the other hand, stand straight and tall with narrow crowns. A deeply set, lateral root system firmly anchors the tree. The red oak thrives better than most other oaks in cold climates, but it is also more vulnerable to drought.

Its common name describes the autumn foliage color, often deep wine-red or orange; twigs and inner bark (and sometimes leaf midribs) are also reddish. Leaves, extremely variable in shape even on the same tree, may remain attached into winter. A dry oak leaf may consist of up to sixty percent tannins.

This tree sprouts vigorously from stumps and roots, providing fairly quick natural reforestation of timbered or fire-ravaged lands.

Associates: Mature red oaks are generally codominant in climax deciduous forests with hickories and other oaks. The tree also occurs in mixed stands with sugar maple, American beech, American basswood, white ash, tulip tree, black cherry, and pines, among others.

Spring, summer. The most destructive disease of red oak is probably oak wilt, caused by the fungus *Ceratocystis fagacearum*. It is marked by fast-dying foliage, often resulting in complete defoliation and death of the tree. Spread of this disease often occurs via the natural subsurface grafting of roots. Sap or picnic beetles *(Glischrochilus)*, feeding on bark wounds, also spread the disease.

The common insect foragers of oaks number at least one thousand species. We'll look at a few of the most notable.

The gypsy moth *(Lymantria dispar)* is the most destructive pest of all northeastern oaks. These hairy, brownish caterpillars annually defoliate millions of forest acres. Peak hatching occurs in early spring. The massed caterpillars feed during the day until half-grown, then feed at night and are often blown to other trees by dropping on silken strands. Despite stiff quarantine regulations in areas of outbreak, this tussock moth continues to expand its range. Imported from France to New England in 1869 by a silkworm entrepreneur, the moths soon escaped. Most healthy trees can survive defoliation for two or three years in a row—death is a rare consequence—but such refoliation is a drain on the tree's resources. A partially defoliated tree reacts by "loading" its leaves with phenol compounds, which stunt caterpillar growth and reproduction. Gypsy moths undergo cyclic highs and

June beetles, big brown buzzing insects attracted to lights at night, eat circular holes in oak and other tree leaves. Seldom active in daylight, they also feed at night.

lows, irrupting in vast numbers about every ten years. An outbreak lasts about three years, until natural control systems (parasites, predators) gain the upper hand. During gypsy moth irruptions, watch for invasions of bird predators, which require ample protein diets for nesting and for feeding young birds. These may include yellow-billed and black-billed cuckoos, Eastern wood-pewees, white-breasted nuthatches, house wrens, red-eyed vireos, American redstarts, yellow warblers, and Northern orioles, among others. A predatory carabid beetle, the European caterpillar hunter *(Calosoma sycophanta)*, may also be numerous.

The oak skeletonizer *(Bucculatrix ainsliella)* makes threadlike mines along the leaf midrib before skeletonizing the leaves. The oak leaftyer *(Croesia semipurpurana)* is a tortricid moth that folds and ties sections of leaves, feeding inside the folds. The common oak moth *(Phoberia atomaris)* is another caterpillar feeder.

Some fifty species of leaf miners feed on oak leaves (see White Oak).

Circular holes in the leaves may indicate the night feeding of adult June beetles *(Phyllophaga)*.

Slender checkered beetles *(Cymatodera)* are brown, spiny-haired predators of oak gall wasps, hunting and attacking them. The larvae invade the galls to feed on wasp larvae.

Late summer, fall. On oak stumps look for brown, leaflike clusters, a gelatinous fungus known as leaf jelly *(Tremella foliacea)*.

A pore mushroom with reddish-orange cap growing beneath oaks may be the bittersweet bolete *(Tylopilus ballouii)*. A large, scaly-capped bolete on poor soil beneath oaks may be *Boletus variipas*.

Two milkcap mushrooms appearing in oak forests are the tawny milkcap *(Lactarius volemus)* and the wrinkled milkcap *(L. corrugis)*. Both of these gill fungi have golden or reddish-brown caps and ooze a milky latex when cut.

Many types and shapes of insect galls are found on oaks—round, bunched, fruitlike, woody, mossy, or woolly. They occur on leaves and twigs, often most visible in late summer and fall. Of some eight hundred species of gall-makers on oaks, virtually all of them are from one family of wasps, the Cynipidae.

One of the most common leaf galls is the oak apple gall *(Amphibolips confluenta)*, round

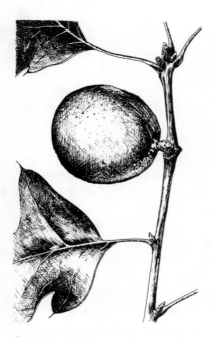

Oak apple galls, brown and dry in the fall, are the most conspicuous examples of the many cynipid wasp galls on oaks. Inside, depending on the wasp species, they are either spongy or partitioned.

Another common gall, found on leaf undersides, is caused by a gall midge (Cecidomyia). *This gall provides an exception to the fact that most oak galls are caused by cynipid wasps.*

and applelike on stems and midribs. On twigs, look for gouty oak galls *(Callirhytis punctata)*, globular and woody. Many gall wasps have alternate generations; the first generation of this species produces blisterlike galls on the leaves in spring. Oak bullet galls *(Disholcaspis)*, hard, grapelike clusters attached to twigs, are also common.

Egg-laying punctures, often in splintered rows on twigs, are made by periodical cicadas *(Magicicada)*; the damage sometimes kills twig ends. This insect appears at regular seventeen-year intervals, with fourteen separate broods each on their own seventeen-year cycle. Look for bunches of dead leaves amid green foliage and for cast skins attached to trunks.

Another prominent pest insect is the walkingstick *(Diapheromera femorata)*, the spindly orthopteran whose body shape mimics twigs. Walkingsticks consume entire leaves except for the main veins, eating in from the edges.

Oakworm moths *(Anisota)*, spiny, striped caterpillars, also devour foliage at this time.

Twigs with leaves still attached that litter the ground beneath oaks are indications of twig

Woody clusters called bullet galls, also produced by cynipid wasps, tend to drop off the twig during winter. Like most stem galls, they are best seen in the fall after the leaves have been dropped.

Cicada egg scars often leave the top portions of twigs torn and ragged. After hatching, the larval insects fall to the ground, there to spend seventeen years preparing to reproduce.

pruners *(Elaphidionoides villosus)*. The ends of the fallen twigs, inside which the long-horned beetle larva grows, are smoothly cut.

Fuzzy, buff-colored patches on trunks are egg masses of the gypsy moth. Touching them may cause a skin rash in allergic individuals.

Acorns showing one or more holes in the nut indicate larval feeding (and exit) of acorn weevils *(Curculio)*. Soft acorns with no exit holes still contain the weevil larva. The acorn moth *(Valentinia glandulella)*, a tiny insect, lays eggs in the weevil-hollowed nuts; the larva emerges in spring.

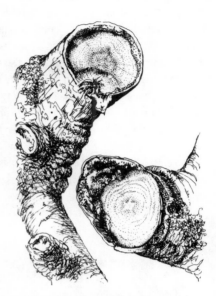

Smooth-cut ends of leafy branches on the ground beneath oaks mark the work of twig pruners. Look for signs of their foliage "thinning" beneath hickory and apple trees, too.

A brown furry patch on a tree trunk is most likely an egg mass of the gypsy moth, oak's most destructive insect pest. Deposited in summer, the masses remain on trees over winter.

Acorns (collectively called *mast*) provide the dominant value of this tree to vertebrate wildlife. Frequent consumers among birds include ruffed grouse, ring-necked pheasants, Northern bobwhites, wild turkeys, red-bellied and red-headed woodpeckers, blue jays, American crows, tufted titmice, white-breasted nuthatches, brown thrashers, rufous-sided towhees, and common grackles (the last species has a palatal keel in the roof of the mouth, enabling these birds to cut acorn shells by direct pressure).

Acorns of the red oak group, though not as palatable to mammals as those of the white oak, are consumed by numerous rodents.

Where both red and white oak acorns are present, gray squirrels tend to bury the red oak acorns and consume the white oak acorns on the spot (see White Oak). In black bear country, look for tangled bear's nests in these trees (see American Beech).

All year. Rough, circular swellings with depressed centers on red oak trunks are probably spiculosa cankers, caused by the fungus *Poria spiculosa.*

Bark sloughing and decay are signs of infection by *Hypoxylon* cankers.

Several fungi (called butt rots) cause decay at tree bases, often entering the tree through old fire wounds. These often show bracket-type conks or abnormal swellings. *Hericium, Polyporus,* and *Pleurotus* species are the most common.

Sap-stained areas surrounding holes in the bark may indicate attack by red oak borers *(Enaphalodes rufulus),* longhorned beetles.

Lore: Bitterly astringent tannin is the compound that makes acorns taste bitter. Repeated boilings, however, will leach out this soluble acid, leaving a tasty nut rich in protein and fat. Native Americans ground these treated acorns into a meal from which they made bread. The Chippewas mixed precise portions of the powdered inner barks of red oak, quaking aspen, and balsam poplar, plus the ground root of Seneca snakeroot, for a powerful heart medicine.

Oak bark is useful for curing (tanning) leather, and oak insect galls were also used for this purpose. Mild tannic solutions also provided a remedy for skin irritations, cold sores, and (taken internally) diarrhea and hemorrhoids.

Red oak's hard, strong wood is a valuable lumber much used for flooring, furniture, and veneer, among other items. All oak lumber of the red oak group is sold commercially as red oak.

Red oak is the state tree of New Jersey.

Oak, White *(Quercus alba).* Beech family. Tree in dry or mesic woods. Recognize white oak, prototype of its group, by its even, rounded leaf lobes that lack bristles and its light gray or whitish scaly bark. Other oaks of this group include swamp white oak *(Q. bicolor),* bur oak *(Q. macrocarpa),* post oak *(Q. stellata),* chinkapin or yellow oak *(Q. muehlenbergii),* and chestnut oak *(Q. prinus).*

Close relatives: Red oaks *(Quercus);* American chestnut *(Castanea dentata);* American beech *(Fagus grandifolia).*

Lifestyle: Thick, squat trees reflect open habitats (in which this oak thrives best), while tall trunks of forest-grown white oaks can reach heights of 150 feet. Old trees (they may live five hundred to six hundred years or older) often show gnarled, twisted limbs. Such trees

Hedgehog galls, common on both white and red oaks, resemble green burs. Each gall contains wasp larvae. Many gall-makers separate sexual and asexual offspring keyed to seasonal timing.

Common galls that appear on white oak include the club gall at twig ends caused by Callirhytis clavula *(left) and bullet galls inhabited by* Disholcaspis globulus *larvae (right). Both are cynipid wasps.*

appear arthritic, their stout, horizontal branches bent in square-angled elbows.

Unlike the red oak group, white oaks produce mature acorns in just one season. Their wind-pollinated flowers are similar, however. Acorn production varies, beginning at about age fifty, with abundant mast crops occurring every four to ten years. White oak acorns germinate (or rot on the ground) fairly quickly and are thus less successfully stored or buried by mammals. A white oak acorn consists of about six percent protein and sixty-five percent carbohydrates, but red oak acorns have a higher fat and tannin content.

With their long taproots and deep lateral roots, these trees are seldom blown over. Leaves turn brownish-purple in the fall, often remaining on the tree into winter. At the top of the tree they tend to be slender and deeply lobed, presenting less surface area than the broader, more shallowly lobed leaves lower down. Though vulnerable to fire, the tree sprouts readily from stumps.

Associates: Sometimes occurring in almost pure stands, white oak more often grows as a codominant climax species with hickories (especially shagbark). It also occurs in mixed stands with white ash, black walnut, black cherry, pines, and other oaks.

Spring, summer. A low, conelike, yellowish-brown herb often found growing beneath oaks is squawroot *(Conopholis americana)*, a plant parasite on tree roots that is closely related to beechdrops (see American Beech).

In addition to insect associates mentioned for red oak, the following also occur on oaks generally but on white oak especially.

A common cynipid wasp *(Cynips)* creates the hedgehog gall, round and prickly, on leaf midribs.

Several hairstreak butterfly species *(Strymon)* feed as green, grublike caterpillars on oak leaves. Juvenal's dusky wing butterfly (see American Hazelnut), also a common caterpillar feeder, fastens down portions of leaf edges.

Two moth caterpillars may sometimes infest and defoliate acres of white oak. The variable oakleaf caterpillar *(Heterocampa manteo)*, a prominent, is variably greenish-yellow. The orange-striped or orange-tipped oakworm *(Anisota senatoria)*, black and spiny with stripes, is a saturniid moth.

Orange-striped oakworms are common foliage feeders in the summer. These moth caterpillars feed in colonies, sometimes causing extensive defoliation of oak.

Rolled or folded leaves may indicate the oak leafroller *(Archips semiferanus)*, a tortricid moth that also defoliates and kills trees.

The solitary oak leafminer *(Cameraria hamadryadella)* and the gregarious oak leafminer *(C. cincinnatiella)*, both tiny moth larvae, create extensive blotch mines on upper leaf surfaces.

Feeding through late summer, oak lace bugs *(Corythucha arcuata)* suck sap on lower leaf surfaces. Look for white, chlorotic flecks on tops of leaves and for premature curling and browning.

Oozing sap and sawdust spilling from holes in trunks of young trees may indicate infestation by the white oak borer *(Goes tigrinus)*, a longhorned beetle.

Fall. Honey mushrooms may abound on trunks infected with armillaria root rot.

White oak acorns vary in taste but are often sweet and palatable. Since mammals

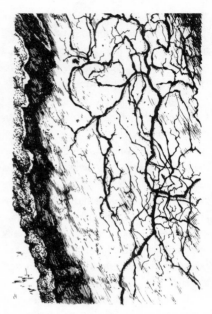

Oak leaves, especially in summer and fall, are full of surprises. This almost devoured leaf, for example, holds clusters of insect eggs, probably laid before insects ate most of the surrounding leaf.

Armillaria "shoestrings" climb the barkless trunk of a partially decayed white oak. The gilled fruiting bodies (honey mushrooms) may be found around tree bases in the fall.

generally prefer them above all acorns, food competition in a good mast year can become intense. White oak acorns germinate quickly, and once sprouted, are difficult to digest, so squirrels tend to consume more on the spot than they retrieve from buried or stored caches.

Black bears, raccoons, Eastern chipmunks, and white-footed mice are also fond of these acorns. White-tailed deer sometimes scrape away snow to get at them; oak foliage is not a preferred browse. Many bird species likewise feed on the acorns (see Red Oak).

Spherical summer nests of twigs and leaves in the tops of trees, constructed by gray and fox squirrels, become more visible in the fall. For winter dens, they prefer tree cavities.

All year. On dead or dying oaks with loose, shedding bark, look for blackish, fibrous, rootlike strands extending up the tree beneath the bark. These are the shoestrings (rhizomorphs) of shoestring or armillaria root rot *(Armillaria mellea)*, outgrowths of a fungus infecting the tree roots. The gilled fruiting body, appearing in midsummer to late fall, is called the honey mushroom.

Flat, circular patches of whitened bark commonly seen on trunks are caused by the smooth or bark patch fungus *(Aleurodiscus oakesii)*, a harmless saprophyte.

Lore: To Native Americans, this was the most important oak. Acorn meal supplied the primary ingredient of a hard, dry bread baked by many tribes. Inner bark was collected in spring, when the tannin concentration (up to eleven percent) is highest, for boiled astringent and antiseptic decoctions useful in controlling dysentery and applying to skin abrasions and hemorrhoids.

Climax forests of ancient northern Europe—called the Hyrcenian Forest by the Romans—were dominated by the closely related English oak *(Q. robur)*. Acorns were phallic symbols of fecundity in many ancient art forms.

White oak wood, with its characteristic medullary rays emanating from the trunk's center, is highly valued for furniture, flooring, and interior trim.

This is the state tree of Connecticut, Illinois, and Maryland.

Osage Orange *(Maclura pomifera)*. Mulberry family. Small tree in bottomland woods, hedgerows, thickets. Identify it by its stout, unbranched thorns, egg-shaped, long-pointed leaves, orange-brown bark, milky sap, and large, wrinkled fruits.

Other names: Hedge-apple, yellowwood, horse apple, bow wood, bodarc, bodock.

Close relatives: Mulberries *(Morus)*; hops *(Humulus)*; hemp *(Cannabis sativa)*; fig *(Ficus carica)*; breadfruit *(Artocarpus communis)*; rubber tree *(Hevea brasiliensis)*.

Lifestyle: Unisexual flowers borne on separate trees emerge after the leaves in spring—male flowers in short, drooping clusters, wind-pollinated female flowers in dense, feathery heads. The green, knobby, grapefruit-size fruit consists of multiple drupes.

This thorny tree forms a low, gnarled crown containing short spur branches of clustered, glossy green leaves. Its roots plunge deep and spread wide. The tree reproduces much more often by sprouting clones than by seed. Osage orange grows fast in full sunlight, is moderately shade intolerant, and lives fairly long. The wood is yellow or bright orange.

The fruit of osage orange, big as a grapefruit, looks like a green brain. It is not readily confused with any other fruit. Few birds or mammals relish or even consume it.

Associates: *Spring, summer.* Relatively few fungus and insect pests plague this tree. Hagen's sphinx moth caterpillar *(Ceratomia hageni)* is a fairly common leaf feeder; the characteristic rear horn identifies it as a sphinx.

The mulberry borer *(Dorcaschema wildii)*, a longhorned beetle, mines into the cambium and wood, sometimes girdling branches.

Loggerhead shrikes sometimes nest in osage orange, using the thorns for impaling prey (see Hawthorns).

Fall. Its curious fruit is not greatly relished by wildlife. Northern bobwhites and fox squirrels sometimes eat the seeds.

Osage orange's chief wildlife value is providing cover for birds and small mammals, especially in hedgerows. Shade-tolerant shrubs and herbs in such areas may offer more in the way of food than osage orange does.

Lore: Native only to Arkansas, Oklahoma, and Texas river valleys, osage orange has been widely planted elsewhere, specifically as "living fences" before the advent of barbed wire. Settlers in St. Louis first obtained it from the Osage tribes, and its use by farmers and ranchers spread rapidly as far north as New England and the northwestern states. Fence posts made of the wood were extremely durable. In Illinois, farmers planted crops when the emerging leaves reached "squirrel's ear" size (about May 10).

Because of its cloning habit, this tree is hard to eradicate once established. Today, however, osage orange hedges are declining as intensive agricultural practices squeeze out the former ample field borders.

The extremely hard but flexible wood, originally used for making bows (French explorers named the tree *bois-d'arc*, wood of the bow) is still prime material for posts and archery equipment. Police billyclubs are also made of it. The bark yields tannin, and a yellow dye can be extracted from the boiled wood chips. The fruits, bitter and full of milky latex, are inedible; in some areas, fruit sections are used as a cockroach repellent.

Phlox, Blue *(Phlox divaricata).* Phlox family. Herb in rich, open woods. Its terminal flower clusters, five pale violet, wedge-shaped petals radiating from a central tube, opposite leaves, and sticky, hairy stem identify phlox. Some seventy species occupy various North American habitats, but this one is probably the most common. The garden or fall phlox *(P. paniculata)*, widely escaped from cultivation, is also frequent.

Other names: Wild blue phlox, wild sweet-William.

Close relatives: Jacob's ladder *(Polemonium van-bruntiae)*; Greek valerian *(P. reptans)*.

Lifestyle: Blue phlox's bisexual flower components are hidden inside the central corolla tube, so this plant obviously requires pollinating insects with specialized mouth parts. After phlox has flowered, the rootstock begins forming horizontal runners *(stolons)*, which extend over the ground and remain there through the winter. New phlox stems will sprout from their tips next spring.

Tell phlox flowers from those of the unrelated wild pink *(Silene caroliniana)* by whether the petals are joined at their bases (phlox) or not (pinks).

Associates: *Spring.* Flowers are pollinated mainly by bumblebees *(Bombus)* and butterflies feeding on the nectar of the slightly fragrant blooms.

Examine the upper stem and flower stems for small trapped insects. The downy, sticky surface often proves a morass for crawling, would-be raiders on the nectaries.

Foliage feeders include two-spotted spider mites *(Tetranychus urticae)*, tiny sap-sucking arachnids that weave mealy webs beneath and between leaves, often causing them to yellow.

The phlox plant bug *(Lopidea davisi)*, orange-red and striped, feeds on new leaves, producing whitish spots, and often deforms buds, stunting the plant.

A common pest of many phlox plants is the stalk borer moth *(Papaipema nebris)*, whose brownish caterpillar bores into stems, causing them to wilt and fall over. A small, round hole in the stem may also indicate its presence.

Phlox is also vulnerable to tiny nematode parasites called eelworms, which kill leaves and stunt plants.

Lore: The Roman scholar Pliny first used the word phlox (derived from a Greek word meaning "fire" or "flame") for a red campion *(Silene)*. Linnaeus then switched the designation to what is now phlox, some say because of the torchlike shape of the buds. The name sweet-William is a misnomer for blue phlox. Named for William the Conqueror, sweet-William *(Dianthus barbatus)* is a variably colored garden annual.

Native Americans made some use of blue phlox, brewing a tea of the plant and drinking it for stomach upsets. They also steeped the roots to make an eyewash solution.

Pine, Eastern White *(Pinus strobus)*. Pine family. Tree in mesic, wet, or dry habitats. This is the only five-needled pine east of the Rockies. Its broad, horizontal limbs, giving the tree a feathery, stacked appearance, are also distinctive.

Other names: Soft pine, northern pine, Weymouth pine (European designation).

Close relatives: Jack pine *(P. banksiana)*; red pine *(P. resinosa)*; Eastern hemlock *(Tsuga canadensis)*; spruces *(Picea)*; balsam fir *(Abies balsamea)*.

Lifestyle: I always think of the white pine as the "wind tree." Not only do this tree's soft needles comb and voice the winds, but its cones are wind pollinated and the tree's very form looks windswept.

White pine grows on a scheme of five: five needles to a cluster, five side buds surrounding a central terminal bud on the shoot, and whorls of five branches surrounding the trunk, one whorl for each year of the tree's life. (As pines age, of course, they lose many of their lower whorls.) Note the distance between whorls. Relatively short spaces indicate an environmental hardship during that year (drought is the most common). Comparing short spaces among several trees will tell you whether that hardship was of general or individual occurrence.

Two sides of each triangular needle are white-lined, and needles remain on the tree for a year and a half. In spring, look for the lengthening terminal bud, or *candle*, the beginning of the current year's shoot. By early summer, annual growth and formation of next year's buds is completed.

White pines begin flowering about age twenty. Both pollen and seed cones occur on the same tree. The wind-pollinated seed cones appear high in the crown and require two years to mature, then drop off in winter and spring. Thus for much of the year, a tree holds two sizes of seed cones. Cone crops vary in abundance from year to year; even-aged stands of trees probably originated in a good seed year. Young trees often thrive best when growing at a distance from older ones even though white pine is moderately shade tolerant. Though it has no large taproot, its lateral roots spread deep and wide, giving it a firm anchor.

White pine grows most rapidly of any northern forest tree, averaging fifteen to eighteen inches per year. Trees in presettlement forests typically lived 250 to 300 years, but today a white pine older than sixty to eighty years is a rare sight because of the lumber's economic value.

This is the largest pine east of the Rockies and, next to the sugar pine *(P. lambertiana)* of California, the largest pine in the United States.

Associates: White pine exists as a codominant species with Eastern hemlock and northern hardwoods in the border zone *(ecotone)* between temperate deciduous and boreal coniferous forests, extending south along the Alleghenies. Whether it can be classed as a climax species is arguable; some ecologists label it a "fire climax." Though long-lived, it often pioneers a forest succession that may eventually result in a northern hardwood climax or mixture. This pine, like many others, is fire dependent for widespread germination; it probably owed its original distribution to naturally occurring fires, which disrupted the uniform forests of red pine, a species with which it often associates. Red pine, however, generally prefers somewhat drier soils.

White pine grows in pure stands or, more often, in mixtures with other conifers and hardwoods. Aldo Leopold noted an affinity between young white pines and dewberry shrubs *(Rubus)*, asserting that trees planted in such bramble patches almost always thrive. In drier or sandy areas, white pine frequently associates with scrubby oaks. Observations in mixed forests suggest that white pine seedlings often occur in greater abundance beneath the canopies of oaks and hickories than elsewhere; a possible reason may involve the activities of squirrels.

Spring, summer. A fungus associate that kills many trees is white pine blister rust *(Cronartium ribicola)*, which requires certain shrubs as alternate hosts (see Currants and Gooseberries). Signs of this most destructive disease include flags of dead needles in the crown and small, oval, blisterlike cankers in the bark, which slowly girdle infected branches and trunks.

Common beneath pines from spring to fall is the fly agaric mushroom *(Amanita muscaria)*, with its red, orange, yellow, or white cap

Dabs of frothy liquid on pine, often at needle bases, contain nymphs of pine spittlebugs. The spittle hiding the insect is actually digested and excreted tree sap.

marked by cottony warts. An energy exchange apparently takes place; the agaric transforms soil nutrients to a form absorbable by pine roots, while the pine provides photosynthetic nutrients.

More than eighty insect species forage on white pine. The bent, "shepherd's crook" appearance of the topmost shoot is caused by larvae of the white pine weevil *(Pissodes strobi)*, a twig borer. The larvae kill the terminal shoot, resulting in upward growth of high lateral branches; one of them eventually replaces the dead leader. A bunchy growth of branches in the topmost crown generally indicates an attack by this insect. These weevils generally attack only trees standing in full sunlight that are younger than fifteen years. A similar "shepherd's crook" injury is caused by an attack of the Eastern pineshoot borer *(Eucosma gloriola)*, a tortricid moth.

The pine webworm *(Tetralopha robustella)*, yellow-brown and striped, creates messy webs near twig ends of young trees. The pine-devil moth *(Citheronia sepulcralis)*, a spiny green royal moth, is another caterpillar feeder. The white pine angle *(Semiothesa pinistro-bata)*, an inchworm caterpillar, is also common wherever white pines exist. Zimmerman pine moths *(Dioryctria zimmermani)* bore into twigs, killing branch tips and entire tops of trees and causing masses of pitch flow.

Brown-tipped needles may indicate the presence of pine needleminers *(Exoteleia pini-foliella)*, small moth larvae.

Nymphs of pine spittlebugs *(Aphrophora parallela)* produce masses of froth on the twigs, from which they suck sap. Their excess spittle secretions may rain over the tree, often resulting in patchy growth of a black, crustlike sooty-mold fungus (Perisporiaceae). Adult spittlebugs are called froghoppers.

Many species of sawfly larvae, resembling caterpillars, feed voraciously on pines. The introduced pine sawfly *(Diprion similis)*, yellow-green and black-striped, is common, as is the white pine sawfly *(Neodiprion pinetum)* and the pine false webworm *(Acantholyda erythro-cephala)*, which webs twigs similarly to the pine webworm.

In midsummer, aborted cones on the ground with holes in their bases indicate the feeding of larval white pine cone beetles *(Conophthorus coniperda)*.

Also in midsummer look for a common cicada called the dogday harvestfly *(Tibicen canicularis)*, a large black and green insect that requires several years to mature. The nymphs feed on pine roots.

Large pines are favored nesting sites for hawks and owls. Sharp-shinned and Cooper's hawks typically build on large branches next to the trunk. Broad-winged hawks may build likewise or in a crotch near the top of the tree. The nests of blue jays, common ravens, American crows, and common grackles may also be seen.

On horizontal limbs and in branch foliage, look for nests of mourning doves, olive-sided flycatchers, magnolia warblers, yellow-rumped warblers, black-throated green warblers, Blackburnian warblers, bay-breasted warblers, pine warblers, evening and pine grosbeaks, purple finches, and pine siskins. Great horned, barred, and long-eared owls often adapt old hawk or crow nests for their own (though barred owls nest more frequently in pine trunk cavities).

Pine candles are delicate and brittle in spring and often break when birds alight upon them or when red squirrels nip them.

Fall. Most pine-associated mushrooms appear on the ground in this season. These include the pinecone mushroom *(Auriscalpium vulgare)*, a small tooth fungus with off-center brown cap, and several boletes or pore mushrooms *(Suillus, Tylopilus)*. Common gill mush-rooms include the goat waxycap *(Hygrophorus camarophyllus)*, brownish gray; Zeller's bracelet *(Tricholoma zelleri)*, orange-brown and sticky; and the brown slimecap *(Chroogom-phus rutilus)*, whose name is self-descriptive.

Numerous songbirds forage for seeds on white pine. Most frequent among them are red-breasted nuthatches, pine grosbeaks, and red crossbills. Other common seed eaters include black-capped chickadees, white-breasted nuthatches, pine warblers, evening grosbeaks, pine siskins, and white-winged crossbills.

White-footed mice, red-backed voles, Eastern chipmunks, and red squirrels are probably the dominant mammal seed eaters. A red squirrel can strip an average-size cone (about forty-five seeds) in two minutes, beginning at the bottom and turning the cone as it feeds. Large piles of stripped cones and cone scales at the base of a pine usually indicate a red squirrel *midden*, where the animal repeatedly feeds and in which it may store caches of unstripped cones.

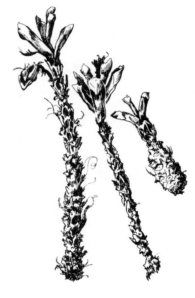

Cones stripped by red squirrels are common beneath large white pine trees. Huge piles of them (middens) often accumulate where the squirrels habitually feed.

Although gray squirrels are not major pine seed consumers, research indicates that their burials of acorns and other nuts in mixed forests serve to encourage white pine germination. The ground disruption from nut-burying activity provides bare seedbeds, as well as seed protection through inadvertent burial.

Winter. Birds and squirrels continue to feed on pine seeds during the cold months. In some areas red squirrels are highly dependent on white pine, not only for food but also for nesting sites and materials.

In late February or early March, certain hawks and owls begin courtship and nesting. Red-tailed and red-shouldered hawks and bald eagles often return to previous nests. The hawks reline them and usually add fresh conifer sprigs; eagles may make extensive additions. Great horned and barred owls, common ravens, and gray jays also begin nesting activity in late winter, the owls often calling loudly at this time.

White-tailed deer frequently browse white pine (not a preferred food) during late winter. The height of the browse line can tell you how hungry they were. Snowshoe hares, porcupines, and squirrels gnaw the bark, sometimes girdling trees.

All year. Foliose lichens are readily apparent on trunks and branches at any time of year. Common ones on pine include species of *Parmelia*, *Cetraria*, and *Parmeliopsis*.

Several needles fused to construct a tube indicate the pine tube moth caterpillar. This insect feeds on the outer ends of the needles, gradually eating down its home.

Some conspicuous insect signs can be seen all year. A silk-lined tube constructed of several needles with the free end cut off indicates the larval presence of the pine tube moth *(Argyrotaenia pinatubana)*, a tortricid that feeds from inside the tube.

Masses of pitch exuding from the trunk are signs of pitch mass borers *(Vespamima pini)*, clearwing moths.

Red squirrels often use white pine branches and crevices as *mycophages*, sites of temporary storage for drying mushrooms before storing them elsewhere.

Check out the bases of large white pines for raccoon scat. These mammals often use pines as daytime resting areas, leaving scats on the ground before they climb. One chilly spring day I saw a raccoon bedded high in an old broad-winged hawk's nest.

Lore: Pollen evidence shows that white pine's distribution was much more extensive some five thousand to eight thousand years ago, during a postglacial warming interval, than now.

White pine needles, rich in vitamins A and C, contain five times as much C as an equal weight of lemons. Young spring needles, chopped fine and steeped, make the best tea. Native Americans used the tree's sweetish, nutritious inner bark as a poultice for sores and wounds and as a flour; dried, it contains up to ten percent tannin plus oils and resins. In solution, it was taken for coughs and colds as an expectorant. The boiled young male cones, the fine, prolific pollen, and the roasted or ground seeds are also edible. All of these tree parts (of any pine species) can provide emergency foods. Natives also used pine pitch for glue, filler, and waterproofing.

Colonial shipbuilding and trade relied heavily on white pine, so much so that New England's early coins bore the image of this tree. Clearing of the vast white pine forests of the northeastern United States in the nineteenth century supported the entire timber industry during that period. Soft and light colored (giving white pine its name), the wood remains one of the most useful and commercially valuable forest products.

White pine is the official tree of Maine, Michigan, and Ontario.

Pine, Jack *(Pinus banksiana)*. Pine family. Small, scrubby tree in dry, sterile soils. Recognize jack pine by its scraggly appearance, its short, two-needled clusters, and its curved cones that may remain on the tree for up to twenty years.

Other name: Gray pine.

Lower dead branches, shaded out by upper ones, may persist on jack pine for years. Though most pine species are fire-adapted to some degree, jack pine's seed release often depends on forest fires.

Jack pines often carry tightly sealed cones, which empty seeds only when the heat of a fire opens them. Some trees may show already opened cones, and many jack pines carry cones in both conditions.

Close relatives: Eastern white pine *(P. strobus)*; red pine *(P. resinosa)*; Eastern hemlock *(Tsuga canadensis)*; spruces *(Picea)*; balsam fir *(Abies balsamea)*.

Lifestyle: Jack pine must have full sunlight to thrive. Notice that the lower, shaded-out branches are frequently dead, though they remain on the tree. Because of this pine's need for sun, so-called jack pine forests are usually quite open, often occurring in "pine plains," savannalike areas of sandy, acid soil. Today this pine mainly occupies the former burned or deforested timberlands where Eastern white pine and red pine once towered.

The paired, blunt needles, often curved or twisted, remain on the tree two to three years. Short male cones produce yellow clouds of pollen in spring. The seed cones, produced every year, require two years to mature. Ripe by autumn of their second season, they may open and discharge seeds or remain closed, sealed by resin, for a decade or more. This closed, *serotinous* condition is probably an adaptation to fire, conserving seeds on the tree until the heat of a forest fire "unglues" the cones. Such sudden harvests of seeds result in prolific reproduction on the fire-cleared soil. The degree of cone serotiny varies widely with location and fire frequency; some jack pine populations show many more open than closed cones.

Pure stands of jack pine may produce tall, spindly trees, but the tree's more typical appearance is short, broad-crowned, and rather bushy and distorted (due mainly to effects of white pine weevils on tree growth). Its root system spreads widely, far beyond the crown width. Young trees grow quickly, maturing in about sixty years, but trees in stands of this age may produce little annual growth.

Jack pine has the most northerly distribution of all the pines, extending south only to the northern United States.

Associates: Pure stands of jack pine are usually even-aged, resulting from seedfall following a fire episode. Jack pine also grows in mixtures with red pine, oaks, and quaking aspen, among others.

Spring, summer. A variety of other plants also characterizes sandy jack pine habitat. The brome grass *Bromus kalmii* is frequent; rough fescue *(Festuca scabrella)*, poverty grass or oatgrass *(Danthonia spicata)*, hair grass *(Deschampsia flexuosa)*, and rice-grasses *(Oryzopsis)* are other common grasses. Bracken fern *(Pteridium aquilinum)* is also a frequent associate.

In midsummer, look for slender ladies' tresses *(Spiranthes lacera)*, slender orchids with small, white flowers spiraling up a spike.

Low, shrubby sweetfern *(Comtonia peregrina)* is a common associate.

Insects that commonly forage on jack pine needles include tufted caterpillars of the pine tussock moth *(Dasychira plagiata)*.

Massed larvae of the jack pine sawfly *(Neodiprion pratti)* and redheaded pine sawfly *(N. lecontei)* resemble caterpillars and are probably the most frequent of many sawfly species that prey on this pine. Look for tufts of partially eaten needles associated with defoliated lengths of twig. Pine sawfly larvae store terpenes from the needles they devour in a croplike sac. If threatened by a predator, the larva may spit these chemicals, which are distasteful to many insects and birds.

The jack pine budworm *(Choristoneura pinus)* is similar in appearance and habits to the spruce budworm (see Balsam Fir).

Webbed and severed needles may indicate the pine needle sheathminer *(Zelleria haim-bachi)*, also called jack pine needleminer, a tiny moth.

A greenish scarab beetle on the needles is probably the pine chafer *(Dichelonyx albicollis)*.

The Saratoga spittlebug *(Aphrophora saratogensis)*, a sap-sucker, produces frothy masses of foam on sweetfern and other vegetation. The adult insects, called froghoppers, migrate to pines but produce no spittle on them.

On young trees, blisterlike nodules in twig crotches are produced by Northern pitch twig moth caterpillars *(Petrova albicapitana)*.

In summer, dead branch tips, especially in the upper crown, may be signs of the jack pine tip beetle *(Conophthorus banksianae)*. Repeated attacks cause crooked, distorted branching. Similar effects result from larval feeding of white pine weevils (see Eastern White Pine).

Another characteristic insect of the jack pine plains is the bronze tiger beetle *(Cicindela lecontei)*. Look for larval burrows, pencil-size or smaller holes in the ground with no excavated earth at their margins.

A ground-nesting bird of dense jack pine habitat (sometimes called "bird of fire" because of its dependence on frequent fire renewal of that habitat) is the Kirtland's warbler. This endangered species currently occupies only a few small, carefully managed areas in Michigan's northern lower peninsula.

Jack pine plains also host such ground nesters as common nighthawks and vesper sparrows.

Red squirrels often begin stripping the cones in midsummer (see Eastern White Pine).

Fall. This is the season to look for distinctive mushrooms on the jack pine plains. A reddish-brown tooth fungus may be scaber hydnum *(Sarcodon scabrosus)*. Yellowish-brown pore mushrooms (boletes) may include a slippery jack *(Suillus subluteus)*, the woollycap *(S. tomentosus)*, and the stubby-stalk *(S. brevipes)*. A large, white mushroom aging to cinnamon color, the pine mushroom or white matsutake *(Armillaria ponderosa)*, may be found, as well as various slimecaps *(Gomphidius)*, thick-gilled olive or reddish-brown mushrooms.

Areas of rubbed-off bark on solitary jack pines six to eight feet tall indicate antler rubs of whitetail bucks. The deer often "attack" shrubs and small trees, especially ones with aromatic bark.

Winter. Rows of neatly cropped needles and buds on twigs are signs of ruffed or spruce grouse feeding.

Lore: Jack pine's soft, weak wood is mainly used for pulpwood, lath, and interior paneling.

Although needles and inner bark can be used for the same food and medicinal purposes as other pines (see Eastern White Pine), little record exists of specific uses by Native Americans. Deforestation and extensive forest fires resulting from lumbering practices have probably increased this tree's prominence in the landscape.

Pine, Red *(Pinus resinosa).* Pine family. Tree in mesic to dry soils, thriving best in sandy soils and gravels. Identify red pine by its long needles in clusters of two, its flaky, reddish bark, and its egg-shaped seed cones. The foliage, unlike that of the jack and Eastern white pines, occurs in tufts at ends of branches.

Other names: Norway pine, hard pine.

Close relatives: Eastern white pine *(P. strobus)*; jack pine *(P. banksiana)*; Eastern hemlock *(Tsuga canadensis)*; spruces *(Picea)*; balsam fir *(Abies balsamea).*

Lifestyle: Red pine requires two years to develop ripe cones, but many of its cones remain on the tree until the summer following the autumn of cone maturity. Seed cones usually appear in the upper crown, the purple pollen cones in the midcrown. In spring, when the pollen cones shed clouds of yellow dust, I have seen puddles become rimmed in gold as the water recedes. If pollen is prolific, however, seeds seldom are; a good seed year generally occurs only once in four to seven years.

The architecture of a pine cone is an admirable structure of bladelike scales and wind channels. Its curves and angles spiral the air currents around the cone, thereby achieving maximum pollen exposure.

New spring needles last more than two years, often falling in their third October. Needles of the Austrian or black pine *(P. nigra),* an imported tree often planted for soil cover or as an ornamental, have a similar appearance. Tell the two apart by bending a needle double. If it snaps clearly in two, it's red pine; Austrian pine needles bend without breaking.

Like many pines, red pine is adapted to fire, germinating best on flame-cleared soils. The thick protective bark is fire resistant. Shade intolerant and thriving in full sunlight, this tree grows fast, sometimes averaging a foot per year until age sixty to seventy, when growth gradually declines. It seldom lives more than three hundred years.

Landowners often plant red pine in rows for its timber value and for reforesting open land. These uniform stands form dense, dark-shaded acreages of wall-to-wall pine and have relatively little value as wildlife habitat. Mature pine plantations are often biological deserts, which host little except pine diseases and pine insect foragers. These pests may become epidemic without the biological controls provided by more balanced plant habitats.

Associates: Before the northeastern forests were cleared, red pine was never as abundant as Eastern white pine, though the two species often occurred together and still do.

Today, the commercial value of white pine and the popularity of red pine for plantings have reversed those proportions, and red pine is the more numerous.

Red pine is intermediate between white pine and jack pine in its soil preference. While the tree can and does grow in pure natural stands, it more often occurs in mixture with the other pines and with northern hardwoods.

Spring, summer. Young trees are subject to a sclerodermic canker disease *(Ascocalyx abictina)*, which thrives during cool, moist spring weather. Scales at the bases of needle clusters are often the first sites of infection. Needles and shoots brown and drop, and elongate cankers eventually form on the trunk and may girdle the tree.

Another common fungus associate is a needle rust, *Coleosporium solidaginis*, that appears as cream-to-orange-colored pustules on needles. Its alternate hosts are goldenrods and asters.

Aldo Leopold noted an apparent association between young red pines and flowering spurge *(Euphorbia corollata)*.

Frequently amid the terminal needle tufts I find the concave and platform webs of bowl-and-doily spiders *(Frontinella communis)*, sheetweb weavers whose name well describes the web.

Shoot borers, sawflies, and spittlebugs are the dominant insect feeders on all pines.

Dead, crooked shoots exuding masses of pitch on young trees often indicate larval feeding of the European pine shoot moth *(Rhyacionia buoliana)*, which hibernates over winter in buds or pitch.

Resembling yellowish caterpillars, redheaded pine sawfly larvae (see Jack Pine) mass on needles, often defoliating young pines. The European pine sawfly *(Neodiprion sertifer)* is another common species.

Pine needleminers, small moth larvae (see Eastern White Pine), feed on the inside of needles, which turn brown. Most needles on a severely infected tree may be mined.

A bowl-shaped web hanging above a flatter one is the construction of the bowl-and-doily spider, often found on red pine needles. The spider waits on the web beneath for insect prey to fall into the bowl.

Pine sawfly larvae, resembling caterpillars, devour needles. They elevate their bodies into S-shaped positions when disturbed. Chemical defenses make these larvae distasteful to bird and insect predators.

A sphinx moth caterpillar that lacks the typical rear horn of sphinxes is the bombyx or northern pine sphinx *(Lapara bombycoides)*.

I have often observed crane flies *(Tipula)*, which resemble large, long-legged mosquitoes (the adult insects do not feed), dancing in flight amid red pine foliage, probably hunting for mates.

Cedar waxwings are among the most common birds nesting in young red pines. Despite the relative infrequency of wildlife in uniform pine plantings, these stands may attract such nesters as red-breasted nuthatches, golden-crowned kinglets, and Blackburnian and pine warblers.

Fall. A common mushroom in red pine stands is a club-shaped, brownish coral fungus *(Clavariadelphus ligula)*, which often appears after heavy rains. Others include the woollycap *(Suillus tomentosus)*, a yellowish, downy-capped pore mushroom, and the winter herald *(Hygrophorus hypothejus)*, a slimy, variably colored gill waxycap.

Bird and mammal seed eaters are generally the same as for the other pines, though the relative infrequency of seed production probably makes this tree less important as a food plant.

All year. Red pine is subject to a condition known as pocket decline and mortality, a large, circular, gradually expanding opening resulting from the decline and death of trees within a stand. Causes remain unclear, but several organisms are often associated with the condition. Among these are two species of black-staining root fungus, as well as pine engraver beetles *(Ips pini)*, red turpentine beetles *(Dendroctonus valens)*, and pine root collar weevils *(Hylobius radicis)*. Pocket decline affects mainly plantation-grown trees.

Beneath shedding bark on dead or dying trees, look for small, oval nests of wood chips constructed by larvae of the ribbed pine borer *(Stenocorus inquisitor)*, a longhorned beetle. The beetles pupate in these nests and, as adults, remain in them over winter.

Lore: Despite its common name of Norway pine, red pine is a native American tree and never grew in Norway. It has been variously claimed that the name originated from Norway, Maine, where it grew abundantly; or that an early explorer confounded it with the Scotch pine *(P. sylvestris)*, which is native to Europe.

Native Americans used this pine along with others for various medicinal purposes (see Eastern White Pine). One of the most charming uses by woodland tribes involved cutting a needle tuft at various lengths to represent a skirted figure. These children's dolls were then placed upright on a flat surface and gently agitated so that they would dance.

Red pine's light, hard wood—often mixed with and sold commercially as white pine, though it is a heavier, stronger wood—is a valuable product for general construction, frames, flooring, and pulpwood.

Red pine is Minnesota's state tree.

Roughly circular rims of shredded debris on the inner side of loose pine bark are the pupal chambers of ribbed pine borers. This is a hand-lens view; the chambers measure about an inch in diameter.

Poison Ivy *(Rhus radicans).* Cashew family. Appears in two forms, a low shrub or a creeping or climbing vine in woods, thickets. Its compound leaf of three leaflets, its aerial rootlets clinging to tree trunks from vines that look like fuzzy ropes, and its waxy-white fruits are key marks. The adage "leaflets three, let it be" will prevent one's contact with poison ivy, but other, harmless plants also show a trifoliate resemblance.

Other names: Three-leaved ivy, poison oak (the latter, sometimes designating the nonclimbing form of poison ivy, is actually *R. toxicodendron,* a more exclusively southern and western species); poison ivy is unrelated to true ivies *(Hedera)* and oaks.

Close relatives: Sumacs *(Rhus)*; cashew *(Anacardium occidentale).*

Lifestyle: Poison ivy forms long-lived, persistent clones in almost any kind of soil but thrives especially well on limy soils and in floodplains. Though the plant is moderately shade tolerant, full sunlight encourages a lush, dense growth.

The greenish-white, insect-pollinated flowers are sometimes bisexual but often unisexual

Which vines on this tree trunk are poison ivy? It pays to be able to recognize this plant in winter, for most parts of poison ivy contain urushiol. Its hairlike rootlets anchor the vine to vertical surfaces.

on the same or different clones. They develop into whitish fruits (drupes) that often persist into winter.

Leaflets, though always in threes, may be toothed or smooth, rounded or pointed, shiny or dull. Indeed, this plant's variability in habit, habitat, and leaf characters has led many a person who "knows" poison ivy into an acutely unforgettable experience. Turning red-gold in autumn, the leaves manifest the bird-attractant scheme known as foliar fruit flagging (see Flowering Dogwood).

In winter, the tree-climbing vines are immediately recognizable by their fibrous, hairlike rootlets that attach to the tree bark.

Associates: Despite its dire reputation among humankind, poison ivy is a fairly important wildlife food plant. Few if any species seem to suffer ill effects from it.

Spring, summer. Flower pollination is mainly accomplished by small bees and flies.

Many insect species feed nonexclusively on this plant. Exclusive feeders include tiny larvae of *Lithocolletis guttifinitella*, a tineid moth, which mine the upper leaves. Two owlet moths, the light marathyssa *(Marathyssa basalis)* and the eyed paectes *(Paectes oculatrix)*, also feed as caterpillars on poison ivy leaves. The adult moths are grayish brown.

Fall, winter. More than sixty species of birds relish poison ivy fruits. Many of these are fall migrants attracted by foliar flagging; others are winter resident species that feed on the fruits when other foods are scarce. Frequent users include ring-necked pheasants, ruffed and sharp-tailed grouse, Northern bobwhites, and yellow-rumped warblers. Ant-eating birds—especially Northern flickers—seem fond of these fruits. Birds mainly account for spread of the plant; the seeds pass undamaged through their digestive systems.

Cottontail rabbits often nip off stems above the snow surface in winter. Such browsing of clones results in abundant branching of the plants in spring, producing thick, dense jungles of poison ivy.

Lore: Merely touching or brushing against a leaf won't give you contact dermatitis; only the sap exuding from a bruised leaf or stem (or droplets in smoke of the burning plant) can. The oily sap found in all parts of this plant (except the pollen), which produces those painful symptoms, is a resin called *urushiol*.

It isn't the urushiol itself that is dangerous, but rather the human body's allergic reaction to it. The oil penetrates to the inner dermis layer of skin, where white blood cells attack it, producing the rash and blisters. Some people seem immune to urushiol (about fifteen to twenty-five percent of the population), but such immunity is notoriously unreliable. Urushiol can, in fact, immunize against itself, but side effects are tricky, so it's not often injected. Urushiol can be spread by means of shoes and clothing as well as animal fur. Century-old herbaria specimens of poison ivy have, on occasion, produced rashes on unwary laboratory botanists. The breaking water blisters on already infected skin are not themselves contagious.

The best home remedy, I find, is to bathe affected areas in tap water as hot as one can stand, then apply rubbing alcohol to the rash. Several Native American remedies, however, may also be used. Crushed leaves of jewelweed or touch-me-not *(Impatiens)*, *Aloe vera*, plantain, and sweetfern, as well as various tannic washes brewed from tree barks, have proven helpful to some. My usual summer case of it is kept restrained by such methods; when in poison ivy's vicinity, I conciliate it, like the Cherokee, by addressing it as "my friend." A severely unfriendly case should, of course, be treated by a physician.

Polygala, Fringed *(Polygala paucifolia)*. Milkwort family. Low herb in moist, rich woods. Its broad, evergreen leaves that resemble wintergreen and its pink-magenta flower consisting of two flaring, lateral sepals and a bushy, fringed central tube identify this plant. About a score of polygala species occupy various northeastern habitats; this is one of the most common.

Other names: Gaywings, flowering wintergreen, fringed milkwort, bird-on-the-wing.

Close relatives: Seneca snakeroot *(P. senega)*; other milkworts.

Lifestyle: Flowers of this polygala superficially resemble pea blossoms. The fringed, central pouch is actually a landing platform for insects, whose weight depresses the pouch and forces the rigid sex organs through a slit at the top and into direct contact with a furry belly. Cross-fertilization is thus achieved.

Like such plants as jewelweeds and violets, polygala also develops another kind of flower that never opens and is entirely self-fertilized. This insurance provision (called *cleistogamy*) produces viable if not genetically diverse seed. Cleistogamous flowers are pouchlike in shape. They are located on tiny, subsurface branchlets that won't be seen unless one carefully hunts for them. The fruits of fringed polygala are small capsules.

Polygala rises from a slender, perennial rhizome, sometimes a foot long. The leaves turn bronze-red on the plant in winter.

Associates: This is mainly a plant of coniferous forests and northern hardwoods.

Spring, summer. Pollination is accomplished primarily by bees.

Investigation of how both aerial and cleistogamous seeds are dispersed has revealed an interesting coaction with at least three ant species. Saclike appendages (caruncles) on the seeds contain an oily liquid appealing to the ants. These insects cut the seeds from the ripe capsules and carry them back to their nests. After consuming the oily appendages, the ants discard the seeds in heaps—where a new bed of fringed polygalas may germinate.

Lore: Fringed polygala's flower looks utterly unlike any other milkwort flower; most others show cloverlike blooms.

Milkworts were so named because of their reputed use in stimulating lactation in nursing mothers and cattle.

Gala, the Greek word for milk, is also the root word for galaxy—the milky way.

Prickly-Ash, Northern *(Zanthoxylum americanum).* Rue family. Shrub in moist woods, thickets, stream edges. Its small, sharp, paired thorns, prickly leafstalks, alternate compound leaves of five to eleven leaflets, and the lemonlike odor of its crushed foliage identify prickly-ash.

Other name: Toothache-tree.

Close relatives: Hoptree *(Ptelea trifoliata)*; rue *(Ruta graveolens)*; unrelated to ashes *(Fraxinus)* and mountain-ashes *(Sorbus).*

Lifestyle: Multistemmed clones of this spiny shrub form dense, formidable thickets. The spines occur at the leaf nodes.

Greenish clusters of unisexual flowers appear on male and female clones before the leaves emerge in early spring. The insect-pollinated female flowers develop into bright red capsules containing two black, lustrous seeds.

Associates: *Spring, summer.* This plant often hosts a number of scale insect species, most of which exude honeydew and attract ants. The ants feed on the honeydew and may react aggressively to disturbance of the massed sap-suckers.

Look for large, brown-and-cream caterpillars on the foliage. These are "orangedogs," larvae of the giant swallowtail *(Papilio cresphontes),* one of the largest North American butterflies. Its paired scent horns *(osmateria)* protruding just behind the larval head produce a strong, disagreeable odor. This subtropical species has gradually worked its way northward to become more common in the northeastern United States. (Owners of citrus orchards, in which these caterpillars are common pests, have been known to shoot the butterflies with birdshot.)

Another caterpillar feeder is the spicebush swallowtail (see Common Spicebush).

Winter. Inspect the stems for wintering pupal forms of the swallowtail butterflies. These are angular chrysalids attached lengthwise to stems by a loop of tough, silken thread resembling a safety belt.

Prickly-ash is apparently not a very important food plant for birds and mammals. Its main value to them is probably as protective cover.

Lore: Native Americans crushed the aromatic root and bark as a remedy for toothache and sore throat. The dried bark was once considered a relief for rheumatic complaints. The fruits, too, found medicinal use as a stimulant and antispasmodic. The lemon-fragrant oil contains berberine (also found in barberries), a mild sedative.

Prickly-ash wood is yellow and hard to cut. It yields a yellow dye.

Raspberries *(Rubus* spp.). Rose family. Prickly or bristly arching shrubs in thickets, edges. Many species and hybridized varieties exist, but the two most common wild plants are black raspberry *(R. occidentalis)* and red raspberry *(R. strigosus).* The first has black fruits and strong, hooked prickles on the ridged, white-powdered stem; identify red raspberry by its round, bristly stem and red fruits. Both species have white flowers and compound leaves that are whitish below.

Other names: Brambles, blackcap *(R. occidentalis),* wineberry *(R. phoenicolasius),* thimbleberry *(R. parviflorus),* cloudberry *(R. chamaemorus).*

Close relatives: Blackberry *(R. allegheniensis);* roses *(Rosa);* cherries *(Prunus);* mountain-ashes *(Sorbus);* hawthorns *(Crataegus);* shadbushes *(Amelanchier).*

Lifestyle: Black and red raspberries both bear white, bisexual, insect-pollinated flowers in spring, but black raspberry fruits generally ripen first. Fruits of both species detach easily from the receptacle, which remains on the fruit stalk, in contrast to blackberry fruits, which detach entirely. Blackberry fruits often dry on the plant, while raspberries fall to the ground when ripe. *Rubus* fruits are not technically berries but aggregates of drupes, each containing a seed.

Cloning raspberry stems rise from a perennial base and last for two years, flowering and fruiting only in the second year. *Floricanes* (second-year stems) often show smaller, less divided compound leaves than *primocanes* (first-year stems). Black raspberry often roots again at the arching tip of the stem; red raspberry does not.

Both plants thrive as pioneering species following fire or land disturbance and can tolerate a wide range of soil acidity (pH 5.5 to 7). Black raspberry can grow in moderate shade, but red raspberry must have full sunlight. Thus, black raspberry will often outlast red raspberry and blackberry, as succession from open to shaded habitats occurs.

Associates: Black raspberry clones often thrive in the vicinity of black walnut trees.

Spring, summer. A spectacular fungous disease of raspberries, sometimes coating entire leaves, is orange rust (see Blackberry).

Raspberries host a number of insect feeders. On leaves, look for green cloverworms *(Plathypena scabra)*, green owlet moth caterpillars. Many other moth caterpillars also forage here.

Japanese beetles (see Wild Grapes) commonly skeletonize leaves and defoliate stems.

Wilted stems indicate insect borers. The most common stem feeder is the raspberry cane borer *(Oberea maculata)*. This longhorned beetle punctures a double row around the stem near the tip, which wilts, and lays an egg between the punctures. Larvae of the rednecked cane borer *(Agrilus ruficollis)*, a buprestid beetle, cause cigar-shaped swellings in stems, which they eventually girdle. Raspberry cane maggots *(Pegomya rubivora)*, grublike fly larvae, kill stem tips, which may break off cleanly as if cut by a knife. Wilting and dying of canes also result from subsurface feeding of raspberry crown or root borers *(Bembecia marginata)*, clearwing moth caterpillars.

A grublike insect inside the fruit is probably the Eastern raspberry fruitworm *(Byturus rubi)*, a beetle larva.

Flower pollinators are mainly bees.

Raspberry fruits provide some of the most important, widely consumed foods for birds. Some of the more common fruit foragers include ring-necked pheasants, ruffed and sharp-tailed grouse, wild turkeys, Northern bobwhites, American woodcocks, blue jays, tufted titmice, veeries, wood thrushes, American robins, gray catbirds, brown thrashers, cedar waxwings, yellow-breasted chats, scarlet tanagers, Northern cardinals, rose-breasted and pine grosbeaks, rufous-sided towhees, fox and Henslow's sparrows, Northern orioles, common grackles, and purple finches.

Eastern and least chipmunks, raccoons, and fox squirrels rank high among mammal fruit eaters.

Dense raspberry thickets also provide nesting and protective cover for many birds and mammals (see Blackberry).

Winter. Look for vertical, zipperlike scars on stems. These are egg scars of the black-horned tree cricket (see Blackberry).

Cottontail rabbits and white-tailed deer browse on the stems (see Blackberry).

Lore: For Native Americans, raspberries provided medicine as well as food. A decoction of the root bark was taken internally for dysentery and externally as an eye wash, said to cure early stages of cataract. Midwives gave expectant mothers a raspberry leaf tea to aid childbirth. During World War II, an obstetric drug called fragerine was discovered in the leaves.

Raspberry flowers produce a nectar that honeybees *(Apis mellifera)* turn into one of the lightest, most delicate and flavorful of honeys.

Familiar uses of the fruits, of course, include jams, jellies, pies, juices, wines. Raspberry-blackberry-dewberry hybrids have produced such market fruits as boysenberries and loganberries.

In medieval plant lore, the raspberry symbolized remorse, and the fruit was apparently little used for food in Europe until the early seventeenth century. Our native red raspberry closely resembles the European red raspberry, *R. idaeus* (some botanists treat both as the same species), that was known to Pliny in the first century A.D.

Redbud *(Cercis canadensis).* Pea family. Small tree in moist woods. Recognize redbud by its untoothed, heart-shaped leaves, its reddish flower clusters in early spring, and its dry seedpods in late summer.

Other names: Judas tree, flowering Judas.

Close relatives: Honey locust *(Gleditsia triacanthos)*; Kentucky coffeetree *(Gymnocladus dioicus)*; sennas *(Cassia)*; black locust *(Robinia pseudoacacia)*; tick trefoils *(Desmodium)*; clovers *(Trifolium).*

Lifestyle: Redbud is typically an understory resident of medium-shaded woodlands or forest edges. Its optimal habitats are stream borders, floodplains, and bottomlands, but it thrives on many soil types and is widely planted as an ornamental. It grows slowly and is relatively short-lived. Redbud's primary distribution is southern, reaching only as far north as southern Ontario and New England.

Redbuds begin to flower when four or five years old. The spectacular flowers appear scattered along the branches before or just after the leaves emerge, about the same time as shadbushes. They are bisexual and insect pollinated, resembling pea blossoms in form. Seedpods often remain on the tree into winter. Under full summer sunlight, leaves in the upper crown often fold, thus reducing the amount of radiation received.

Unlike other plants of the legume family, redbud produces no nitrogen-fixing root nodules. This tree typically divides its trunk near the ground, showing a broad, rounded or flat crown. It has the zigzag branching characteristic of trees with no end buds on their twigs.

Associates: Other tree species in typical redbud habitats commonly include American elm, American basswood, and Northern hackberry.

Spring, summer. Bees are the chief pollinators.

Several moth species feed as caterpillars on the foliage. The redbud leaffolder *(Fascista cercerisella)*, a gelechiid moth, folds and ties leaves together with silk. Grape leaffolders and grape skeletonizers (see Wild Grapes) are also fairly common.

Curved holes or slits in the leaves may indicate the nighttime feeding of rhabdopterus beetles *(Rhabdopterus praetextus)*, small and blackish bronze.

Henry's elfin butterflies *(Incisalia henrici)*, small and brownish, visit redbud flowers.

Late summer, fall. Redbud seeds are not important wildlife foods. A few songbirds consume them, as do Northern bobwhites.

Lore: The association of Judas with this tree comes from the belief that Judas Iscariot hanged himself from a Eurasian species of redbud *(C. siliquastrum).*

The hard wood is heavy but relatively weak. The red roots yield a dye. Flower buds and young seedpods are edible as are the flowers, which may be added to salads.

Redbud is the state tree of Oklahoma.

Roses, Wild *(Rosa* spp.). Rose family. Trailing or climbing shrubs in thickets, edges. Most wild roses have prickly stems, compound leaves with three to eleven leaflets, winged leafstalk bases, pinkish flowers with five showy petals, and red, fleshy fruit cases called *hips.* About twenty species exist in the northeastern and north-central United States. Many species hybridize with each other. Many, such as the sweetbrier or eglantine *(R. eglanteria)*, are alien species escaped from cultivation. Multiflora rose *(R. multiflora)*, an Asian native, is frequently planted for erosion control and wildlife hedges. Native upland roses include the pasture or Carolina rose *(R. carolina)*, the prairie rose *(R. setigera)*, and the smooth rose *(R. blanda).*

Other names: Common, low, or dwarf rose *(R. carolina)*, climbing or Michigan rose *(R. setigera)*, early or meadow rose *(R. blanda).*

Close relatives: Cherries *(Prunus)*; blackberry and raspberries *(Rubus)*; mountain-ashes *(Sorbus)*; hawthorns *(Crataegus)*; shadbushes *(Amelanchier).*

Lifestyle: The sharp spines of roses are outgrowths of the stem bark. Slightly curved in most roses, they may be adaptations for climbing as well as a defense against herbivores.

The fragrant and spectacular bisexual flower has a thick, central cluster of pollen-bearing stamens, turned slightly outward from the pistils. This makes self-fertilization less likely and also guides an incoming, presumably pollen-laden insect to the prominent, sticky stigma first.

The rose hips that develop and redden are not themselves fruits but urn-shaped receptacles containing the fruits, which are dry, bony seed structures called *achenes*.

Unlike the stems of *Rubus* brambles, rose stems are perennial.

Associates: *Spring, summer.* Almost all parts of these plants provide some insect a favored food.

On leaves, nonexclusive moth feeders include the stinging rose caterpillar *(Parasa indetermina)*, a sluglike, striped caterpillar whose large spines can sting. A tortricid moth caterpillar *(Argyrotoxa bergmanniana)* folds single rose leaves and pupates inside the fold. *Nepticula rosaefoliella*, a tiny moth caterpillar, makes serpentine mines in the leaves.

Massed sawfly larvae resemble caterpillars; some specialize in defoliating roses. The bristly roseslug *(Cladius isomerus)*, greenish-white with bristles, skeletonizes leaves, as does the curled rose sawfly *(Allantus cinctus)* and the roseslug *(Endelomyia aethiops).*

Round pieces notched from rose leaves indicate leafcutter bees. The bees cut pieces from other species as well, but rose seems their favorite. The leaf sections provide nest lining in hollow twigs.

Stippled and slightly curled leaves may indicate feeding of rose leafhoppers *(Edwardsiana rosae)*, creamy yellow in color.

Among beetle foragers are Japanese beetles (see Wild Grapes) and rose leaf beetles *(Nodonota puncticollis)*, small and shiny green or blue.

Oval or circular sections cut from the margins of rose leaves mark the work of leafcutter bees *(Megachile)*. The leaf sections go to line the nests of these bees in twig cavities or inner stems of various plants.

Rose stems and foliage are subject to the sapsucking of many aphid species. A frequent associate of the aphids is the common black garden ant *(Lasius niger)*, which guards groups of aphids and feeds on the honeydew they exude.

On rose flowers, holes eaten in the petals are probably the work of rose curculios, also called rose snout beetles *(Rhynchites bicolor)*, bright red weevils that feed in the unopened buds, sometimes killing them.

Diplolepsis wasps create variously shaped galls on rose stems. Two common ones are shown here. Note the exit holes in the galls made by the emerging adult insects.

Rose chafers *(Macrodactylus subspinosus)*, tan beetles with spiny legs, feed first on the flowers, then on the foliage. These insects contain a heart poison known to have killed birds that ate them.

European earwigs *(Forficula auricularia)*, small, beetlelike insects with forcep tails, feed on rose stamens and petal bases.

Tiny yellowish insects crawling around the base of petals may be flower thrips *(Frankliniella tritici)*, also called wheat thrips. They migrate daily to flowers from grasses and weeds and often cause distorted buds and blossoms.

Bumblebees *(Bombus)* are the primary pollinators. Other bees also collect pollen. A brown and greenish scarab beetle *(Trichiotinus piger)* feeds on the pollen as well.

Stem-boring insects include small carpenter bees *(Ceratina)*, also called pith borers, whose larvae hatch and develop in tunnels mined in the stem. Larvae of rose stem girdlers *(Agrilus aurichalceus)*, greenish buprestid beetles, make spiral mines around the canes, which swell and sometimes split at these points. Rose stem sawflies *(Hartigia trimaculata)*, wasplike horntails, puncture the canes in which they lay eggs; the developing larvae cause shoots to wilt.

Rose thickets are favored nesting sites for gray catbirds, Northern mockingbirds, brown thrashers, yellow warblers, and Northern cardinals.

Fall, winter. Rose stems host more than fifty gall-making insects, most of which are tiny wasps of the genus *Diplolepsis*. Some of these galls are globular, others mossy, bristly, or tapering. Though formed in spring and summer, they are most visible after the leaves fall.

Birds' nests, now vacated by their builders, are often adapted as nest foundations or feeding platforms by white-footed mice. Piles of chewed-apart rose hips or seed remnants in these nests indicate mice have fed here.

Birds and small mammals consume rose hips and seeds as winter foods after preferred foods are snow-covered or depleted. Though high in vitamin nourishment, the hips are low in fat content. Common winter feeders are ring-necked pheasants, ruffed and sharp-tailed grouse, American robins, and Northern mockingbirds. Cottontail rabbits and meadow voles frequently gnaw the stems.

Dense rose thickets are widely used as protective cover for many small mammals.

Lore: Three rose hips, it is said, contain as much vitamin C as a single orange, up to sixty times as much as a lemon, and the hips are also richer by weight than oranges in calcium, phosphorus, and iron. The only problem is in the eating: most hips contain very little flesh in proportion to seed and have only a slight citrus taste. They can be used in quantity, however, for making an excellent beverage and, when mixed with apples, a jam.

The fresh petals are also edible raw and can be candied or made into a jelly. Leaves of *R. eglanteria*, which smell somewhat applelike when crushed, can be steeped for a tea. Native Americans used decoctions of the inner bark and root for treatment of various minor ailments.

The main commercial use of roses (besides the marketing of new hybrid garden varieties) has been the processing of petals for the manufacture of essential fragrant oils, or attars, for perfumes and other aromatic products.

Associated with Venus, the goddess of love, roses have adorned history since the earliest times. The Latin phrase *sub rosa*, meaning "in secret," translates literally as "under the rose." This usage derives from the Roman practice of hanging a rose over the door of a chamber, thereby binding to secrecy anyone who passed beneath it. "Rosary beads," writes Mary Durant, "originally represented the Virgin's crown of roses, or rosarium, as her garden was called in Medieval Latin." A crown of roses, of course, would also be a crown of thorns.

The rose is England's national flower. Iowa, New York, and North Dakota share the rose as state flower, and Alberta claims it as official provincial flower.

Sassafras *(Sassafras albidum).* Laurel family. Shrub or tree in woods, edges. Variably lobed or unlobed leaves, green twigs, furrowed red-brown bark, and spicy fragrance of crushed leaves, twigs, and bark identify this plant.

Other names: Ague tree, saxifrax, cinnamon wood, saloop, smelling stick.

Close relatives: Common spicebush *(Lindera benzoin)*; bays *(Persea)*; avocado *(P. americana)*; cinnamon *(Cinnamomum)*; camphor tree *(C. camphora)*; anise *(Pimpinella anisum).*

Lifestyle: Sassafras is a cloning plant; the stems rise along the wide-spreading lateral root system. Seedlings are shade tolerant, but they don't survive unless a disturbance opens the canopy to full sunlight. They are thus predominantly edge plants.

Individual clones are unisexual. Flowers of both sexes resemble each other and have male and female parts, but female parts are abortive on male flowers and male parts are sterile on the female ones. The drooping, greenish-yellow flower clusters emerge with the leaves in spring.

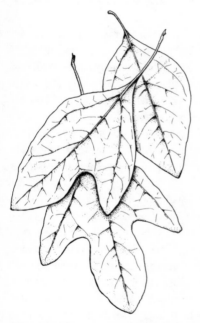

These three leaves from the same tree highlight the shape variability of sassafras leaves. All three basic shapes can be found on most sassafras trees, though lobed forms predominate on younger stems.

Sassafras leaves appear in three distinct shapes, usually all on the same tree: oval, two-lobed like a mitten, and three-lobed and symmetrical with broad, rounded sinuses. Younger trees generally show more lobed leaves than older trees. In the fall, the leaves turn spectacular shades of orange, pink, and red, providing a good example of foliar fruit flagging (see Flowering Dogwood).

The dark blue, berrylike fruits cupped atop bright red stalks are drupes.

Sassafras grows fast in the sun. It is not long-lived, partly because over time it becomes shaded out. This mainly southern tree reaches its northern limits in New England and the southern woodlands of Ontario and the Great Lakes region.

Associates: Except where it colonizes fencerows and old fields, sassafras is generally found along edges and in openings of dry to mesic oak woodlands.

Spring, summer. Most flower pollination is accomplished by flies.

The spicebush swallowtail butterfly and the promethea or spicebush silkmoth (see Common Spicebush) are common caterpillar feeders. Also, look for the small necklace moth *(Hypsoropha hormos)*, an owlet moth, the tulip-tree beauty (see Tulip Tree), and a minute tortricid, *Cenopis saracana*, which crumples leaves.

The sassafras or yellow poplar weevil *(Odontophus calceatus)*, a small, black snout beetle, eats holes in new spring leaves. Its larvae also produce blotch mines in the leaves.

Fall, winter. Sassafras fruits, though high in fat content, are usually not produced in sufficient quantity to make the plant a major wildlife food source. At least eighteen species of birds, however, do feed on them. Northern bobwhites and wild turkeys are the main game birds. Other consumers include pileated woodpeckers and several flycatcher species, which are otherwise mainly insect feeders: the Eastern phoebe, great crested flycatcher, and Eastern kingbird. Red-eyed vireos and gray catbirds also eat the fruit.

White-tailed deer browse twigs and foliage, while cottontail rabbits nip twigs and gnaw the bark.

Winter is a good time to look for the distinctive cocoons of promethea moths (see Common Spicebush).

Lore: The key ingredient (eighty percent) of aromatic sassafras oil, present in every part of the plant, is safrole, a substance also present in nutmeg, mace, and camphor. It is a weak carcinogen of the liver; in 1976 the Food and Drug Administration declared any food containing it unlawful to market interstate.

Sassafras tea, steeped mainly from the root or root bark, has been a favorite drink for centuries. Sassafras once formed the primary root ingredient of root beer, and safrole was also used in chewing gums, toothpastes, mouthwashes, and soaps. Taken in moderation, whether as tea or chewed bark or leaves, sassafras is pleasant and harmless.

The leaves, when chewed, promote salivation, and young leaves have long been used as a soup and gumbo thickener. As a medicinal, sassafras tea is an all-around folk remedy like witch hazel; everyone says it's good for you, but nobody can say how and why. Native Americans often used it for soothing minor ailments and for its mildly antiseptic and stimulant properties.

In early colonial days, its reputation as a medicinal plant was much higher than it is today. The first forest product to be exported from the New World (in 1603) was sassafras bark. Pioneers also used the bark as a source of earth-tone dyes.

The word *sassafras* is apparently Spanish in origin, dating back to the tree's discovery by Florida explorers in 1577, but its original meaning is lost. In 1492, Columbus was said to have sniffed the nearness of land by the scent of sassafras.

Its soft, weak wood has little commercial value, though its durability in contact with the soil has given it some utility as fence-post material. Sassafras does not make a good fuel wood because it pops and shoots sparks.

Shadbushes *(Amelanchier* spp.). Rose family. Shrubs or small trees in woods, thickets, edges. Shadbushes have toothed, alternate leaves, clusters of white flowers in early spring, and small, dark blue, applelike fruits. Foliage color is often a deep blue-green. Botanists disagree on whether there are many species or simply many variable and hybridized forms. Two of the most common recognized species are the Allegheny or smooth juneberry *(A. laevis)* and the downy juneberry *(A. arborea).*

Other names: Serviceberry, juneberry, shadblow, sarvis, saskatoon *(A. alnifolia),* May cherry, Indian pear.

Close relatives: Hawthorns *(Crataegus)*; mountain-ashes *(Sorbus)*; cherries *(Prunus)*; roses *(Rosa)*; blackberry and raspberries *(Rubus).*

Lifestyle: Those spectacular white flowers shaped like five-bladed propellers appearing on edge or forest understory shrubs before hardly a leaf unfolds in spring are probably shadbush blooms (though some species flower a bit later). Flowers are bisexual and insect pollinated, producing clusters of blueberry-colored pomes in summer.

Shadbushes, slow growing and relatively long-lived, are quite moisture and shade tolerant, occupying a wide range of dry to mesic habitats (a few species also occupy swamps and wet woods).

Note the long, pointed buds, often two-tone red and green with twisted tips. Warm weather in late fall sometimes causes the new spring buds to flush out prematurely. The bark resembles that of American hornbeam.

Swollen, fungus-infected fruits and crusted twigs are marks of a common rust that requires both shadbush and red cedar trees to complete its destructive life cycle.

Associates: *Spring.* Flowers are pollinated mainly by the earliest small bees of spring, notably the various andrenid and halictid species.

Peak hatching of the destructive gypsy moth (see Red Oak) coincides with shadbush flowering. These caterpillars feed on shadbushes along with many other species.

Summer. Swollen, distorted fruits and twigs marked with powdery fungal outgrowths represent the fruiting stage of a *Gymnosporangium* rust. Its alternate host is red cedar *(Juniperus virginiana).*

Broad mines in the leaves may indicate larval feeding of the shadbush leafminer *(Nepticula amelanchierella),* a tiny moth.

At least twenty-two bird species relish shadbush fruits. Prominent feeders include veeries, hermit thrushes, gray catbirds, cedar waxwings, and Northern orioles.

Among the eleven or more mammal species that feed on the fruits, bark, and twigs are black bears, beavers, fox and red squirrels, white-tailed deer, and moose.

Lore: Few plants have provided such a widely used seasonal clock as shadbushes, a function reflected in many of their common names. On the eastern seaboard, colonial fishermen timed the spawning runs of shad fish by the flowering of this plant. Shadbush flowering also marked the time of burial services for colonists who had died during the winter, hence *serviceberry.* In our own day, foresters beleaguered by gypsy moth outbreaks also use this clock.

Fruits of many species are sweet and tasty; a few, though not harmful, are dry and tasteless. Native Americans used them abundantly for food. The Crees dried and mixed them with venison and bear meat to make pemmican. "Take some juneberries with you" was a common farewell among the Chippewas. They and other tribes also mixed decoctions of the root and bark for medicinal tonics.

Shadbush berries are among the most overlooked and neglected wild fruits. They can be used in any way that one would use fruits of blueberries.

Solomon's Seal *(Polygonatum biflorum).* Lily family. Herbs in moist woods, thickets. Parallel-veined leaves on an arching stem, paired greenish-yellow flowers dangling beneath the leaves, and dangling blue-black berries in the fall identify Solomon's seal. The false Solomon's seals *(Smilacina)* show similar leaves, but their white flowers (and the fruits) occur in terminal clusters. Also closely similar in form are the twisted-stalks *(Streptopus).*

Close relatives: Trilliums *(Trillium)*; bellworts *(Uvularia)*; Canada mayflower *(Maianthemum canadense)*; greenbriers *(Smilax)*; trout lilies *(Erythronium)*; onions *(Allium).*

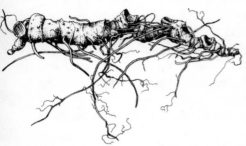

The jointed, horizontal rhizome of Solomon's seal bears circular scars on the top side, marking the sites of former leafy stems. Some say these scars give the plant its name.

Lifestyle: The bell-like bisexual flowers of this spring ephemeral are six-parted and insect pollinated. Note that the tubular female style is much shorter than the six pollen-bearing anthers, an arrangement that probably helps prevent self-fertilization. Flower location beneath the leaves protects them from wind and weather.

Stems rise from a perennial rhizome that produces a circular scar atop the rootstock after each season's growth so that one may age a plant by its number of scars.

Solomon's seal thrives in slightly acid soil. It usually grows as a solitary plant, not in colonial groups, though several may be found together.

Associates: *Spring.* Often you may find both true and closely related false Solomon's seals growing in proximity.

The flowers seem particularly adapted to pollination by bumblebees *(Bombus)*, though other insects also frequent them.

A tortricid moth caterpillar, *Clepsis melaleucana*, often feeds on the leaves.

Summer. Various birds consume the berries, thus aiding the plant's distribution, but Solomon's seal is not a major food plant for wildlife.

Lore: Though the berries are inedible, the young shoots can be eaten raw or cooked, and the fleshy rhizome can also be boiled and served like a potato. This plant, however, is not usually so numerous that it can tolerate regular harvesting for food. Iroquois and other tribes dried and ground the rhizome to make a sort of "potato bread." The Chippewas made a decoction of it, sprinkling it on hot stones and inhaling the vapors to relieve painful headaches.

The conventional explanation for this plant's ancient name refers to the round scars on the rhizome that, with some imagination, resemble the impressions created by signet rings for wax seals. But English herbalist John Gerard, writing in 1597, believed that the name involved the root's "singular vertue" to "seale up greene wounds." Naturalist Mary Durant has suggested that since *Solomon's seal* originally referred to the Star of David emblem with its six points, the flower may well have been named for this resemblance and then forgotten. Her theory sounds as plausible as any.

Spicebush, Common *(Lindera benzoin)*. Laurel family. Shrub in moist woods, bottomlands. Its aromatic leaves and twigs, smooth, untoothed leaves, yellow flowers in spring, and red fruits in autumn identify spicebush.

Other names: Wild allspice, spicewood, fever-bush, snap-bush, snapwood, Benjamin-bush.

Close relatives: Sassafras *(Sassafras albidum)*; bays *(Persea)*; avocado *(P. americana)*; cinnamon *(Cinnamomum)*; camphor tree *(C. camphora)*; anise *(Pimpinella anisum)*.

Lifestyle: This common understory plant of bottomland forests is often passed unnoticed when not in fruit or flower. Dense clusters of lemon-fragrant yellow flowers, mostly unisexual on separate clones, appear in early spring before the leaves. They have no petals, but the six yellow sepals attract a variety of insect pollinators. On male flowers, note with a hand lens the pollen-containing anthers that open by uplifted valves.

By late summer the scarlet, shiny drupes appear, and the leaves turn bright yellow before dropping. Roots are shallow, and the brittle twigs snap easily.

Spicebush tolerates high water tables and moderate shade. The resinous oil found in all parts of the plant contains benzoic acid, a useful compound usually derived from the related Asiatic tree *Styrax benzoin*.

Associates: Look for spicebush among lowland trees such as American elm, Eastern cottonwood, and Northern hackberry.

Spring, summer. Moist spicebush habitats are good places to hunt for orchid species. Watch especially for the long-bracted green orchid *(Coeloglossum viride)*, the putty-root *(Aplectrum hyemale)*, and the more southerly Wister's coralroot *(Corallorhiza wisteriana)*.

The flowers are mainly pollinated by early solitary bees, by ladybug beetles (Coccinellidae), and by bee flies (Bombyliidae).

Inspecting curled leaf edges or leaves folded along the midrib may reveal the caterpillar of one of our largest, most impressive butterflies, the spicebush or green-clouded swallowtail *(Papilio troilus)*. The smooth, green caterpillar shows four eyespots on its humped forepart. As it grows, it moves to successively larger leaves (it takes about three to complete its larval stages), folding them over as shelters when not feeding. Another large green caterpillar that feeds on spicebush is the promethea or spicebush silk moth *(Callosamia promethea)*. It has red tubercles, and the blackish adult male flies in late afternoon.

Fall, winter. Visible after the leaves have fallen is the brownish, angular chrysalis (pupal form) of the spicebush swallowtail butterfly. It is fastened vertically to a twig or branch by a looped silken girdle. Cocoons of promethea moths are spun inside a rolled dead leaf and suspended by a tough silken cord.

Though consumed by many birds, the fruits are especially relished by the veery and wood thrush.

Lore: A mildly astringent and stimulating tea may be steeped from the leaves, twigs, and bark. Native American women drank it to ease the discomfort of menstrual cramps, and it was said to induce sweating and help break fevers. The dried, powdered fruits (minus the seeds) provided a popular substitute for allspice in colonial households, but they should not be eaten in quantity.

Early land surveyors regarded spicebush as an excellent indicator of fertile soil.

Spring Beauty *(Claytonia virginica).* Purslane family. Herb in moist woods. Its five white or pink petals lined with darker pink veins and its single pair of linear, grasslike leaves identify this spring ephemeral. The Carolina spring beauty *(C. caroliniana),* occupying somewhat drier habitats, shows similar flowers but much wider leaves.

Promethea moth cocoons, commonly seen in winter on spicebush, sassafras, and cherry trees, hang from a tough, pliable, silken binding that reinforces a projecting twig.

Other names: Claytonia, Quaker ladies, patience.

Close relatives: Purslane *(Portulaca oleracea)*; moss-rose *(P. grandiflora)*; fameflower *(Talinum teretifolium).*

Lifestyle: The flowers range from white through shades of pink. Bisexual and insect pollinated, the male and female parts mature separately, thus reducing the likelihood of self-fertilization. Typically a mature female stigma receives pollen from a younger flower that is still producing it. The flowers, which close at night and during cloudy weather, last only about three days. The pink veins leading to the flower center guide insects to the nectaries; strongly reflected ultraviolet light from the male filaments does the same job.

The fruit is a capsule that explosively ejects its seeds—often as far as two feet—by suddenly inrolling valves.

Spring beauty rises from small, perennial, bulblike corms; the plants often densely carpet the ground. By late spring, the stems have died back, and the plant lives underground the rest of the year.

Associates: Spring beauty usually appears in flower a few days later than hepaticas, about the same time as bloodroot.

Spring. Chief pollinators include bumblebees *(Bombus)*, the solitary bee *Andrena eriginiae*, bee flies (Bombyliidae), and butterflies.

Only the bulblike corms have much wildlife food value. These are often dug and consumed in spring by Eastern chipmunks and white-footed mice. In the western United States, the Northern pocket gopher is a primary consumer.

Lore: The corms are edible not only to rodents but to humans as well. Stripped of their skins and prepared in potato fashion, they are tasty. Many must be dug to make a meal, however, and they should be collected only where abundant.

Spruce, White *(Picea glauca)*. Pine family. Tree in upland forests, rich soils. Recognize white spruce by its steeple shape, its short, stiff, singly attached needles, its rough twigs, and its pendant, one- to two-inch seed cones. Other common spruces include two widely planted species—Norway spruce *(P. abies)*, a European tree, and Colorado blue spruce *(P. pungens)*, a western species—and black spruce *(P. mariana)*, which resides in northern bogs.

Other names: Cat spruce, skunk spruce.

Close relatives: Balsam fir *(Abies balsamea)*; Eastern hemlock *(Tsuga canadensis)*; pines *(Pinus)*.

Lifestyle: This northern conifer lives in a variety of sites, soils, and forest types. Its needles, spirally arranged on the twig but often curving around so that they appear crowded on the upper side, are often bluish green owing to a "bloom" or whitish cast that coats them. When crushed they emanate a pungent, disagreeable odor, a sure sign of this species. Needles remain on the tree five to ten years.

Both male and female cones appear on the same tree in spring. The wind-pollinated seed cones mature by autumn and drop soon after opening. Abundant cone crops occur only once every four to six years, usually simultaneously over a large area. This irregular seed production may inhibit populations of seed-eating wildlife from growing too large. Thus, in years when abundant seed crops do occur, the chances for germination are increased.

Associates: White spruce rarely grows in pure stands. Most often it occurs in mixed forests with balsam fir, pines, and northern hardwoods.

Clipped spruce needles may indicate feeding by spruce grouse or snowshoe hares. A cropped-off twig could indicate feeding by deer, rabbit, or porcupine.

Spring, summer. Several orchid types frequent spruce forests. These include coralroots *(Corallorhiza)*, rattlesnake plantains *(Goodyera)*, and Northern twayblade *(Listera borealis)*.

This tree's foremost insect enemy is the spruce budworm, a tortricid moth caterpillar that irrupts in periodic outbreaks and may defoliate thousands of acres (see Balsam Fir). But budworm irruptions may be spruce's way of maintaining itself against the aggressively competitive balsam fir, which is budworm's preferred food; that is, balsam depletion by budworm may benefit spruce.

Sawfly larvae, which feed in masses on needles, resemble caterpillars. Especially common are the European spruce sawfly *(Diprion hercyniae)*, green with white stripes, and the yellowheaded spruce sawfly *(Pikonema alaskensis)*, yellow-green with a brown head.

Grayish webbing between needles on twigs may indicate the presence of spruce spider mites *(Oligonychus ununguis)*. Spruce needle miners *(Epinotia nanana)*, tiny moth larvae, also web needles together after mining their interiors.

Spruce-nesting birds may become especially common during years of spruce budworm outbreaks. These may include black-backed woodpeckers, boreal chickadees, ruby-crowned kinglets, Swainson's thrushes, Cape May warblers, yellow-rumped warblers, bay-breasted warblers, blackpoll warblers, purple finches, and white-winged crossbills.

Fall. Beneath spruces and other conifers, waxy-gilled mushrooms, generally brownish or white, may be waxycap *(Hygrophorus)* species. Most appear from late summer to early winter.

Frequent spruce seed eaters among birds include boreal chickadees, red-breasted nuthatches, and red and white-winged crossbills.

Red and gray squirrels clip off cones, then rip them apart and consume the seeds on the ground.

Two common galls on spruce are produced by adelgids, aphidlike insects: Eastern spruce gall at twig bases (left) and Cooley spruce gall at twig tips (right). These galls often remain on dead twigs.

Winter. Spruce is not a favored browse for moose and white-tailed deer, though it was apparently a diet staple for the now-extinct mastodon. Game biologists consider spruce a "stuffing" species, upon which a deer can feed and starve with a full belly. Browsed spruce twigs generally indicate a lack of more nourishing foods in a deer range. Spruce needles, on the other hand, are a favored year-round food of the spruce grouse; look for partially clipped twigs. Snowshoe hares and porcupines clip off needles and gnaw the bark.

In the northern breeding range of white-winged crossbills, these birds sometimes nest in spruces during the dead of winter following autumns when seed cones are especially abundant.

All year. Many aphidlike insects produce galls on spruce. The Eastern spruce gall aphid *(Adelges abietis)* creates pineapplelike galls at the base of new shoots (similar galls are caused by larvae of spruce gall midges, *Phytophaga piceae*). The Cooley spruce gall aphid *(A. cooleyi)* forms conelike galls at twig tips (the latter are more common on ornamental spruces). Both insects are actually adelgids, not aphids.

A typical sumac clone consists of multiple stems rising from a unisexual root system. The persistent fruit clusters reveal this clone as female. Can you identify the possible mother stem?

Lore: Native Americans found many uses for spruce. The pliable rootlets provided lace binding for birchbark canoes, and the thick, resinous pitch made a good patching glue. The inner bark can be eaten as a nourishing emergency food. The Chippewas steamed a decoction of the twigs for rheumatic aches, and the Crees ate small, green cones to treat sore throat. Old woodsmen chew "spruce gum," as I still do on occasion, as a chewing-gum substitute. Today, it is even sold to tourists, packaged in little boxes as a flavor treat of the North.

Spruce is a primary source of pulpwood. The soft, light wood also provides excellent material for piano sounding boards, musical instruments, boatbuilding, and interior finish.

Sumac, Staghorn *(Rhus typhina)*. Cashew family. Shrub or small tree in dry soil, edges, openings. Alternate compound leaves and velvet-hairy twigs topped with red-plush fruit clusters are good identity marks. Similar species include winged or shining sumac *(R. copallina)* and smooth sumac *(R. glabra)*. Poison sumac *(R. vernix)* is found only in wet habitats.

Other names: Vinegar tree, velvet sumac.

Close relative: Poison ivy *(R. radicans)*.

Lifestyle: Its antlerlike branching and fuzzy twigs (like a deer in velvet) account for staghorn sumac's name. This is often one of the first shrub-size plants to become established in old fields and open land.

Count the age of a stem by the number of branching angles from the top of a branch to the bottom of the stem. The merging crowns form a canopy of tropical-looking foliage that turns brilliant red in early fall, an example of foliar fruit flagging (see Flowering Dogwood).

Each sex rises in a separate clone; a solitary sumac stem is rarely seen. Sex ratios differ as plant succession proceeds. Male clones often outnumber female ones in early and late successional stages, with female clones more numerous in midsuccession.

Flower clusters are greenish yellow, and the female ones are insect pollinated. The erect, fruiting candelabras consist of multiple dry, oily drupes, each seed thinly enclosed in a red-hairy covering high in ascorbic and malic acids, vitamins C and A, fat, and tannin. These clusters often remain on the plant through winter, fading in color, becoming mined with insects, and gradually crumbling away.

Sumac thrives best in open sun but tolerates light shade. Individual stems, containing a milky latex, are often short lived, but parent clones may survive for many years.

Associates: Early successional species that often invade sumac clones include black cherry, red cedar, hawthorns, and sassafras.

Spring, summer. Female flowers are mainly bee pollinated, but look for two longhorned beetle species on the flowers: the notch-tipped flower longhorn *(Typocerus sinuatus)*, black and yellowish with spots, and the banded longhorn *(T. velutinus)*, reddish-brown and striped. Both are pollen and nectar feeders.

Several moth caterpillars specialize on sumac foliage, including the dark marathyssa *(Marathyssa inficita)*, an owlet moth, and the showy emerald *(Dichorda iridaria)*, an inchworm or looper. The sumac caterpillar or spotted datana *(Datana perspicua)* is a striped prominent that feeds in colonies and elevates both ends of the body when disturbed.

Reddish, fruitlike galls, sometimes large on leaf undersides, are caused by sumac gall aphids *(Melaphis rhois)*.

Leaves rolled into conelike or spiral tubes may indicate feeding by witch-hazel leaf-folders (see Witch Hazel).

Any sizable clone of sumac shows plenty of dead stems, and several kinds of carpenter bees and wasps make hollow chambers in the soft, decayed pith for laying eggs. Sand or mud partitions indicate wasp work. Some wasp species (notably *Trypoxylon*) stock the chambers with spiders, which the larvae will consume after hatching, and several eumenid wasps collect and stock caterpillars. Yellow-faced bees *(Hylaeus)* construct brood cells in the pith. Small carpenter bees *(Ceratina)* make chambers partitioned by wood chips and then enclose pollen in the chambers. (The latter bees must enter the twig by a cut or broken end. One investigator attracted them by cutting off a number of sumac stems; in a month, seventy-five percent of the cut stems were occupied by the bees.)

Fall, winter. Almost one hundred species of birds are known to consume sumac fruits. They are only important as a secondary and supplemental food, however; extensive feeding usually indicates that more preferred fruits are unavailable. Among the most frequent feeders are ring-necked pheasants, ruffed grouse, wild turkeys, Northern bobwhites, Eastern

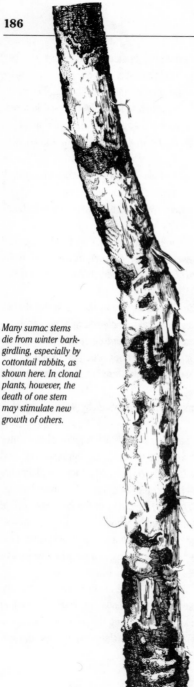

Many sumac stems die from winter bark-girdling, especially by cottontail rabbits, as shown here. In clonal plants, however, the death of one stem may stimulate new growth of others.

phoebes, American crows, Eastern bluebirds, hermit thrushes, American robins, gray catbirds, brown thrashers, European starlings, and Northern cardinals.

Birds and mammals generally account for the distribution of clones. Studies have shown that sumac seeds in cottontail rabbit pellets germinate at a much higher rate than uneaten seeds.

Sumac bark is a favored food of cottontails in winter, and many stems are girdled by them. White-tailed deer often browse stems and foliage.

During winter, crumble some of the fruit clusters; you'll find them mined, tunneled, and loaded with insect frass (wastes). Winter is also a good time to look for wasp cocoons inside hollowed dead twigs, as well as egg chambers and residues left by other insect occupants.

Lore: In need of campfire wood, I once learned the hard way that sumac is better suited for an artillery show than for a peaceful blaze. A piece of sumac stem can be used as a "blower" to coax flames from other fuel. Such pith-hollowed sections were often used as spikes for tapping maple trees during sap season.

The fresh, red fruit clusters in the fall can be rubbed and steeped in cold water, then strained to make a refreshing, citrus-tasting drink relished by Native Americans. The Micmac tribe made a fruit tea for sore throat, Menominees brewed a solution from the tannic bark for hemorrhoids, and the Chippewas drank a tea made of the flowers for stomach pain. Yellow and gray dyes were also extracted from the inner bark, pith, and roots. The tannin content of bark, leaves, and flowers accounts for their astringency and their use as materials for tanning leather.

Sumac roots with attached stems, when carved and sanded, make fine walking sticks or canes because of the right-angled root–stem connection.

Sweetfern *(Comptonia peregrina)*. Bayberry family. Low shrub in dry, sandy soils. Its dense, fernlike, aromatic foliage is the best identity mark.

Close relatives: Sweetgale *(Myrica gale)*; Northern bayberry *(M. pensylvanica)*; common waxmyrtle *(M. cerifera)*.

Lifestyle: It's not a fern but a knee-high, woody shrub that often covers acres of semiopen ground in acidic, soil-impoverished habitats.

The flowers are wind-pollinated catkins, unisexual on the same plant. The fruit, a nutlet inside a bur, resembles a common tip gall found on meadowsweet *(Spiraea)*.

This densely cloning plant branches profusely. Its roots, like those of the pea family, host nitrogen-fixing bacteria. Thus sweetfern improves the soil as well as binds it.

Note the yellowish resin dots on the narrow, lobed leaves. These are the source of their spicy odor. Dried leaves often remain on the plant through winter.

Associates: Sweetfern often associates with jack pine and also with Northern bayberry. It is typically a resident of oak and pine plains.

Spring, summer. Several moth caterpillars are common on sweetfern. A rear-horned one may be the pawpaw sphinx *(Dolba hyloeus)*. The wayward nymph or sweetfern underwing *(Catocala antinympha)* often stretches parallel to the foliage and twigs when feeding. The double-lined gray *(Cleora sublunaria)*, the chainspotted (or chain-dotted) geometer *(Cingilia catenaria)*, a looper, and the crinkled flannel moth *(Megalopyge crispata)* also occur. Webbed terminal leaves often indicate *Acrobasis comptoniella*, a tiny webbing moth larva. Insect nymphs with bright red abdomens may be Saratoga spittlebugs (see Jack Pine).

Grouse feed to some extent on the buds and catkins, but the only extensive foliage browser is white-tailed deer.

Fall. The seeds apparently have little if any wildlife food value. Cottontail rabbits may gnaw the stems.

Lore: Its leaf somewhat resembles the leaflet of a spleenwort fern *(Asplenium)*, hence its common name.

A tea brewed from the dried leaves is pleasantly spicy and astringent. Native and pioneer Americans used the green leaves as a tonic and diarrhea treatment, as a remedy for worms, and as a wash for poison ivy rashes. A strong solution is indeed one of the best natural remedies for skin ailments. The nutlets are also edible.

Sycamore *(Platanus occidentalis)*. Planetree family. Tree in moist soil, bottomlands. Its maplelike (but broader) leaves, mottled bark that flakes off in scaly patches, and ball-shaped fruits are distinctive marks.

Other names: Buttonwood, buttonball, American planetree.

Close relatives: London planetree *(P. x acerifolia)*; Oriental planetree *(P. orientalis)*.

Lifestyle: Sycamores attain the most massive girth of any American deciduous tree, reaching ages of five hundred to six hundred years. Fast growing and shade intolerant, a young sycamore may grow to seventy feet in seventeen years. Its root system is rather shallow in lowland habitats but goes much deeper in upland soils. Often it divides into two or more trunks near the ground, and its massive branches form a wide-spreading, irregular crown. Mature trees usually develop hollow portions and areas of decay, making them vulnerable to wind and ice damage. Large sycamores can be recognized in any season by the patchwork of brown, green, and cream-colored mottled patterns on the bark.

Stalked unisexual flowers of both sexes appear on the same tree at leaf emergence. Male flowers are small and dark red in the twig angles, and wind-pollinated female ones are greenish at twig ends. The round fruit, consisting of multiple achenes, often remains on the tree through winter before breaking into separate nutlets. Abundant fruiting occurs almost every year. Seeds do not germinate, however, unless deposited on very moist soil with lots of sunlight and minimal competition. The tree sprouts readily from cut or burned stumps and from stem cuttings.

Note the hollow base of the leaf stem, which forms a protective cap over the devel-

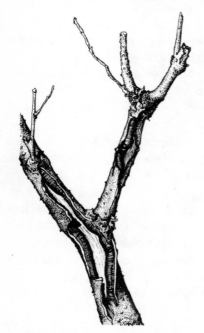

Sycamore branches infected by the common anthracnose fungus, which defoliates them in early spring, often show cankers like these. Unless infection is frequent, the tree usually survives.

oping winter bud. Leaves and fruits of sycamore produce an allelopathic herbicide that leaches into the soil when they drop. This substance inhibits competition from grasses and other plants beneath the tree.

Associates: Sycamore may grow in more or less pure stands along water courses, but ordinarily it occurs in mixtures with willows, Eastern cottonwood, silver maple, American elm, and other lowland species.

Mineral nutrients from the decayed leaves provide a rich bed for earthworms.

Spring, summer. A cool, wet spring can result in infection by an anthracnose fungus *(Gnomonia platani).* The most visible sign is sudden dieback and defoliation of branches just as the leaves begin to expand, a symptom often confused with frost injury. Infection also produces browning of leaves and small cankers on the twigs, which cause buds and tops of twigs to die. A tree infested for several successive years often has a bunchy, distorted appearance of branches and twigs.

A common foliage feeder is the sycamore lace bug *(Corythucha ciliata)*, a gregarious, lacy-winged insect that sucks sap from leaves (usually the undersides), causing them to stipple and turn white. The sycamore plant bug *(Plagiognathus albatus)*, brownish and spotted, produces small yellowish or reddish spots on the leaves. Two tiny moth larvae that mine in sycamore leaves are *Phyllonorcycter felinella* and *Nepticula platanella*, the latter creating large blotch mines on leaf undersides. Silken tents between veins on leaf undersides may indicate larval *Ancylis platanana*, a tortricid moth.

A yellow caterpillar with long, whitish hairs and projecting orange hair "pencils" is probably the sycamore tussock moth *(Halysidota harrisii)*, also called sycamore tiger moth.

The cavities and hollows found in many older sycamore trees make favored denning sites for several mammals, including opossums, squirrels, and raccoons. They're also useful to hole-nesting birds, such as wood ducks, owls, and Northern flickers. In certain areas, yellow-throated warblers site their open nests high on a horizontal branch.

Fall, winter. Sycamore offers relatively little food for birds and mammals. Purple finches and goldfinches are apparently the main seed eaters, and fox squirrels also consume the seed. Twigs are sometimes nipped by muskrats and white-tailed deer. Winter dens may shelter several tree-climbing mammals.

Lore: Sycamore wood is heavy and hard but not a good construction material because it's difficult to work and has a tendency to warp. Butchers favor it, however, for blocks.

Native Americans sometimes used hollowed trunks for enormously heavy dugout canoes. The trees can be tapped for sweetish sap in early spring, but the quantity and quality of syrup is inferior to that of sugar maple. In emergency situations, such tapping can provide an instant source of pure water.

The tree was probably named by early colonists who noted its leaf resemblance to the English sycamore maple *(Acer pseudoplatanus)*, an unrelated species. The sycamore tree of the Bible is actually the sycamore fig *(Ficus sycomorus)*, also unrelated. Most urban plantings are of the hybrid London planetree because of its resistance to anthracnose.

Tick Trefoils *(Desmodium* spp.). Pea family. Slender herbs in moist or dry woods. Often growing to four feet tall, trefoils have three-part leaves, loose terminal clusters of small white or pinkish flowers, and flat, chainlike, bristly seed pods that readily adhere to clothing. Some twenty-five species occur in the eastern and central United States; most of them prefer woodland or thicket habitats. The most conspicuous species is the Canadian or showy tick trefoil *(D. canadense)*.

Other names: Sticktights, tick clover, beggarweed, beggarticks.

Close relatives: Bush clovers *(Lespedeza)*; clovers *(Trifolium)*; vetches *(Vicia)*; locusts *(Robinia)*.

Lifestyle: Bees must force entrance into the bisexual flower, which has a pollen trigger. Depressed, the lateral, winglike petals cause the lower united petals to snap down and release a cloud of pollen upward, thus powdering the bee's belly. The small, chainlike seed pods that stick like Velcro are familiar to all woods walkers.

These perennial plants typically flower in summer. Despite their height, most are easily passed by.

Associates: *Summer.* Bees are the chief pollinators. Caterpillars of the Eastern tailed blue *(Everes comyntas)*, sluglike and dark green, often feed in the flower heads. The hoary edge or frosted skipper *(Achalarus lyciades)*, dark green with orange spots, is another butterfly caterpillar that feeds on trefoil.

Larvae of a leaf-mining buprestid beetle, *Pachyschelus laevigatus*, make broadly linear tracks beneath the leaf epidermis.

Fall. These seeds are dispersed by attaching to mammal hair or fur and hitching a ride (a stratagem known as *epizoochory)*. Thus, the plant depends on animal mobility for its success.

The seeds are not eaten to any large extent by birds or mammals. Northern bobwhites are apparently the foremost consumers.

Lore: Wearing corduroy trousers afield is probably the best defense against acquiring mats of the clinging seed pods as you walk. A small pocket comb can strip these hitchhikers from clothes.

Trefoils, like other legumes, increase soil fertility. By means of nitrogen-fixing root nodules, *Rhizobium* bacteria convert atmospheric nitrogen to soil nitrogen, which is then accessible to plants.

Cherokees chewed the root for mouth or tooth inflammation.

Toothworts *(Dentaria* spp.). Mustard family. Herbs in rich, moist woods. Recognize these spring ephemerals by their opposite leaves, each divided into three leaflets, their terminal clusters of white (fading to pinkish) four-petaled flowers, and their slender, ascending seedpods. The most common species are the two-leaved toothwort *(D. diphylla)* and the cut-leaved toothwort *(D. laciniata).*

Other names: Pepperwort, pepper-root, crinkle-root, crow's foot, wild horseradish.

Close relatives: Bitter cresses *(Cardamine)*; mustards *(Brassica)*; winter cress *(Barbarea vulgaris)*; watercress *(Nasturtium officinale)*; radish *(Raphanus sativus).*

Lifestyle: A four-petaled, cross-shaped flower often belongs to the large mustard family. Although most mustards favor wet or open, sunny ground, toothworts are among the few that thrive in woodlands. These perennials rise from fleshy rhizomes that show pointed, toothlike (hence the name) projections or constricted, necklacelike tubers.

Flowers are bisexual and insect pollinated, though self-fertilization does occur. A spot at the base of each petal reflects strong ultraviolet light, visible to bees. A flower lasts about four days. *D. laciniata* blooms earlier and lasts longer than *D. diphylla*, which generally flowers only briefly in May.

Associates: Cut-leaved toothwort appears at about the same time and places as trout lily and the early violets.

Spring, summer. Small pollen-collecting bees (andrenids, halictids) are the chief pollinators. On the foliage, look for solitary, velvety green and yellowish-striped caterpillars. These may be larvae of a butterfly group called whites *(Pieris)*, most of which feed on plants of the mustard family. The mustard white *(P. napi)* and West Virginia white *(P. virginiensis)* are two common feeders on toothworts.

White-footed mice are the main seed eaters.

Lore: The peppery rhizome can be chopped or ground and used as horseradish or a pungent addition to salads.

Trailing Arbutus *(Epigaea repens).* Heath family. Ground-level trailing shrub in dry woods. Recognize trailing arbutus by its woody stems, its leathery, heart-shaped, hairy leaves and twigs, and its white or pink five-petaled flowers.

Other names: Mayflower, ground laurel, shadflower, winter pink, gravel-plant.

Close relatives: Wintergreen *(Gaultheria procumbens)*; blueberries *(Vaccinium)*; laurels *(Kalmia)*; heaths *(Erica)*; heather *(Calluna vulgaris)*.

Lifestyle: Its spice-fragrant flowers, among spring's very earliest, are mostly unisexual on separate plants. Male flowers have a touch of light yellow. Despite their insect-attracting fragrance, the flowers often remain hidden beneath dead leaves and surface litter. Leaves stay evergreen beneath the snow, and new ones develop in late spring.

This cloning plant is often found in large, creeping mats, its woody stems prostrate. Its presence generally indicates dry, acidic soil of low nutrient value.

Associates: This plant frequently resides in pine forest habitats. Also look for it in company with mountain laurel, moccasin flower, and round-lobed hepatica.

Spring, summer. Bumblebees *(Bombus)*, especially early-ranging queens, seek the abundant nectar produced by the flowers; these insects are their common pollinators.

Look for ant activity on the opened seed capsules in late spring or summer. Ants are attracted to the sticky, berrylike, placental tissue of the capsule, and they are probably important dispersers of the seed (an ant-plant coaction known as *myrmechory*).

Lore: The name arbutus comes from the Latin name for the unrelated European strawberry tree *(Arbutus unedo)*, said to bear leaf and flower resemblances to *Epigaea*.

The raw flower tube is edible, even tasty. But please sample this flower with eyes only; trailing arbutus is a protected plant in many states. Even picking the flower stems may loosen the roots and cause the plant to die.

An astringent decoction made of the leaves (which contain arbutin) has been used for urinary disorders and kidney stones.

Trailing arbutus is the state flower of Massachusetts and the floral emblem of Nova Scotia. It is said to have heralded spring to the winter-beleaguered Pilgrims of 1621.

Trillium, Large-flowered *(Trillium grandiflorum)*. Lily family. Herb in moist woods. Three broad leaves and three showy petals mark all the trilliums, of which some ten species exist in our area. This species, the largest, most common, and most variable, has a white flower that often turns deep pink as it ages.

Other names: White trillium, common trillium, wake-robin, white wood lily.

Close relatives: Greenbriers *(Smilax)*; Solomon's seals *(Polygonatum)*; bellworts *(Uvularia)*; Canada mayflower *(Maianthemum canadense)*; trout lilies *(Erythronium)*; lilies *(Lilium)*; onions *(Allium)*.

Lifestyle: The spectacular bisexual flowers rise from perennial rhizomes, making the spring woodland floor seem carpeted with lilies. The flowering of a trillium, however, requires much longer than for most wildflowers. For at least six years, the plant produces only one-leaf and three-leaf forms before flowering for the first time. From then on, the plant blooms every spring if the habitat remains stable. A single flower lasts about two weeks before turning pink.

The fruit, technically a berry, is a swollen, ridged capsule that bends to one side as it matures. Seed pressure splits it, and the seeds fall out in clusters. Two winters in the soil are required, the first to release root dormancy, the second to release the shoot block. A germinating seed, following a winter in the soil, develops only a small root and won't even send a shoot above ground the first spring.

Often a giant flower or a flower showing an anomalous form will be seen. One April I found a flower consisting of nine petals set in three layers. Such anomalies are believed to result from an infection caused by mycoplasmalike bacteria.

Associates: *Spring, summer.* The most abundant colonies of this trillium occur in beech–maple forests. Trout lily is a frequent associate.

A commonly observed crab spider on the flowers is *Misumena vatia*, the goldenrod or flower spider, a predator on insects that visit the flower. Whitish with two red side stripes, it migrates to goldenrods in summer, where it turns yellowish.

The main pollinators are bees and butterflies.

A tortricid moth caterpillar, *Clepsis melaleucana*, feeds on the leaves.

When the seeds spill, ants are attracted to an appendage on the seed where it was attached called the *strophiole*. Ants carry the seeds to their nests, where they eat the strophioles, thus helping to disperse the plant.

On the whole, however, the seeds and foliage of trillium are generally unimportant foods for wildlife in Eastern forests.

Lore: Native Americans used decoctions of the rhizome for various ailments, including ear infections and rheumatism, and as external dressings for inflammation. Trillium species were often used to control bleeding during childbirth. The effect of the solution is mainly astringent.

Very young leaves are edible as salad greens but become bitter as they age. This plant is protected by law in some states, however, so should not be picked. Even clipping the leaves and flowers can quickly kill the rhizome, which has taken many seasons to become productive.

The large-flowered trillium is the floral emblem of Ontario.

Tulip Tree *(Liriodendron tulipifera).* Magnolia family. Tree in fertile woods. Its truncated, four-lobed leaves, tuliplike orange-green flowers, conelike fruit clusters, and tall, columnar trunk identify tulip tree.

Other names: yellow poplar, tulip poplar, whitewood, saddle-leaf tree.

Close relatives: Magnolias *(Magnolia)*; the tree is unrelated to poplars *(Populus).*

Lifestyle: This is the tallest eastern tree, sometimes reaching a height of 150 feet or more, and second only to sycamore in trunk diameter. It's unique in so many ways that it is one of the easiest trees to recognize.

Its showy, bisexual flowers appear after the leaves unfold, usually high in the canopy and hard to see unless a branch falls. Loaded with nectar, they attract many insects. Conelike clusters of long, flat samaras develop, breaking apart at maturity; some may remain on the tree over winter. When fresh, they have a clean, lemon fragrance.

Roots plunge deep and wide. Tulip tree is shade intolerant, grows fast, and sprouts readily from the stump when burned or cut. Older trees often develop large, hollow butts. Though it can grow on almost any mesic soil, the tree is sensitive to frost, which largely re-

Soaring tulip tree, one of the tallest American trees, is also notable for the unique shape of its leaves and its tuliplike flower. A cross-section of its seed cluster (inset) shows the stacked samaras.

stricts its distribution to south of lower New England and the Great Lakes. Sometimes during a winter thaw, you can hear these trunks "sound off," as if being hit by a baseball bat.

The leaves, unlike any other tree's in shape, wear remarkably well, having few insect foragers, and turn clear yellow in the fall. Because of their long, angled leafstalks, they flutter in the breeze. Their emergence in spring is especially interesting: from terminal buds shaped like duck bills, successions of bills within bills uncurl and unfold, revealing a marvel of leaf packaging.

Notice the bark. Its vertical, crosscut fissures have been likened to a series of parallel mountain ridges with deep gullies in their sides.

Associates: Beech–maple and bottomland forests are the most typical habitats for this tree, which occurs in mixed stands.

Spring, summer. The white or late morel mushroom *(Morchella deliciosa)* sometimes appears abundantly beneath tulip trees, usually after the other morel species are gone.

Probably the most common foliage feeder is the tulip-tree aphid *(Macrosiphum liriodendri)*; green and often abundant on leaf undersides, it secretes copious amounts of honeydew, which attracts ants and causes the unsightly growth of black sooty mold (Perisporiaceae). Ladybird beetles (Coccinellidae) are the aphids' chief predators.

The tulip-tree or liriodendron scale *(Toumeyella liriodendri)*, one of the largest scale insects and also a honeydew producer, clusters in dark brown masses along twigs and branches.

Holes and blotch mines in leaves may be signs of the tulip-tree leafminer, also called sassafras weevil (see Sassafras). Long, threadlike mines may be the work of *Phyllocnistis liriodendrella*, a tiny gracilariid moth. Also on leaves look for galls produced by gnat larvae: *Cecidomyia tulipifera* causes swellings in the midleaf vein, and *Thecodiplosis liriodendri* produces brown spots with yellowish borders.

A large green saturniid moth caterpillar, the tulip-tree silkmoth *(Callosamia angulifera)*, feeds on the leaves; though nowhere common, it is always worth watching for. Much more common is the tulip-tree beauty *(Epimecis hortaria)*, an inchworm moth caterpillar. Tiger swallowtail butterflies (see Black Cherry) are often seen flitting high in the treetops. Their caterpillars also feed on tulip tree.

Flower pollination is accomplished by beetles, flies, and bees.

Fall, winter. Though not preferred wildlife foods, tulip-tree seeds are consumed by several bird species, chiefly Northern cardinals and purple finches.

White-footed mice and squirrels—especially red squirrels—consume the seeds. I once spent a fall afternoon watching a red squirrel move from branch to branch. It clipped off seed clusters, bitten close to the base, and dropped them for later collection. Red squirrels also strip off pieces of bark for nests.

Lore: Livestock relish the aromatic twigs of young trees. Inner bark of the root and trunk, intensely acrid and bitter, is the source of the alkaloid tulipiferine, a heart stimulant. Powdered bark and seeds were sometimes used by Native Americans for rheumatic and digestive problems and as a remedy for worms. They also made dugout canoes from the trunks. Today, tulip-tree honey is a delicacy.

The light, soft wood has much commercial value because it is easily worked and doesn't split readily. Paneling, interior and exterior trim, and veneers are some of its uses. It's the favorite material for hat blocks as it doesn't absorb moisture.

Of ancient origin, tulip tree and its close relatives once occupied a much wider range in Europe and Asia as well as North America. This group is considered one of the most primitive among seed plants. Fossils of tulip-tree species date from the Upper Cretaceous

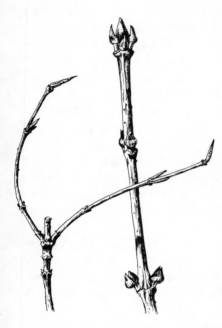

Nannyberry (left) has long, slim buds, while mapleleaf viburnum (right) shows roundish, stemmed buds. Opposite leaves and branching occur in all viburnums.

period (seventy million to one hundred million years ago), but all species except for one in central China and this one were wiped out by Pleistocene glaciation.

This is the state tree of Indiana and Tennessee.

Viburnums (*Viburnum* spp.). Honeysuckle family. Shrubs or small trees in woods, thickets, edges. All viburnums (about a dozen species exist in our area) have opposite leaves, and most have small, white flowers and small, fleshy fruits containing single flat seeds. Flowers and fruit occur in flat-topped clusters. Viburnums include hobblebush *(V. alnifolium)*, the arrowwoods, the blackhaws, the wild-raisins, and cranberry viburnum *(V. trilobum)*. This account focuses on nannyberry *(V. lentago)* and mapleleaf viburnum *(V. acerifolium)*, two of the most common woodland species.

Other names: Sheepberry, nannybush, sweet viburnum *(V. lentago)*, dockmackie, arrowwood *(V. acerifolium)*.

Close relatives: Snowball tree *(V. opulus)*; elderberries *(Sambucus)*; honeysuckles *(Lonicera)*.

Lifestyle: Nannyberry and mapleleaf viburnum differ much in general profile, leaf and bud shapes, and typical habitats. The first often grows to small tree size. It has long, slim buds, finely toothed leaves marked with black dots beneath, and winged leafstalks. It is moderately shade tolerant and prefers open edges and moister ground than the second species. Mapleleaf viburnum is typically a low or head-high shrub. It has roundish, stalked buds and lobed, maplelike leaves also dotted beneath. This forest understory plant is much more shade tolerant and can occupy drier sites than nannyberry.

Both species form clonal thickets, have bisexual, insect-pollinated flowers, and bear bluish-black drupes. Recognizing mapleleaf viburnum in the fall is easy: the leaves turn a unique shade of pinkish-magenta and the fruits are red before turning dark. Nannyberry leaves also turn purplish-red. This shrub may become somewhat sprawling as branches arch over and rest on the ground. The wood has a rank, unpleasant smell.

Associates: Look for nannyberry clones in thickets near American elm, Eastern cottonwood, maples, ashes, and beech. Mapleleaf viburnum prefers mature oak–hickory and beech–maple forests.

Spring, summer. Nannyberry foliage hosts several moth caterpillars including the unsated sallow *(Metaxaglaea inulta)* and the horrid zale *(Zale horrida).* Both are owlet moths.

On mapleleaf viburnum, rose-tinted sluglike caterpillars attended by ants may be larvae of spring azure butterflies, also called common blues (see Flowering Dogwood).

Nonspecific viburnum feeders include the azalea sphinx moth caterpillar *(Darapsa pholus),* large and green with a projecting rear horn. A tiny casebearer moth larva, *Coleophora viburnella,* constructs flat, toothed cases of plant materials on leaves and twigs.

Fall. Though widely consumed by various birds and mammals, viburnum fruits are seldom taken in great abundance, perhaps because of their low fat content. Foremost feeders are ruffed grouse, brown thrashers, cedar waxwings, Eastern chipmunks, and red squirrels. White-tailed deer browse on the twigs.

Lore: To humans, the edibility of viburnum fruits varies with the species. Some, such as nannyberry, are edible right off the plant, others need lots of sugar and boiling, while still others taste acid and bitter. A bark decoction of mapleleaf viburnum was used by Native Americans as an emetic.

Violets *(Viola* spp.). Low herbs in dry or moist woods, meadows, wetlands. Some seventy-seven species range throughout North America; most of them are blue-flowered, but there are also yellow, white, and a few purple, pink, and red species. Violets come in one of two groups: the stemmed species, in which leaves and flowers grow on the same stalk, and the stemless group, in which each grows on separate stalks. Most violets have heart-shaped leaves (a notable exception is birdfoot violet, *V. pedata).* The flowers are five-petaled, the lowest petal heavily veined and extending back into a spur. The most common blue, yellow, and white violets are, respectively, the common blue violet *(V. papilionacea),* the downy yellow violet *(V. pubescens),* and the Canada violet *(V. canadensis).* But the species continually hybridize; trying to identify a violet (especially a blue one) "by the book" often becomes an exercise in frustration.

Close Relatives: Pansy *(V. tricolor);* green violet *(Hybanthus concolor);* not related to African violet *(Saintpaulia ionantha).*

Lifestyle: It's the most visible beginning, this low, blue flame in the woods. I think of it as a pilot light that ignites the entire burst of resurrection we call spring.

Violets have two kinds of flowers, one rarely seen. The colored petals of early spring attract pollinating insects, directing them inside the flower by lines called nectar guides. Yet this obvious flower is probably less important to the plant's reproduction than the later, hidden flower. It grows low and close to the root, never opens, and thus exposes no pollen for cross-fertilization. The seed produced from this self-contained flower carries genes only from its sole parent.

Violet plants seem extremely picky about where they will grow. Two plants from separate colonies that look exactly alike may not thrive or even grow in each other's microhabitat.

This fastidiousness may be both a survival mechanism and a result of inbreeding. Because the violet that germinates from a self-pollinated seed is a genetic repeat of its sole

The common blue violet, one of our most familiar wildflowers, is often overlooked once the showy flower itself is gone. But violet's most important flowers never open and are self-fertilized.

parent plant, it is already precisely adapted to its own microhabitat. For a genetically distinct plant produced from two parent violets, the situation would be hit-or-miss. Thus violets show that it is sometimes advantageous for an organism not to evolve. The violet's dual means of reproduction guarantees its success in most circumstances.

Seedpods open explosively, sometimes shooting the seeds three or four feet—and sometimes not scattering them at all but holding them in the splayed pods.

The sight of violets reflowering in the fall is not unusual. Day length is the trigger. When the tilt of the planet in relation to the sun is exactly the same in the fall as it was in the spring, day length is also the same, thus releasing the hormone that stimulates flowering.

Associates: *Spring, summer.* Violets rely mainly upon the solitary bees as pollen vectors. Other insect visitors include syrphid flies, bee flies, butterflies, and moths. Bumblebees *(Bombus)* sometimes bite through the nectar spur of the flower, taking the payoff without performing the service.

Irregular holes in the leaves generally indicate caterpillar feeders, most notably two genera of fritillary butterflies *(Speyeria, Boloria)*. The dark, spiny caterpillars feed only at night. During the day look beneath the fed-upon plant, in the leaf litter, where they hide.

A moth with translucent, pale-yellow wings is probably the beggar *(Eubaphe mendica)*, whose caterpillar is an inchworm.

Curled, distorted leaves result from feeding of the violet gall midge *(Phytophaga violicola)*, a tiny fly larva. Wormlike larvae ("leatherjackets") of certain crane fly species (Tipulidae) also feed on leaves at night.

Violet sawfly larvae *(Ametastegia pallipes)*, resembling bluish or greenish caterpillars, skeletonize leaves from below, then eat holes through them. Blistered leaves result from their egg laying.

Large, ragged holes in leaves combined with trails of slime are signs of the spotted garden or giant slug *(Limax maximus)*, a night-feeding mollusk.

Ants collect seeds from the open pods and carry them to underground nests. It is the oil gland portion (caruncle) of the seed that attracts them. Investigations have shown that violet seeds manipulated by ants germinate faster, producing healthier plants, than seeds that simply fall to the ground.

Though not a major wildlife food plant, violet foliage is relished by cottontail rabbits. Wild turkeys consume the tuberous rhizomes. Seed eaters include ruffed grouse, mourning doves, and dark-eyed juncos. Pine and white-footed mice also eat the seeds.

Lore: Most wild violets have only subtle fragrance if any. Rich in vitamins A and C, the leaves may be nibbled raw, used as a salad or cooked green, and when dry, steeped for a tea. Flowers can be candied or made into jam, jelly, or syrup. Some of the yellow violets can be mildly cathartic and have been used as a gentle laxative. Native Americans used a rhizome decoction as an expectorant remedy for coughs and bronchitis. Used as a poultice, violet plants apparently have remedial effects on certain skin cancers, a subject of continuing research.

The sweet violet *(V. odorata)*, blue and fragrant, is a common garden species native to Europe. It was the sacred flower of ancient Athens. Blue violets, the traditional nosegay flowers, symbolized faithfulness between lovers.

Exposed to acid or alkaline solutions, the petals of many blue violets react like litmus, turning red in acid and yellow in a base.

In North America, the common blue violet is the state flower of Illinois, New Jersey, Rhode Island, and Wisconsin and the provincial flower of New Brunswick.

Virginia Creeper *(Parthenocissus quinquefolia)*. Grape family. Climbing vine in woods, thickets. Recognize this woody high-climber by its five, fan-splayed leaflets, its disk-tipped tendrils, its greenish, clustered flowers, and its blue-black, grapelike berries. Very

The disk tendrils of Virginia creeper securely anchor this climbing vine to almost any vertical surface. They are so persistent that they often remain attached long after the vine itself dies.

similar is the thicket creeper *(P. vitacea)*, which lacks the adhesive disk tips on tendrils.

Other names: False grape, American ivy, five-leaved ivy, five-fingered ivy, woodbine (properly the name of woodbine honeysuckle, *Lonicera periclymenum*).

Close relatives: Boston ivy *(P. tricuspidata)*; grapes *(Vitis)*; American ampelopsis *(Ampelopsis cordata)*; pepper vine *(A. arborea)*.

Lifestyle: The greenish, insect-pollinated flowers, borne opposite the leaves, are usually bisexual; when unisexual, both sexes appear on the same plant. Berries, high in fat content, often remain on the plant into winter.

Its branched, adhesive tendrils distinguish this genus from all others. Secreting a cement-like substance, the clasping disks on the tendril tips form only after the tendril touches a support. They often continue to adhere long after the vine dies. So strong are these modified flower stalks that five tendril branches can hold a weight of ten pounds. Where the vine climbs on smooth masonry, the disks can in time erode and crumble its surface.

Spectacular red foliage announces Virginia creeper in late summer and early fall; it is one of the first plants to turn color as the seasons change. This brilliant display is believed to attract birds, which consume the fruits and thus disperse the seeds (see Flowering Dogwood).

Virginia creeper, a sun lover, is nonetheless moderately shade tolerant and can occupy many habitats. In general appearance it is often confused with poison ivy, which always has three leaflets.

Associates: Often this vine will take over a dead tree, such as a disease-killed American elm, and use it as a support, thus giving the tree an interesting new appearance. Poison ivy is a frequent associate.

Spring, summer. Many of this vine's common insect feeders may also be found on grapevines (see Wild Grapes).

Whitened or grayish foliage may indicate the feeding of Virginia-creeper leafhoppers *(Erythroneura ziczac).*

Threadlike mines in leaflets result from the feeding of *Phyllocnistis ampelopsiella*, larvae of a tiny moth.

The grape cane girdler *(Ampeloglypter ater),* a small, black snout beetle, tunnels in the canes, creating stem galls.

Bees are the chief flower pollinators.

Late summer, fall. Bird consumers of the nutritious berries are numerous. The fruit is a favorite of woodpeckers, including red-bellied, downy, hairy, and pileated, plus Northern flickers and yellow-bellied sapsuckers. Among other frequent feeders are great crested flycatchers, Eastern bluebirds, Swainson's and wood thrushes, American robins, brown thrashers, red-eyed vireos, and fox sparrows. Fermented fruits on the vine occasionally intoxicate birds.

Mammal consumers include striped skunks and red foxes; white-tailed deer browse on twigs and foliage.

Lore: Though nutritive to wildlife, these berries are not for human consumption. Eaten in quantity, they can be fatal. The stem, however, provided food for the Chippewas. They cut it in short lengths, then boiled and peeled it, eating the sweet, saplike substance that jelled beneath the bark. The cooking water could be boiled down to a syrup.

An old reference recommends an application of the crushed leaves to trunk and branches as an effective insecticide against the woolly apple aphid *(Erisosoma lanigerum),* a pest of apple and other fruit trees.

Walnut, Black *(Juglans nigra).* Walnut family. Tree in rich, moist edges, open woods. Black walnut has feather-compound leaves with seven to seventeen narrow, toothed leaflets that smell spicy when crushed. Its large nuts with green husks are also aromatic.

Close relatives: Butternut *(J. cinerea);* English walnut *(J. regia);* hickories *(Carya).*

Lifestyle: Late to leaf out in spring and early to drop leaves in the fall, this tree stands like a black, furrowed skeleton for much of the year. Its massive, sharply divided trunk, heavy branching, and zigzag twigs give it a distinctive profile. A shade-intolerant species, it grows fast, plunging a deep taproot and deeply set lateral roots (usually one to two times the crown radius). Walnut does not tolerate soil acidity or extremes of temperature and moisture; it thrives best in moist, sandy loams and alluvial soils.

Walnut secretes a brown-staining substance called juglone, an allelopathic quinone that inhibits the growth of many plants (including walnut seedlings) and seems to stimulate the growth of others. Heaviest concentrations occur in the buds, nut hulls, and roots, lesser amounts in leaves and stems. Decaying leaves and hulls plus rain-drip from the tree result in large quantities of juglone beneath the tree. So powerful is this substance that sometimes the tree's root pattern can be traced on the ground by noting where one kind of plant replaces another. Its roots also tend to increase the soil alkalinity in their immediate vicinity.

Flowers—the male catkins drooping, the wind-pollinated female spikes at the ends of terminal twigs—appear on the same tree after leaf emergence. Seldom produced on trees younger than age twenty, nuts may remain on the tree for a time after the leaves drop. The green husks dry and turn brittle and brown, exposing the hard-shelled, deeply corrugated nut, which requires a season of freezing and frost-cracking in the ground before germination can occur.

Associates: Juglone is toxic to many plant species. But black raspberry (though not blackberry) thrives, and most fruit trees other than apple are not affected. Forage grasses and mints also thrive; poor pasturage and hay crops are sometimes much improved by planting walnut borders. The precise role of juglone in benefiting the tree remains unknown.

Black walnut typically occurs in mixtures with other deciduous trees. Where present in forests, it is often the tallest (and perhaps oldest) dominant tree, owing to its sunlight requirement.

Spring, summer. A common fungous disease, sometimes causing defoliation, is bull's-eye spot *(Cristulariella pyramidalis).* Look for targetlike spots on the leaves and, on their undersides, small, white sporophores shaped like Christmas trees.

Insects that feed on walnut include many that also feed on butternut and hickories. Only those that are most common on this species are cited here.

Conspicuous among the caterpillars is the larva of the luna *(Actias luna),* one of the largest, most spectacular saturniid moths. Luna

A moiling mass of walnut caterpillars about to become larger caterpillars experiences a kind of communal ecdysis (skin shedding) that will leave the old skins matted on the trunk.

caterpillars are fat, green, and bristled.

The walnut sphinx caterpillar *(Laothoe juglandis)* is green or reddish.

A foremost leaf forager is the walnut caterpillar, also called the walnut datana *(Datana integerrima)*, black with white hair tufts, which feeds gregariously. When the larvae are disturbed, they elevate the front and rear parts of their bodies, forming a circle or letter-C shape. The caterpillars all molt together; massing on a branch or trunk, they leave a deposit of cast skins and hair. These caterpillars are often heavily parasitized by *Phorocera claripennis*, a fly.

Several underwing moth species *(Catocala)*, tapered fore and aft, the elm spanworm (see American Basswood), and the maple looper, *Parallelia bistriaris*, are also common.

Narrow, whitish mines in the leaves may indicate feeding of *Nepticula juglandifoliella*, a tiny moth larva.

Walnut lace bugs *(Corythucha juglandis)*

These walnut shells show characteristic gnawing by squirrels, in this case fox squirrels. The number and placement of gnawed openings indicate the feeder's identity.

stipple foliage, and black walnut curculios *(Conotrachelus retentus)* feed on young shoots. Inspect half-grown nuts that drop prematurely; crescent-shaped cuts in them are curculio egg scars.

Feltlike galls on leaf undersides may signal walnut blister mites *(Aceria erinea)*.

Late summer, fall. Adult black walnut curculios feed on the leafstalks before hibernating for the winter.

Conspicuous on branch ends in summer and fall are the unsightly silken nests of the fall webworm (see White Ash).

The nut burials of squirrels generally account for the tree's distribution. Fox and gray squirrels gnaw the nut from both sides, leaving two large holes. Red squirrels gnaw from one end, and flying squirrels gnaw four circular side openings.

Lore: Walnut is the nut of the gods. The genus name *Juglans* is a contraction of *Jovis glans,* "nut of Jupiter."

There is no more highly valued timber tree in North America. A walnut tree must be at least seventy years old to produce a forty-foot saw log, which yields about one thousand board feet of lumber. Such logs may sell for $5,000, but single trees have sold for as much as $20,000. The heavy, hard wood is especially sought for fine furniture, cabinet work, interior finish, veneers, and gunstocks. It is also a good fuel wood; its smoke fragrance has been likened to tea leaves. The bark has been used in tanning, and a yellow-brown dye can be made from the nut hulls. The hulls can also be used to stain leather and wood, and pieces of walnut shell can be used to polish metal.

Because of their commercial value, large walnut trees are becoming increasingly rare; this species was formerly much more abundant than it is today.

Native Americans, in addition to using the nuts for food, threw the green husks into water for poisoning fish in order to catch them (now an illegal practice). Nuts eaten in quantity may produce a laxative effect. When the nuts are crushed and boiled, they produce an excellent vegetable oil. Trees can also be tapped in spring for a sweet sap that will boil down to syrup.

Wintergreen *(Gaultheria procumbens).* Heath family. Low, creeping shrub in acid soil of dry or moist woods. Its shiny, evergreen leaves, white, dangling flowers, and dry, red berrylike fruits identify this plant, as does the wintergreen taste of leaves and fruit.

Other names: Checkerberry, creeping or redberry wintergreen, teaberry, mountain tea, ground tea, groundholly, deerberry, boxberry, spiceberry, partridgeberry (properly *Mitchella repens*, Bedstraw family); the name is also sometimes ascribed to the shinleafs *(Pyrola)*, spotted wintergreen *(Chimaphila maculata)*, and one-flowered wintergreen *(Moneses uniflora).*

Close relatives: Trailing arbutus *(Epigaea repens)*; blueberries *(Vaccinium)*; laurels *(Kalmia)*; Indian pipe *(Monotropa uniflora).*

Lifestyle: The small, waxy, bell-like flowers appear in early summer and last to early autumn. Bisexual and insect pollinated, they produce fleshy berrylike capsules that remain bright red on the plant through winter.

The visible plant is actually twig growth from the creeping, horizontal, usually subsurface stem. New leaves grow from the perennial stem before the flowers appear, and with the onset of cold weather, the leaves sometimes turn red. Wintergreen often indicates a low-nutrient, dry, acidic soil.

Associates: This is mainly a plant of coniferous forest habitats, though it also occurs in mixed oak and pine woodlands. A frequent plant associate is blueberry.

All year. Few insects, birds, or mammals seem to forage on this plant. Ruffed grouse eat both leaves and fruit, however, and white-tailed deer and black bears browse the wintergreen foliage.

Lore: The aromatic oil, a terpene that gives wintergreen its distinctive taste and odor, can also be tasted in twigs of yellow and black birches. Oil from both wintergreen and birches was once distilled to produce oil of wintergreen, used for flavoring and as anti-rheumatic medication (it also contains methyl salicylate). For a medicinal headache remedy, fresh leaves are steeped to make a solution that also has astringent and diuretic properties. Wintergreen tea, a well-known beverage to Native Americans, is a favorite woodsman's drink, usually made with the dry leaves.

The fruits, rather mealy and more weakly flavored than the leaves, can be eaten raw or added to salads or pies.

Witch Hazel *(Hamamelis virginiana)*. Witch hazel family. Shrubs in mesic to dry woodlands. Recognize this forest understory shrub by its wavy-edged leaves with uneven bases, its yellow flowers in autumn, and its woody seed capsules that usually persist on the plant throughout the year.

Other names: Winterbloom, snapping alder, spotted alder.

Close relative: Gums *(Liquidambar)*; unrelated to hazelnuts *(Corylus)*.

Lifestyle: Moderately shade tolerant and slow growing, witch hazel typically displays a growth form of several crooked stems that together produce an irregular open crown. Each clump is one plant.

When most other plants are dispersing seed, witch hazel is just beginning to flower. From September to December, even as they drop their leaves, these shrubs flame into yellow torches. Flowers, clustered in threes and showing four narrow, twisted petals, are bisexual and insect pollinated.

At the same time that flowering occurs, seedpods from the previous year's flowers are popping open, shooting out two black seeds. This artillery begins on a day when temperature and humidity are just right; hearing the popping explosions and tracing the arcs of bombarding seeds requires the luck of being there at the right time. Seeds are commonly shot a distance of ten to twenty feet.

Pollinating insects are often in short supply when frosty weather sets in, and the flowers can and do self-pollinate. Actual fertilization of the pollinated ovules, however, does not occur until spring (a process somewhat analogous to delayed implantation of the fertilized ovum in certain mammals). Seeds then develop during the "normal" season. A high rate of fruit abortion—half or more of all developing capsules—may occur in spring. These aborted fruits may be self-fertilized ones, thus controlling the degree of inbreeding, but positive data are lacking.

Individual plants differ widely in annual flower and fruit abundance. Plants in full sun

On the twig above the leaf, the spiny witch-hazel budgall resembles a small bur. On the leaf, witch-hazel leafgall aphids form toothlike projections. Both of these aphid species migrate to birch trees.

usually bear more fruits than shrubs in shade. The seeds themselves usually lie dormant on the ground for two winters before germinating.

Associates: Witch hazel is a typical resident of oak–hickory and mixed deciduous forests. I have seen it fairly often too in riverbank and open, infertile, savanna habitats.

Spring, summer. Two galls are common, both caused by aphids. The witch-hazel leafgall or conegall aphid *(Hormaphis hamamelidis)* forms cone-shaped galls on upper leaf surfaces. The spiny witch-hazel budgall aphid *(Hamamelistes spinosus)* produces oval, spiny galls on the twigs. Both species spend much of their life cycle on white birch.

A leaf folded once or more along a lateral vein is probably the feeding haven of a witch-hazel leaffolder *(Episimus argutanus)*, a tortricid moth caterpillar. A leaf rolled from the top down may hold another tortricid, the witch-hazel leafroller *(Cacoecia rosaceana)*. *Caloptilia superbifrontella*, a gracilariid moth, rolls the leaf into a cone.

Lithocolletis hamameliella, a tiny moth larva, makes whitish blotch mines on leaves.

Other caterpillars may include the mustard sallow *(Pyreferra hesperidago)*, the three-spotted nola *(Nola triquetrana)*, the figure-seven moth *(Synedoida grandirena)*, and a dagger moth, *Acronicta hamamelis*, which rests in a fishhook position. All are noctuid moths.

Holes in unopened seed capsules are signs of a weevil larva, *Pseudanthonomus hamamelidis*. Witch hazel is its only known host plant.

Fall. Mustard sallow caterpillars are often more abundant in fall than in spring.

Since the peak flowering period occurs at a season when most pollinating insects have retired, how is cross-fertilization accomplished? Research into this matter has shown that the chief pollen vectors are small gnats, particularly fungus gnats *(Bradysia)*, and small parasitoid wasps. According to botanist Diane De Steven, witch hazel is "opportunistic in its use of whatever insects are active in the fall, and its long flowering period allows opportunities to take advantage of favorable conditions when they occur." My own observations confirm frequent visits to flowers by American hover flies *(Metasyrphus americanus)* and tachinid flies (Tachinidae).

Bird and mammal seed eaters are not numerous. Ruffed grouse and fox squirrels are apparently the most frequent consumers. White-tailed deer browse twigs and foliage.

Lore: Witch hazel oil, distilled mainly from the twigs, is one of those all-purpose healing remedies sanctified by long tradition if not medical science. It is still an over-the-counter item in drugstores. Most physicians don't find much to recommend or condemn in its use as a mildly astringent lotion for minor abrasions and skin irritations—it contains tannic and gallic acids. Native Americans used decoctions of leaves and twigs as liniments and on poultices. The Iroquois made a tea of the leaves, sweetened with maple sugar; they also drank it unsweetened as a diarrhea remedy. The seeds are said to be edible but aren't very tasty.

Another ancient tradition is the use of forked witch hazel branches as divining rods for "water witching." Its adherents swore on its ability to point underground water, coal, tin, and copper lodes, as well as lost household items.

If the plant's common name originated from its supposed "witching" powers, it did so by a round-about route. *Witch* is a corruption of the Anglo-Saxon word *wych* (related to the word wicker), meaning "bending." Because the leaves resemble those of the English elm *(Ulmus procera)*, the shrub was named wych-elm, then wych-hazel, and eventually witch hazel. (Wych elm today labels a genuine elm, *Ulmus glabra*.)

Yew, American *(Taxus canadensis)*. Yew family. Evergreen shrub in moist and wet woods. Flat, stalked, firlike needles, a straggling or sometimes prostrate growth form, scaly, reddish bark, and red, berrylike fruits identify this conifer.

Other names: Canada yew, ground hemlock.

Close relatives: Japanese yew *(T. cuspidata)*; English yew *(T. baccata)*; torreyas *(Torreya)*.

Lifestyle: Often forming dense, hip-high thickets in the understory of coniferous or northern hardwood forests, yew is a midlevel evergreen. The needlelike, dark green leaves, though spirally arranged on the smooth twigs, are twisted at the base so that they appear two-ranked, as in the tree conifers.

This species carries unisexual, wind-pollinated flowers on the same plant (on most other yews, each sex occupies a separate plant). The erect ovule develops into a hard, bony seed cupped in a berrylike, bright red aril. Both seed and foliage contain taxine, which is a toxic alkaloid. Like balsam fir, yew produces a strongly defensive hormone that retards the pupation of certain insect larvae that may venture to feed on the evergreen needles.

Yew thrives best in cool, dense shade and is extremely sensitive to heat and drought.

Associates: Yew grows in just about any woodland where moisture and shade conditions are right. In lowland areas white cedar is a common tree associate.

Spring, summer. Enlarged or distorted twig ends indicate the feeding of taxus bud mites, also called yew bigbud mites *(Cecidophyopsis psilaspis).* Up to one thousand mites may infest a single bud.

Several insects feed voraciously on yew foliage. Discolored needles, waxy-white secretions, and masses of white-woolly insects on branches reveal the presence of taxus mealybugs *(Dysmicoccus wistariae).*

Copious honeydew, together with black sooty mold (Perisporiaceae) that grows upon this insect secretion, are signs of the Fletcher scale *(Lecanium fletcheri),* a soft, immobile scale insect.

Notched and bitten-off yew needles are signs of the destructive black vine weevil. Rarely seen, it feeds mostly at night. The larval beetles, feeding underground, are the actual killers.

Probably yew's foremost insect pest is the black vine or taxus weevil *(Otiorhyncus sulcatus),* a dark snout beetle. Adult insects feed on innermost needles at night, leaving notches, scallops, and cut-off tips. The root-feeding grubs, however, do the real damage, causing the shrub to yellow and die.

Within their breeding range, black-throated blue warblers frequently nest in yew thickets.

Fall. Birds are probably the main seed dispersers, though no single fruit-eating species is a dominant consumer. Birds that eat fermented fruits may become intoxicated.

All year. Yew is a favored browse of white-tailed deer and moose. In areas with large deer overpopulations, the shrub is virtually extirpated.

Yew thickets also provide excellent protective cover for several grouse species.

Lore: The strong, resilient wood was a frequent choice of Native Americans for bowmaking. In Europe, the English yew was also used for this purpose (the word *taxus* comes from an ancient Greek word meaning "bow"), especially by English archers. This yew was often planted in churchyards as a symbol of mourning and is still commonly seen in European cemeteries.

The red, fleshy aril enclosing the seed is edible, but the seed itself, as well as the foliage, contains a dangerous heart depressant and should never be eaten. These seeds pass intact through the digestive systems of most birds and mammals. Although deer and moose readily consume the foliage with no ill effects, other ruminants—notably cattle—have been killed by it.

Taxol, a substance derived from yew bark, shows increasing promise in treating ovarian and breast cancers.

Glossary

Achene. A one-seeded, dry fruit that does not split open along suture lines, as in buttercups, sycamore.

Adaptation. An evolved process, structure, or activity by which an organism becomes apparently better suited to its habitat or environment, or for particular functions.

Allelopathy. One organism's inhibition of another by secreted chemicals.

Alluvial. An adjective referring to any sediment deposited by flowing water.

Alternation of generations. The reproductive scheme of nonflowering plants, whereby the sexual generation alternates with an asexual generation.

Anther. The pollen-bearing part of a stamen.

Aril. A fleshy covering that encloses a seed, as in American bittersweet.

Autogamy. Self-pollination, an optional method of reproduction in many plants.

Berry. A pulpy or fleshy fruit with seeds embedded in the pulp.

Biennial. A plant with a two-year life span, usually fruiting in the second year.

Bisexual flower. A flower having both male and female sex organs; also called a perfect flower.

Boreal forest. The northern forest of North America consisting chiefly of conifers.

Canopy. The uppermost level of foliage in a forest, consisting of aggregated tree crowns.

Caruncle. An area of oil glands on certain seeds, such as trout lily and violets, attractive to ants and other ground insects; also called *elaisome*.

Cleistogamy. A form of autogamy; the process of self-pollination in certain basal or sub-surface flowers that remain closed, as in violets, fringed polygala.

Climax forest. A mature forest that is the final, stable result of plant succession for an area.

Clone. A plant or group of plants, produced by asexual or vegetative reproduction, which has the same genetic makeup as its parent.

Coaction. An interaction between two or more organisms.

Conk. The fruiting body of a woody or bracket fungus, usually on dead or infected trunks.

Corm. A bulblike, vertical underground stem.

Drupe. A fleshy fruit with a hard or stony pit, as in cherries, dogwoods.

Edge. The transition or border zone between forest and open land, characterized by interspersed trees, shrubs, and herbs; also called an ecotone.

Epicormic branching. Small, stunted branches arising from dormant buds on a trunk or large branch. This often occurs as a compensatory result of unusual stress on the plant.

Follicle. A dry fruit that splits open by valves or slits along one side, as in wild columbine.

Fruiting body. In fungi, the reproductive portion of the plant produced above ground from its subsurface mycelia; that is, a mushroom or conk.

Gall. A localized growth on a plant induced by a fungus or by egg laying or feeding of certain mites and insect larvae, especially aphids, gall gnats, and gall wasps.

Gametophyte. In plants exhibiting alternation of generations, the plant produced by a spore and giving rise to male and female sex cells, which produce an asexual spore-bearing plant.

Habitat. The total set of environmental conditions in which an organism exists.

Herb. Any nonwoody, usually low plant (excluding fungi) that dies back each year.

Hybrid. The offspring of a cross between two different though closely related species; usually this offspring cannot itself reproduce.

Inquiline. An organism of one species that inhabits the nest or abode of another, such as nongallmaking insects that occupy galls.

Mast. Nuts, especially acorns, beechnuts, and hickory nuts, in a collective sense; usually refers to wildlife food.

Mesic. A habitat or environment of medium moisture; not overly dry or wet.

Microhabitat. A subdivision of a habitat, such as a stump, small patch of ground, or mud puddle, to which certain organisms may become specifically adapted.

Mycelia. The threadlike masses of a fungus from which arises a reproductive fruiting body.

Mycorrhiza. A symbiotic relationship of a subsurface fungus with vascular plant roots. The fungus aids, and in many cases is vital to, nutrient absorption by the roots.

Perennial. A plant with at least a three-year life span, usually flowering annually.

Petiole. The stalk of a leaf.

Pistil. The female seed-bearing flower organ, consisting of ovary, style, and stigma.

Pome. A fleshy fruit with a papery core, as in apple, shadbushes.

Rhizome. An underground, horizontal, rootlike stem that produces stems and roots.

Samara. A dry, winged fruit that does not split open along suture lines.

Serotiny. Late development or blooming.

Spore. A one-celled asexual reproductive organ borne on sporangia, used mainly in referring to flowerless plants; spores produce sexual gametophytes.

Sporophyte. In plants exhibiting alternation of generations (clubmosses, ferns), the spore-producing plant that grows from a gametophyte.

Spring ephemeral. A forest herb that completes its above-ground growth and flowering before full tree canopy development occurs in spring and dies back as shading increases. Most spring ephemerals rise from perennial rhizomes.

Stamen. The male pollen-bearing organ of a flower, consisting of anther and filament.

Stigma. The pollen-receiving part of the female flower pistil.

Symbiosis. Any intimate coexistence between different organisms; includes parasitism, commensalism, and mutualism.

Unisexual flower. A flower having either male or female sex organs, but not both. Dioecious plants bear each sex on different individuals; monoecious plants bear each sex separately on the same individual.

Vegetative reproduction. Any replication of a plant not directly resulting from seed or spore germination, as in cloning or sprouting from stumps, rhizomes, or twigs.

Witches' broom. An abnormal growth of numerous weak shoots toward the branch tip of a tree or shrub, symptomatic of fungous or viral infection, mite infestation, or combinations of these.